Alas

MW01098389

Alaska Frontier Surgeon is a nicely written and detailed account of how an energetic and talented son of missionary parents became the first physician in a remote part of Alaska. It is an engaging story of his daily life as the lone provider of modern medicine to the island communities on Kodiak.

—*George S. Rhyneer, M.D.*
Retired Alaskan Cardiologist

• • •

I give by highest recommendation to *Alaska Frontier Surgeon* for a great read. You will find it enthralling! Doctor Robert Holmes Johnson has woven a history of one of Alaska's great pioneer families into a history of the development of Kodiak Island from a sleepy fishing village to the vibrant economic powerhouse it has become today. All of this is written in the context of the family background and the course of world events during the 20th century and the impact of those events on Kodiak and the people who lived on Kodiak Island.

This book takes you through the 20th century, across three continents including the entire continental United States and Alaska, and covers the human family aspects from birth, youth, romance, war, peace, disappointment, success, struggle, illness, overcoming adversity, victories and death. Everyone will find something of interest in this book. This is a story about real people who committed their lives to making the world a better place for their fellow man in the areas of health, education and humanitarian interests. They were very successful in these endeavors and Kodiak Island is the beneficiary of their committed lives.

Arthur Holmes Johnson put aside his doubts and concerns and focused on confidently providing the best health care he could for people regardless of the circumstances. One gutsy determined man made a lasting impact on Kodiak Island and Alaska for many generations to come. Enjoy the book!

—*Jerome M Selby,*
former Mayor of the Kodiak Island Borough, 1983-1998 and 2004-2013

• • •

A beautifully written story of the maturing of a man told in his own words from his youthful journals kept throughout his life. This is the story of a man who left his mark for many generations to come on his chosen community, Kodiak, Alaska. A. Holmes Johnson was a product of his birth, his time and his decisions, as are we all. This book leaves us pondering our own lives, relationships, and purpose.

—*Nancy Kemp,*
Member and Past President of the Kodiak Historical Society

• • •

Can one rejoice twice? First, for A.Holmes Johnson coming to Kodiak in 1938 and second, for his son rendering his father's diaries and letters into *Alaska Frontier Surgeon.*

It was a pleasure to read about a man who did not believe in idleness, or complaints, but in working for a common good.

In addition to being a busy doctor and surgeon in a remote community, he put immense energy into the making of Kodiak today. There is hardly an area he didn't touch upon: School Board, Art and Music, Library, City Planning, Borough government, Red Cross, and service organizations. Rotary's motto of 'Service Above Self' is well exampled by A. Holmes Johnson who accomplished a lasting impact upon the early community of Kodiak.

Congratulations to his son, Dr. Robert Johnson, for compiling this interesting history of an earlier Kodiak.

—*Ann Barker*
Kodiak Video Magazine

• • •

If is often said that each Alaskan pioneer has a fascinating story to tell and the biography of Dr. Arthur Holmes Johnson, and his wife Fostina Bishop Johnson, as written by their son, "Dr. Bob" Johnson, is no exception. What is exceptional is the loving humor and wit with which the Johnsons are remembered and their story told by their son, himself no small presence in Kodiak.

From Dr. A. Holmes Johnson's first Alaskan experience as a cannery physician in 1937 over the course of a long, colorful and sometimes establishment-shaking career as a frontier physician in Kodiak, Alaska, the doctor's son narrates a touching, often laugh-out-loud funny and always fascinating look at the challenges, hardships and friendships that lured and endeared this frontier family to life in remote Alaska.

From the very beginning, where Dr. Bob describes his grandmother "as a devout Christian, who believed thoroughly in the Bible as she saw it. Her three children were indoctrinated as thoroughly as she could manage" to the very last, "I'm really the lucky one, as I will not have to grieve when my loved ones go first…" you will not be able to put this book down and will come to know and respect these complex characters who put their mark so indelibly on Kodiak's history.

—*Barbara Bolson, Director,*
Kodiak College/UAA

ALASKA FRONTIER SURGEON

Arthur Holmes Johnson, M.D.
Pioneer Kodiak Physician

Robert Holmes Johnson, M.D.

Sprucehaven Publishing
Kodiak, Alaska

Published by Sprucehaven Publishing
Editor: Ellen Wheat
Cover & text designer: Jeanie James, Shorebird Creative
Proofreader: Karen Olson
Publication management: Aftershocks Media/Epicenter Press
Distribution: Aftershocks Media

Library of Congress Control Number: 2014934261

ISBN: 978-1935347378

10 9 8 7 6 5 4 3 2 1
Printed in the United States of America

To order single copies of ALASKA FRONTIER SURGEON, mail
$17.95 plus $6 for shipping to:

Sprucehaven Publishing
PO Box 945
Kodiak, AK 99615

Dedication

In memory of the remarkable man
whose story unfolds in its pages,
this book is dedicated to my wife, Marian,
for her help, and her patience
during its writing,
and to the members of the immediate
and extended Johnson Family,
as a reminder of their heritage.

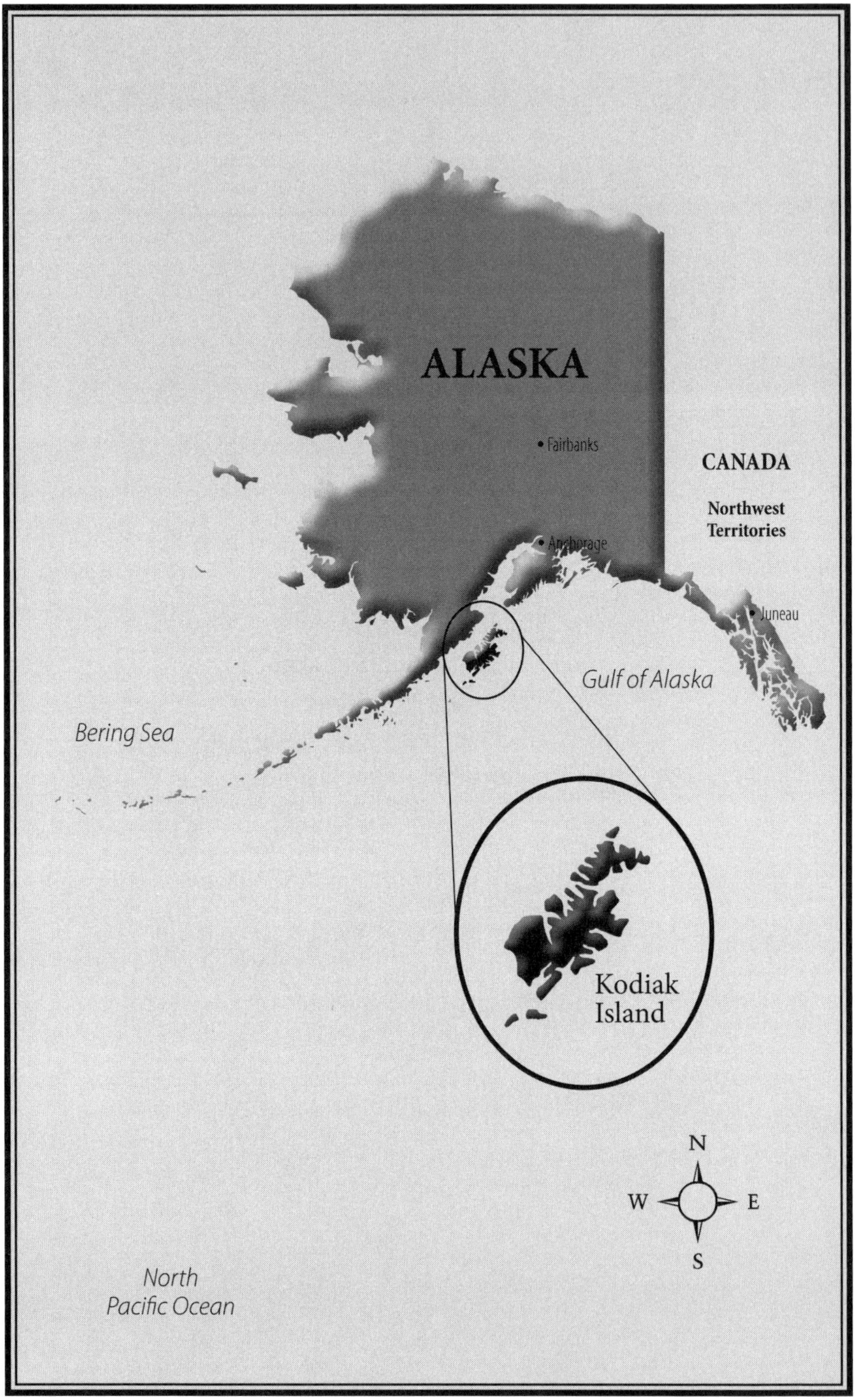

ALASKA

• Fairbanks

CANADA

Northwest
Territories

• Anchorage

• Juneau

Gulf of Alaska

Bering Sea

Kodiak
Island

North
Pacific Ocean

N
W E
S

Arthur Holmes Johnson, c. 1920.

Table of Contents

Preface

Prologue *1*

Chapter 1: The Early Years *7*

Chapter 2: Morningside College and the National Guard *11*

Chapter 3: To Africa *17*

Chapter 4: Old Umtali Mission *25*

Chapter 5: Duty Calls *33*

Chapter 6: Off to War *41*

Chapter 7: Oxford *49*

Chapter 8: Medical School *59*

Chapter 9: The Romance *69*

Chapter 10: A New Life Begins *77*

Chapter 11: The Great Depression *85*

Chapter 12: A Summer Up North *93*

Chapter 13: The Move to Alaska *101*

Chapter 14: A New Practice *105*

Chapter 15: The Transition *117*

Chapter 16:Hospital Practice *131*

Chapter 17: Difficult Years *147*

Chapter 18: The Workload Grows *165*

Chapter 19: Solo Practice Continues *179*

Chapter 20: A Vacation *191*

Chapter 21: Back to Work *195*

Chapter 22: Shared Practice *205*

Chapter 23: Solo Practice, Once Again. *215*

Chapter 24: Staying With It 219

Chapter 25: Voyage of the Windbird 227

Chapter 26: World Without End 239

Chapter 27: A New Leaf 251

Chapter 28: The Vacation 261

Chapter 29: Semi-Retirement 267

Chapter 30: Rotary District Governor 281

Chapter 31: The Good Friday Earthquake. 289

Chapter 32: The Final Chapter 297

Epilogue 303

About the Author. 307

Index. 309

Preface

THIS IS THE STORY OF MY FATHER, Arthur Holmes Johnson (1894–1964), who was raised by English-born Methodist Episcopalians and became the first physician to set up permanent practice in Kodiak, Alaska, in 1938.

As a physician and town activist, he left a major imprint on his remote Alaska community. The story is based on the diaries my father kept throughout his life and on his correspondence with family members. Excerpts have also been taken from the diary and letters of my mother, Fostina Bishop Johnson. The process of writing the manuscript was facilitated by my wife, Marian Johnson, who is a consummate reader and helped me edit copies of the manuscript as it evolved.

Raised in a religious milieu, and working with his father in a Methodist mission in Africa, my dad absorbed the missionary spirit. Eventually, however, he shed the religious trappings and was compelled to simply live a life of service to mankind.

I write as a disembodied narrator throughout his bachelor years, but after my arrival on the scene, I become part of the story and write as his son.

Prologue

ARTHUR HOLMES JOHNSON stood at the rail of the ship's deck, leaning into the brisk wind that was laced with salt spray. The ship was steaming northeast along the southern shore of the Alaska Peninsula. It was late August 1937, during the Great Depression, and he had just completed a summer as a cannery physician at Bristol Bay to earn some good money. When the season ended, he boarded a company ship bound for Seattle, to rejoin his family in Portland.

A day after passing through Unimak Pass from the Bering Sea, the ship's course brought them along the eastern shore of a large, mountainous island in the Gulf of Alaska. Above them loomed towering peaks, the higher ones still capped with snow, some bearing glaciers that gleamed in the sunlight. Long, finger-like fjords penetrated the depths of the slopes, and to the north the hills became covered with dense spruce forests. Tucked in a large bay on the northeast end of the island lay the village of Kodiak.

The ship docked at the wharf, in a channel formed by one of the smaller spruce-covered islands in front of the village. Stepping off the ship, Arthur found himself in a picturesque little fishing town, basking in the warm, late summer sunlight. The breeze gently ruffled his hair and swept through tall grasses growing in uncultivated fields. It was a picture of tranquility—winding dirt roads, many cabins each with its own vegetable garden, cattle grazing peacefully here and there, and children at play. The town had five or six hundred residents, mostly of Native heritage. There was one salmon cannery at the harbor's edge, which looked like it supported everyone who lived there.

Superimposed on the serenity of this spot were the sounds: the swish of gentle waves on the shore and the shouts of happy children, as well as the songs of many wild birds: the cackle of magpies, the chortle of ravens, the penetrating screech of circling bald eagles far overhead, and the piercing cacophony of hundreds of seagulls circling over the fish waste being dumped from the cannery dock into the bay.

Arthur was taken with the island and the ambience of the village. When he learned there was no doctor in residence, his missionary background surfaced and stirred his imagination. The quiet place beckoned to him. When the ship stopped in Juneau before heading south, he was met by a doctor with the Public Health Service. When Arthur inquired about Kodiak and expressed his interest in the place, the doctor said that the remote village needed a doctor and encouraged him to consider setting up practice there. He indicated that he could help him by authorizing payment for the Natives. And he also said that with a doctor present, the chances of the Territory building a hospital would be good.

The Depression had not treated Arthur well. He wanted to become independent and cease being a financial burden to his father. Most of all, his background had spawned a deep-seated need to be needed. This sylvan setting, where he could provide what was needed, was very tempting.

Back home in Portland, Oregon, he talked with his wife and young son about the prospect of moving to Kodiak. Considering their financial state, it seemed like a good option. A decision to launch the family on an Alaskan adventure was made with very little debate and with the blessing of his parents. He wrapped up his Portland medical practice in the next several months, and set off for Kodiak, in January 1938.

✳ ✳ ✳

ARTHUR HOLMES JOHNSON, a first-generation American, was born on October 18, 1894, in Mapleton, Iowa, to Ebenezer Samuel Johnson and Sarah Tilsley Johnson. A brother, Darlow Samuel, born in England on November 20, 1885, preceded him, and a sister, Dorothea, followed, born in Iowa on July 23, 1901.

Ebenezer Samuel Johnson, c. 1920.

His father, Ebenezer Samuel Johnson, was from England, and had two brothers who became Anglican ministers. He was a newspaper reporter in London before coming to America, with Sarah, his wife, at age twenty-three. After coming to this country, he was admitted to the Northwest Iowa Conference of the Methodist Episcopal Church. First a circuit pastor in Iowa, he eventually became a bishop, and headed the Methodist African Mission where he served for twenty years. He was described in his obituary as "tall, imposing, charismatic, an educator; he was revered by all his peers."

Sarah Tilsley Johnson, c. 1920.

Arthur's mother, Sarah, was a devout Christian, who believed thoroughly in the Bible as she saw it. Her three children were indoctrinated as thoroughly as she could manage. They were expected to attend Sunday school, church, all the church doings, and to observe Sunday as a day of rest. In their young years, they were surrounded by the missionary spirit, which infused in each of them a need to be of service.

Darlow, Arthur's older brother, became a Methodist minister, married, and moved from pastorate to pastorate as they were required to do. He fathered four children, and cared selflessly for them, for his flocks, and for his parents.

Samuel Darlow Johnson, and his wife Alta, c. 1940.

His younger sister, Dorothea, spent most of her adult life in Cape Town, South Africa, the Bishop's home during his mission years. She had two children by each of two husbands, became an accomplished gardener, philosopher and poet, and a woman of remarkable depth and sensitivity.

Dorothea Johnson and her first son, Hilary Graham Botha, c. 1935.

Under his parents' jurisdiction throughout his elementary years, Arthur learned not only the beliefs of the religion, but faith in the goodness of his fellow man, appropriate social behavior, good manners, a pleasant personality, and a willingness to make himself useful. These qualities, and his intelligence, served him well as he ventured forth to embrace the world.

Being of an adventurous spirit, as he matured he developed wide-ranging interests and became somewhat of a rebel. He had a thirst for knowledge and for experience, and took summertime as an opportunity for adventure. He would, on occasion, somewhat proudly refer to himself as the "black sheep" of the family.

According to available records, the adventures of Arthur Holmes Johnson began in 1912, during the summer of his seventeenth year.

Chapter 1

The Early Years

1912– 1914

JUST SEVENTEEN, Arthur departed in June 1912 on the Northwestern Railroad from Sioux City, Iowa, to spend the summer in Nebraska's cattle country. He, like many boys his age, had an abiding romantic interest in cowboys. To him, they represented the epitome of rugged individualism and independence, and he yearned for a taste of that adventurous lifestyle.

After traveling 230 miles, he arrived at Valentine, Nebraska. He was met by Beebe, a young minister, whose pastorate included north-central Nebraska. Within days, he and his friend headed south on a dusty road in a horse-drawn buggy. "No one seemed to think twenty miles is much out there—nor fifty," he noted. The road was "surely fierce," and "mostly sand, one or two inches thick, and was just a trail across the prairie." Only a few houses and fewer fences were seen on the way to a rancher's house, where they were given supper and a bed for the night. Rancher Young "owned more than 10,000 cattle and I do not have any idea how many horses."

About Nebraska, he wrote, "The weather here is very changeable, warm in the daytime and quite cold at night. The country is different from that in Iowa. It is sandy, but how sandy you could never realize unless you had seen it for yourself. The hills are slightly higher, and the vegetation is composed of desert prairie grasses. Wildflowers abound, and some of them, especially the dwarf cacti, are very beautiful. The soil is too sandy to do any farming, so the industries are cattle and horse raising, and haying in the valleys. A person can often see a thousand cattle in one bunch, grazing the open prairie."

They continued on to a ranch owned by Reece Daniels, who said he had all the men he needed, but suggested that they ask at a ranch owned by a Mr. Bussy. They rode on horseback, and found Mr. Bussy in one of his corrals, watching his son rope cattle. He wanted someone who could be firm with horses and could manage a team-driven plow. Arthur, supremely confident, was sure he could handle the job, and was told that he would do, and that he could come to work in two weeks. This would be "at thirty-five per," which probably meant 35 cents a day. Arthur described the ranchers as a special breed, who did not consider themselves farmers, and were genuinely hospitable. "They put on nothing extra, are very frank and open, and you instinctively feel, and know, that their hospitality is natural. They work when they work, during haying season, but otherwise, do what it pleases them to do."

One day they watched wild horses being tamed: "I cannot describe it, or the sensation that it gives one, watching those wild horses, doing their utmost to unseat their rider, out there on the wide, far-reaching, desert sand. You have to see it, to appreciate its wild, free aspect."

One day, Yankee Robinson's Circus came to town. Everyone knocked off work, and people came "in their rigs" from all around the country to see it. The Sioux Indians from the Rosebud Reservation had set up camp on the outskirts of town the day before, and they supplemented the circus entertainment with war dances. The men in full regalia performed a vigorous dance, within a ring formed by the women who cheered them on.

He continued to help ranchers, breaking mules and horses one day and helping brand calves the next. He said it was "hot as blazes in the scorching sun." He could lasso nearly as well as the old timers, and was conceded to be the fastest calf wrestler of the lot. He felt that he was becoming a "pretty good cowboy."

On July 2, Beebe left for his home in Johnstown for a visit, and asked Arthur to take his place as pastor. A few weeks later, he preached his first sermon at two services, taking for his text Matthew 11:29, "Take my yoke upon you and learn of me, for I am meek and lowly in heart and ye shall find rest unto your soul." There was fine attendance, and four or five men who had never been inside a church before—ranchers he had helped—came to hear him.

The following day, he went to work for Mr. Bussy. His routine included rising at 4:30 a.m., milking the two cows, and cleaning the barn before breakfast. After breakfast, he overhauled and greased the hay rakes. Then he roped his team, the fastest and most fractious horses, to pull his twelve-foot hay rake so he could keep up with three drivers, two of whom pulled seven-foot mowers and one a six-foot mower. Then he drove again to the field and raked until noon, then stopped for dinner. He roped two fresh horses for his team after lunch, harnessed them, drove again to the field, and raked until eight o'clock in the evening, then ate supper, milked the cows, and retired, rarely before nine o'clock. "Do you wonder that the bed felt good?" he wrote. He was "on the trot all the time," and he was always driving lively beasts, which caused him to break three fence posts and to twice break the rake in the first week.

On Friday evening, after the day's work, there was an ice cream social at the farmhouse to benefit the church. People began to arrive at 9 o'clock, and were still coming at eleven. They didn't leave for their homes until sometime between 1 and 2 o'clock in the morning. He got two hours of sleep that night and had to work all the next day. On Wednesday, the following week, he ran into a nest of bees and fled, only to be stung twice coming back for the team. Apparently that, the punishing schedule, and the Friday night party, were "straws that broke the camel's back," for he quit as soon as he found there was a place for him at a ranch owned by a Mr. Daniels, where his friend, Beebe, was working.

The hayfield at Daniels' was far from the ranch house, so they worked from a camp, consisting of a tent in which the crew slept, another for the horse tack and equipment, a sod house that contained the kitchen and dining room, and a corral. He got up at 6 o'clock for breakfast, then the crew rounded up the horses, which were allowed to run free at night, and herded them into the corral. The horses were skittish, and each had to be roped, harnessed (gingerly), and attached to the hay rakes. The men raked until 12 o'clock, then dispensed with the teams and ate dinner, after which they roped and harnessed fresh horses, and raked again until 6 o'clock, then had supper and went to bed at 9 o'clock.

On August 2, he spent the morning practicing lassoing, "especially fancy throwing, at which I am becoming quite proficient."

"On the morning of the eighth, my team bolted. I happened to be driving one of the worst pair of broncos on the place, and whenever they started something, they usually had the idea that they were going to finish it. I held on to them until they pulled me off the seat. I then straddled a foot lever, and continued to hold until the double-trees broke, and the neck yoke snapped from the tongue, letting it down, and, at the same time, pinning me by the stomach and small of the back between the lever and the rake itself. Of course, I could not control the horses any longer, and they ran off. I could not move, so I yelled for assistance, which came in the form of my friend, Beebe, who heard me from where he was stacking hay, half a mile away, and ran over to free me. I was never so glad to see anyone in all my life. I was carried back to the tent, rubbed with ointment, and soon improved."

The rest of the summer, Arthur spent "breaking broncos to ride and drive, and herding cattle in the fall roundup."

* * *

IN THE SUMMER OF 1913, Arthur and three fellow students got the idea that they might combine a western adventure with a money-making scheme. Montana, they were told, was populated by many god-fearing folks and should be a good place for bright young men to earn a commission selling bibles. Intrigued, Arthur and his friends boarded a local train and departed Sioux City for Montana. At the end of the summer, Arthur went home broke. He had sold nary a bible, because the areas he visited had already been canvassed by college students and folks weren't buying. He then obtained a job in a department store in Sioux City. Luckily, the $50 he earned at the department store restored a little of his pride.

* * *

ARTHUR'S BROTHER DARLOW decided to follow the advice of Horace Greeley, to "Go west, young man," so he and his bride, Alta, accepted a Methodist pastorate in Drain, Oregon, in 1914. Arthur agreed to follow them and accompany some of their household goods and animals—Billy the dog, a pig, and some chickens—on a freight train across country. The journey began in Sergeant Bluffs, south of Sioux City, in a boxcar of the Missouri Pacific Railroad. En route, he and his charges spent two days on a Montana siding, waiting out a raging early spring blizzard. In Drain, Oregon, Arthur and Darlow became co-editors and printers of the city's newspaper, the *North Douglas Herald*, in addition to Darlow's duties as Methodist minister.

Chapter 2

Morningside College and the National Guard

1915–1916

B Y EARLY FEBRUARY 1915, Arthur's family had moved from Mapleton to Storm Lake, Iowa. Now twenty years old, Arthur boarded the train, to return to Morningside College, a Methodist liberal arts college, for a second year. When he arrived in Sioux City, he took a streetcar to his room at Patrick's boarding house, where he would live. His roommates, John and Jim Kalp and Earl Hicks, "could not be surpassed as gentlemen, the rooms were furnished in modern style," and Mrs. Patrick said the whole house was open to "her boys." Apples were on the table for them at all times.

Morningside College, Sioux City, Iowa, 1915. Wikipedia.

That year, Arthur took trigonometry, psychology, English, chemistry, education, physical training, chemistry lab, and military drill (national guard) in the evening. This ambitious program required that he apply himself. He also ran track, gave speeches, sang in quartets and choruses, and on Sundays he attended church, afternoon men's meetings, Epworth League (a religious and social organization), and often evening services. He rarely missed a play, concert, or guest lecture held at the university. Add movies, tennis, card games, parties, working at a printing office, working at the restaurant, helping at the boarding house (which gained extra treats), and one would think he had little time left over for enjoying the company of young ladies which are, however, mentioned frequently in his diary.

In early March, his father, whom he referred to as the Bishop, came to Sioux City for a meeting of the Committee on Instruction at Morningside. The two of them visited the university to meet with his chemistry professor. His father was disappointed to learn that Arthur was not doing too well, and pressed him to tend to the business of learning. Arthur determined to do so.

Morningside College Glee Club

Morningside College Glee Club,
Arthur (top row, sixth from right), 1916

✳ ✳ ✳

AFTER COMPLETING HIS SECOND YEAR in college, Arthur, now twenty-one, was called up by the Iowa National Guard to serve on the Mexican border. Between 1910 and 1916, Mexico was embroiled in a violent upheaval, with opposing political and military forces vying for control. In 1913, President Taft stationed a large military force along the Rio Grande River to protect Texans from violence. This show of force caused more violence. When Woodrow Wilson became president in

1913, he refused to recognize the revolutionary government of Mexico, and sent in 4,800 additional troops under the command of General Pershing. The violence continued to intensify. In June 1916, Arthur was ordered with the Illinois National Guard to mobilize, and 12,000 troops were sent to San Antonio, Texas, and a small cavalry contingent to Brownsville.

He trained at Camp Dodge in Des Moines, and then embarked for Texas by train. His father, major of the regiment, was on board. Arthur, sergeant of the guard, was busy keeping order on the train. They traveled through Sapulpa, Oklahoma, the oil city of the Southwest, and crossed the Red River, into Texas, encountering many cotton fields in first bloom. Here and there, he saw solitary brick chimneys, remains of burned cabins, and scattered old, unpainted frame buildings, usually with one window and a brick chimney for a fireplace. Some of these housed Negroes and poor whites, who lived there in obvious poverty. The train eventually emerged into the great American desert, "absolutely level, as far as the eye can see, and dotted with cactus, mesquite, and some sage brush." They then reached Brownsville, the southernmost town in Texas, to end their journey.

Arthur's father, the Bishop, chaplain and Major,
Iowa National Guard, Mexican Border War, 1915.

Brownsville was about fifty miles up the Rio Grande from the Gulf of Mexico. The encampment was on the river, two miles east of town. Shortly after arrival, they set about clearing the desert over a large enough area to pitch several thousand tents, and then camp routine began. Their task was to protect the citizens of the region from forays by Poncho Villa, a counterrevolutionary who had been deposed by Mexico's current president, Carranza. They were not allowed on the banks of the river, because sharpshooters on the Mexican side were on the lookout for likely targets.

*Company B Camp, Sergeant Arthur Johnson's temporary home
in Brownsville, Texas, 1916.*

Brownsville was very interesting, Arthur noted, with its Spanish architecture, tropical vegetation, and preponderance of Mexicans, who outnumbered whites five to one. Everyone spoke Spanish! Camp life took some adaptation to the environment. It was "hot as blazes" all the time, and there were many unaccustomed inhabitants, such as: chameleons, who change color to match their surroundings; poisonous scorpions; all kinds of snakes, especially rattlers; sand lizards, parrots, and locusts, which make a shrill peculiar, and penetrating noise, especially at night; horned toads in abundance; and tarantulas. And the country was subject to voluminous dust storms, hurricanes, and drenching rainstorms.

In September, Arthur's father "found it necessary to get to his Episcopal duties in Africa, so he resigned and left for Sioux City and the East Coast to settle his affairs in this country. The heat, the dust, the rain, the mud, the mosquitoes, the spiders, and multiple other flying and crawling insects of unknown description, coupled with the lack of action, began to wear thin for Arthur. He was ready to give it up but no one was being discharged, so he was resigned to bear with it.

In November, Arthur received a telegram from his father telling him that he had been given an honorable discharge, and that the Secretary of War had sent the certificate to headquarters. He immediately went to claim it, and was told that he must "certainly have pull with the government, for many had requested discharge and none had been granted." He telegraphed his father to inform him that he was leaving the next morning for Des Moines.

At home in Des Moines, after Thanksgiving, he helped his parents pack for the voyage to Africa, where he looked forward to unknown adventures, as secretary to the Bishop, in the service of the Methodist Episcopal Mission in Africa.

Chapter 3

To Africa

1916–1917

ARTHUR, NOW TWENTY-TWO, and his parents, the Bishop and Sarah, boarded the train in Sioux City on December 8, 1916. The trip to New York would be the first leg of the journey to Africa, where his father would be in charge of the Methodist Episcopal Mission. From New York, they would travel by sea to Africa via England. These were somewhat perilous times. The Great War (World War I, 1914–1918) was in progress in Europe, and German submarines were plying the seas and sinking ships. Their precise destination and their safety could not be known, and this might have led to some anxiety. Arthur referred to feeling "unsettled," but he looked forward to the experience without any fear, an emotion he said he had never experienced.

Their ship arrived at the docks in Liverpool the day before Christmas after eight days at sea. They were boarded by federal officers, separated into two groups—English and aliens—and asked many questions, before being allowed to disembark. Ashore, they were interrogated by Customs officials. In England, they traveled by train to villages where the Bishop's relatives lived, and spent time in each location. When meeting each family, Arthur learned that many of his cousins were away at the war.

* * *

AFTER SEVERAL ATTEMPTS to book passage from England to Africa, they were at last informed that they would sail on February 3, 1917. Germany had promised just two days earlier to "redouble their efforts to torpedo every ship that entered or left England." But having heard nothing to discourage them, Arthur and his parents departed

London for Tilbury Dock, thirty miles to the east, near the mouth of the Thames River where it joins the English Channel, and boarded their ship, the RMS *Balmoral Castle.*

Arthur's passport (first page), for the passage to England en route to Africa, where he was to serve as secretary to the Bishop, 1916.

The RMS Balmoral Castle, 1917. Arthur and his parents sailed on this ship from England to Africa at the height of the German U-boat attacks during World War I.

They did not travel far. In the morning they found themselves in the midst of a veritable fleet of ships, from ocean liners to fishing boats, assembled off Goodwin Sands, just outside the mouth of the Thames. One of His Majesty's cutters was busy boarding each unrecognized vessel, to confirm its identity, and all were awaiting clearance to enter or depart. They did not proceed until the following morning. The ships steamed very slowly east, with a mine seiner escort on each side, while torpedo boats sped to and fro ahead of them. They passed close to the white cliffs of Dover, where Dover Castle could be seen glistening in the sun, and continued at the same pace. About 5 o'clock, as they were passing St. Catherine's Point, on the southernmost end of the Isle of Wight, they were flashed by a destroyer, after which the ship turned completely around and steamed in the opposite direction at good speed until signaled by another destroyer, at which time they resumed their previous course. Later, Arthur learned that a big freighter, toward the rear of the fleet, had struck a mine. They had been directed to its aid, but another ship reached them, so they were advised to resume course.

The next morning, during Arthur's early morning walk on deck, the ship entered Plymouth Sound and they were greeted by flashing lighthouses from various projecting points of land, casting long shadows in the dawn, and surrounded by craft of all kinds. There was a light breeze, and, as the day grew brighter, the sun finally touched the wavelets, "creating a thousand sparkling lights." They anchored, and it was soon light enough to see the fleet surrounding them—ocean liners, battleships, cruisers, cutters, and sloops. The swift greyhounds of the sea, the torpedo boat destroyers, were passing to and fro, protecting England's shore or her vessels.

The ship lay in Plymouth harbor five days. Soldiers came on board on one of the days, some bound for garrison duty in India, others for active duty in Mesopotamia. There were 1,600 in all, officers and cadets in first class, sergeant-majors and quartermaster sergeants in second class, and others in special troop steerage.

One afternoon, all preparations having been made for emergencies, lifeboats provisioned and swinging from their davits at the ready, and lifeboat drills having been held daily, they were as ready as could be, and it looked like they might be preparing for departure. This, in spite of the fact that there had been two ships sunk just outside the harbor during the day. In late afternoon, a destroyer from outside the harbor sent several long messages to the ship, and at 8:30, they hoisted anchor, blacked out the ship, and got under way. They were given instructions to wear their life vests and to be ready to abandon ship at any time. During the night, the *Balmoral Castle,* accompanied by a torpedo boat destroyer, separated from the fleet, and set course for New York, and then followed a circuitous course across the Atlantic to avoid U-boats. They traveled south six days before turning east again, to approach the African coast. They visited Freetown, in Sierra Leone, a British possession, before continuing on to Cape Town, South Africa.

On March 13, as the morning fog cleared, they found themselves cruising past several flat-topped mountains into Cape Town harbor. As they rounded the point, a beautiful bay unfolded before them, and they beheld the city, nestled at the foot of Table Mountain. The mountain was draped with white fog, the way it is often seen in the morning.

After the ship docked, Arthur's parents called on an acquaintance of his Uncle William. Arthur took the baggage to register the family at a hotel in Sea Point, a coastal suburb of Cape Town. There he strolled out onto the veranda, where "the vista and a warm ocean breeze created an immediate ambience of peace. The building was set back well from the road, and in front was a garden containing a fountain, beautiful trees, and bushes, where neat little phoebe-like birds flitted about. All sorts of colorful tropical vegetation abounded."

Cape Town, South Africa, and Table Mountain,
from the town side of Lion's Head, 1917. photo by Eve Andersson.

The next morning, he took a remarkable tram ride around the Lion's

Head, which began as a winding route through the streets of Cape Town, meandered higher and higher up the inside slope of the Lion's back. Higher they climbed, until they could look almost straight down into the town, then 2,000 feet down over a granite cliff to the sea.

Arthur thought Cape Town was a beautifully situated little city. Attractive villas were visible in all of the outskirts and suburbs, often resembling old Spanish architecture. The inhabitants were all good-looking and healthy. The black folks were mostly what was called "colored"—a mixture of Negro with white. There were so many Dutch in the South African Union, the circulars and bulletins were printed in both Dutch and English.

On Friday, the seventeenth, they were ready to board the train, which would take them 1,400 miles to Salisbury, the capital of Rhodesia, and from there an additional 150 miles to the city of Umtali. The final destination would be the Old Umtali Mission, a short distance beyond Umtali.

* * *

THEY BOARDED THE TRAIN in the morning. In the afternoon, watching the passing countryside, Arthur saw many graves alongside the tracks. These were a testimony to the Boer War, as were the blockhouses, built at intervals, to protect the roadbed. The next day, they passed through much interesting and scenic country. There were mountains everywhere, much like the Rockies in Montana and Wyoming. Unlike the Rockies, however, there were no tunnels, and the train wound around the hills and traversed the steep slopes, doubling back on itself, so that they could look below and see the track over which they had just come, and above to see where they were going.

Leaving the mountains, they came into the great Karroo, a vast, nearly flat country, with small, scattered, flat-topped mountains (kopjes) visible at some distance on both sides. In this area, the stations were small and not very far apart, and farm buildings were scattered about the landscape. There were no fences, and roads were merely tracks over the veld. On one of the iron telegraph poles, Arthur noted a parrot that cocked his head to watch the train pass. Iron poles were necessary, because Africa hosted hoards of white ants that would demolish wooden poles.

Early the next morning, Arthur saw his first Native family on the open veld, cooking their breakfast over a small campfire, little children running around naked, seemingly comfortable, although he felt it was rather chilly. Midday, well into the Karroo, they passed through De Aar and soon they left the kopjes behind and entered really flat country stretching to the horizon. They reached the Oranje River in the late afternoon. There, they crossed what was reported to be the best bridge in Africa on their way to Kimberly, where there were diamond mines.

On Monday, the nineteenth, they left the Karroo and came out into Khama country, which was more like Iowa, with tall waving grass and shrubs, and gentle, rolling hills. They were seeing all of this at the best time of the year, since it was just at the end of the growing season in the Southern Hemisphere. In four months, all would be dry, brown, and dusty, and certainly not as pleasant. At small towns along the way, little Native boys ran along by the train, trying to sell food. Often men and women would come to meet the train, the women with great loads on their heads, the men with skins and curios to sell to the passengers. Many wore charms and bracelets on wrists and legs, which, for the black people, were to protect their limbs from injury. Arthur noticed that the Natives were lean, attractive, and carried themselves upright. But there were quite a few with sore eyes, some with distended abdomens, and an occasional lad with a tubercular hip.

They reached South Matabeleland, in Rhodesia, about dark. Here they were met by Mr. Gates, District Superintendent of Missions from Umtali, who drove them to their hotel, where a good bath and change of clothes removed the dust and cinders of the journey. Arthur's parents soon became occupied with missionary officials, so Arthur took one of his usual reconnaissance strolls around the city, and found it very up-to-date. The roads were good, the buildings new and in good condition, and the botanical gardens were quite beautiful.

It was in Bulawayo that he learned that Rhodesian tea was even a more extensive custom than in England. There was tea at 7 o'clock in the morning, tea at 11 o'clock, the usual 4 o'clock English tea in the afternoon, and there was often a nightcap tea before retiring. Tea was served with each meal, and also at every house at which one made a call of over five minutes duration.

The next day, Mr. Gates, having learned of Arthur's experience as a printer, told him that a printer was "one of the chief needs in their mission work" at that time. Arthur said he could not help, because he was employed as secretary to his father for the year and he would be returning to go to medical school thereafter. But Mr. Gates was persistent. He showed how few translations there were for the Chimanyika people, on whom their work in Rhodesia was centered. They had only one old hymnal, two primers, and a catechism. This shortage held their work back, because only the people who came into direct touch with the mission could hear the gospel, whereas if they had a printed literature, Christianity could spread much faster. There was an obvious need, too, to inform those in the mother country of their work in order to raise funds for mission work.

Arthur resolved that he would look for a book on bookbinding, and, if he found one, he would take the job offered by Mr. Gates. He went shopping the next morning, visited three bookstores, and finally, on a shelf near the third store's exit, he found a volume called *Bookbinding*. He purchased the book, and told the district superintendent, on returning, that he would take the job.

The director of the British South Africa Company called in the forenoon, and invited the family to join his wife on a drive that afternoon, an offer they readily accepted. His wife and car arrived after lunch, and they began a 30-mile trip to Matopos, where Cecil Rhodes was buried. Rhodes was a British mining magnate and politician in South Africa, who founded the De Beers Diamond Company and the State of Rhodesia. South Africa's Rhodes University was named after him, and his estate still funds Rhodes Scholarships to Oxford University. At the grave, they left the car and went up a hill on foot. The grave was on the top of a great mountain of solid rock, in the midst of a natural cathedral of giant rocks that formed a circle around it. The grave was hollowed out of solid rock, and covered with a simple bronze plate, bearing the inscription, "Here lies the body of Cecil Rhodes."

Thursday morning, they packed and departed. The Bishop traveled north on a rather long, tiresome ride to a conference he was holding in the Belgian Congo, before returning to his work in Rhodesia. Sarah, Mr. Gates, and Arthur boarded the train for Umtali. There they were taken to the Gates's home, where they met his wife and two very sweet daughters, Harriet and Mary, ages eight and five. Arthur fell in love with them at once.

Monday, having survived April Fool's Day without any incident, they departed, about 9 o'clock, on the last leg of their journey. They took the auto stage, "a most beautiful ride, up and around the mountains, with varying scenery at every turn and new vistas of receding hills opening up at every new rise and, after topping the divide, an entirely new set of mountain scenery, and a new valley, spreading before us." They disembarked at the Christmas Pass Hotel, which is just halfway to Old Umtali, and continued on by four-mule cart that had been sent from the mission to meet them.

Chapter 4

Old Umtali Mission

1917

OLD UMTALI MISSION was nestled at the foot of Hartzell Mountain, the buildings surrounded by trees of many varieties, flowering shrubs, rose bushes, climbing vines and winding pathways, resembling a beautiful park or a botanical garden. This site was the center of the mission activities in Rhodesia, the location of the Central Training School, and it would be their home for the rest of the year. On this spring day, they arrived in time for morning tea, at the home of Mr. Robert, head of the agricultural department, and father of year-old twin boys. This was followed by dinner at Mr. James', head of the school, and, after an afternoon looking over the office and equipment, they had supper at the Roberts' home.

Old Umtali Mission, Rhodesia, near Hartzell Mountain, 1916.

Mr. Roberts continued his orientation the next day, driving him over part of the farm that was operated by the mission, and explaining features of his work. The following day, Arthur went to work. He ran off several printing jobs, such as letterheads and other items that had been waiting some time, and began to get acquainted with the abilities of the four men who would assist him: Titus Marange, the nephew of a king of the Mashona tribe; Mupsuk, a son of Marange; Jason, a *murume* (married man) with a strong sense of humor; and Tom, a cousin of Titus. They were the pick of the school, and Arthur liked them at first meeting, particularly Titus, who was quite dependable and, in the field, one of the best interpreters.

Native pastors and teachers at the mission conference, Old Umtali Mission, Rhodesia, assembled to welcome the Bishop and his wife, 1916.

A great many folks, both white and black, called to see the lady whom the black folks talked of as Mrs. Bishop. Arthur was referred to as *mwana wa Bishop*, or child of the Bishop.

In the first week, Arthur began to acclimate to the place and to his duties as printer for the mission. He ran off another two pages of the *Advance*, which was a quarterly publication for the patrons of the mission. When completed, this would be a "classy" sheet of twenty pages with half-tone illustrations. The mission was in the process of completing a sixty-page, illustrated booklet on their work in Rhodesia, of which 4,000 copies were to be made, a stupendous job for their resources "but by no means, impossible." Bulletins were needed for Saint Andrews, the Umtali white church, and 4,000 Sunday school lesson leaflets in Chimanyika each week. Besides those, there was job work for the mission, such as letterheads, billing forms, receipts, checks, and work tickets. During the year of his service, three new publications in the vernacular were planned. This was a lot to accomplish, the anticipated year's work nearly doubling all printing done since the beginning of the Rhodesian Mission Press.

Sunday, Arthur attended the Native service in the morning, which was really the only service during the day, except for a religious songfest in the afternoon. The church was full, with missionaries and other white people sitting on the platform, men on one side of the auditorium and women on the other, with children on the front seats. Mr. Howard preached through an interpreter, and the hymns were sung in Chimanyika. Arthur could pronounce the words correctly but had no idea of their meaning, except for his familiarity with the hymns in English. Midweek, in the afternoon, he overhauled and cleaned the Chandler and Price printing press to insure its continued operation.

Native students at the Old Umtali Mission, 1917.

Native Assembly Day soon arrived, which was an annual gathering of the Christian Natives from the kraals of the Rhodesian mission, each of which had a Native teacher who was trained in the Central School in Old Umtali. This gathering was special, for it was to be their first welcome for the Bishop. Although he had visited throughout the territory, many had not had the opportunity to sing him a welcome, a custom they followed with great enthusiasm. They had been arriving in kraal groups of varying sizes for two days. In the larger groups, the men with their assegais and hatchets led, and the women followed with their blankets and ground grain in a pack on their heads.

"A chariot had previously been made, and decorated with red, white, and blue bunting. When they arrived, the Bishop and his wife were helped into the chariot, which was then pulled by a team of forty Old Umtali school lads through the people-lined pathway. Each kraal, as the chariot approached, broke into their favorite song with vigor, and what a welcome it did make. Such was the triumphant procession of colors and humanity, straight to a large arch over which there were great letters, WELCOME BISHOP JOHNSON. This was decorated in patriotic bunting, and over all waved the Stars and Stripes and the Union Jack of Old England."

The business of the conference began later in the morning, with a service in which fifty-seven infants were baptized. Then the Bishop received those desiring membership into the church: there were 250 probationers and 200 full members. There followed two communion services, which lasted until suppertime, because the Natives did not wish to leave until they had heard the Bishop speak. The Bishop was a tall, imposing figure of a man, yet gentle, whose charisma transcended language, and his influence among the Natives was considerable. His sermon was delivered through David Mandisozda, the best interpreter, and held his great audience in rapt attention.

The Bishop at the Old Umtali Mission annual conference baptism, 1917.

The conference lasted a full week, closing on May 10, at which time Arthur concluded that everything was going well for the mission, and that they, and he, could look forward to a successful year. This, after he had wrestled with the "call to arms" he felt, upon learning that his country had declared war on Germany and was coming to the aid of England. He concluded that he was obligated to complete his work in

Africa and that, at the end of the year, should his country still be at war, he would enlist immediately.

A week later, the *Advance* having been completed, the pages needed stapling before mailing and the staples, ordered from the States a year previously, had still not arrived. This meant that they had to be sewed, which was tedious and time-consuming work, but they made their deadline.

His father traveled a lot, mostly to hold conferences all over Africa. He was to leave on May 19, for Beira, on the east coast, where a boat would take him to Inhambane, to conduct a conference, following which he would travel around the Cape to Angola, on the west coast, for the last conference of the year. Sarah, who accompanied him on many of these trips, would be staying with Arthur for a while, since travel on the coastal vessels was often uncomfortable. She would meet him, eventually, in Cape Town.

Arthur had learned that Miss Borland, an elderly Swedish nurse who was responsible for the operation of the dispensary for the Natives of Old Umtali and the surrounding area, was to leave on furlough the end of May. He was asked to take on this responsibility, which would mean "much study and anxiety, especially with all my other work. But such an institution cannot be closed and, since it is in line with my forthcoming life's work, I will be benefited by aiding the sick in such small ways as I can." On Monday, May 28, the keys of the dispensary were turned over to him and his initial medical work began.

Thatched Native dwelling in Rhodesia, typical of the time, 1917.

* * *

AT A TIME WHEN ARTHUR WAS ANTICIPATING seven long more months of heavy responsibility at the mission, his diary includes the text of a letter written June 3 to the district superintendent of the Rhodesian Mission: "Dear D.S. I received a letter from the States yesterday which told of how all of the single men hastened to join the colors at the first call. My friends there are all joining up and I cannot happily live here in this safety and calm. I feel that I simply must do my bit. Can you not please let me go and join the German East Campaign? Of course my work has been laid out here for the coming year, but at the time of my promising to come here, the U.S. was not in the war, and seemingly had small chance of getting in. I would dislike leaving this work unfinished and in the lurch but, if it is at all possible, I most earnestly desire to be released."

Arthur had set clinic hours at 9:45 to 10:15 a.m., apparently not expecting a lot of business, but, one day, he was called early to see a baby too sick to await call. He worked with the baby until it was better and returned to the office, returning later to the clinic where he had a number of patients waiting. He saw those with syphilis, stomachaches, coughs, colds, cuts, dysentery, and measles. Then he took care of a number of other printing jobs, ordered some materials, and, just before dinner, took care of a lad who had run a nail into his foot.

In another letter to his brother Darlow he wrote, "There is so much to do, and so many anxieties, and so great incompetence on my part. The dispensary work is a source of worry. When all goes well it is a joy, but when I get something that I have no idea how to treat, or someone I know is too sick to get better, then I begin to feel so sorry for my lack of knowledge." He went on to describe syphilis as a terrible disease, and that he had seen some people with sores all over their bodies, including their faces, so that they were hardly recognizable as human. He had four syphilitic patients who lived in separate huts up the hillside and came in each morning for treatment. The mercury treatment, he said, was very hard on them and had to be administered very carefully, and when their teeth got loose or there was too much salivation, it had to be stopped. He had one woman who was a mass of sores, "even inside of her mouth and down her throat." This was tertiary syphilis and was, virtually, terminal, and, he said, "I am afraid I can do nothing for her, but I hate to tell her so and send her away. She came from twenty-five miles away, in the hope of being cured. I am really afraid every time I go up there that she will be dead. I wish I knew more what to do."

A bare two weeks after the departure of Miss Borland, on a day when the district supervisor came out from town, he wrote, "What will one not do on a mission field?" He then proceeded to document the capacities in which he had functioned that day: (1) as a doctor, he had about thirty folks in the dispensary; (2) as a mailman, he took care of the post office while Mr. James was sick; (3) as a printer, he set up a letterhead and ran off four more pages of minutes, and planned a statistics page; (4) as business editor of the African *Advance*, he went over the next issue with the editor-in-chief, and picked out the negatives to be used for cuts; (5) as photographer, he printed and toned the *photo*s; (6) as custodian, he put up about eight pounds of books and school supplies; (7) as maintenance man, he directed the sprinkling, rolling, and marking of the tennis court; and (8) as butcher, he assisted in dispensing with two pigs.

Three days later he was called in the wee hours of the morning for a "confinement case." The missionary women were to take care of such calls while the nurse was away, but, owing to a difficult delivery, the nurse sent for Arthur, thinking he would know enough to be of more help. He knew very little, but "had read up on a little bit of everything" and possessed the nerve and common sense to accept the call. When he arrived, he found one leg of the baby delivered and the other tucked in the back of the baby's pelvis. With difficulty he managed to extract the leg but, because of weak contractions, was unable to deliver a live baby. "As a happy sequel to the story, this was a twin and the other was born alive, which pleased the mother, for the Natives have a suspicious dread of living twins and often kill one themselves if they are born alive."

Chapter 5

Duty Calls

1917–1918

I N MID-JULY, Arthur reviewed several college papers from Morningside, and discovered that two military companies had been formed at the college since war was declared, and many of his friends were joining up. "America is surely in it, and I am going to do my part." He wrote to Mr. Gates and told him that he would finish the booklet and the next *Advance,* and then would leave for the States. He also wrote to his father, explaining that his "true duty" was with the United States "during this awful war for the peace of the world and the redemption of humanity."

Eager for his parents' responses, Arthur kept busy at his multiple tasks. On the last day of August, the villa donkey, which had been getting meaner, threw Miss Quinton, one of the workers, into a tree, causing a concussion and a scalp laceration. She was able to get herself to the dispensary, and Arthur, although feeling a little anxious, succeeded in acting as though this were a run-of-the-mill problem, and cleansed and closed the wound, which was deep enough to expose the skull. Miss Quinton was much relieved when he finished. The donkey's mean behavior continued, and when it had subsequently thrown two others, Arthur took it upon himself to put his cowhand experience to work, mounted the beast, and rode him until he became docile.

A week later, he found Miss Quinton's wound to be healing well. He took advantage of the visit to enlist her services in mending the frayed top edge of the tennis net and found two old pairs of khaki trousers for material. He even sat down and helped her sew which, after they had worked together a few minutes, led her to comment that he sewed "nearly as fast and just as neatly as she did," and went on to say, "How is it that you do everything like a master—fixing pianos and typewriters, making carts, fixing heads, cleaning up a room, acting the fool, giving serious talks, etc., and even sewing!"

As he waited, Arthur was getting restless. He wrote, "At no time in my life have I been so unsettled as to the future. All I know is that I will start for America next month. Whether I will cross the Atlantic to the east coast or the Pacific to the west coast, I have no idea. Whether the folks, one or both, will accompany me, I know not. I am not sure whether I will be able to get a commission, nor my rank if I do. I am not at all certain what branch of armed service I will be able to enter, although I very much prefer aviation. I have no idea when I will get to France, nor if the war will end in one year or twenty. If I get to France, I may be killed or not, or I may be badly wounded so that I will have to change my life work. Therefore I do not know whether I will be able to attend Johns Hopkins for my surgical training or whether I will spend the remainder of my life good for nothing. I cannot see how anyone can be in a more uncertain frame of mind."

On Saturday, October 13, Arthur received a telegram from his father informing him of his and Sarah's arrival in Cape Town, after which he packed all of his earthly goods for departure on Monday. He finished up all business, traveled to Umtali, and boarded the train for the Cape. The posters he saw when he had a few hours to stroll the streets in Kimberly gave a sense of the urgency associated with the war: "Fight for Liberty—Your Forefathers Did! Do a Man's Part—Go and Fight! A Place at the Front Awaits You."

* * *

THE TRAIN ARRIVED IN CAPE TOWN Saturday morning, October 20, after a five-day journey. His mother and father met him, and he joined them at their hotel. Walking the streets, he saw wounded soldiers everywhere, most being Australians on furlough or on their way home. Many had lost limbs, and he saw one who had lost both legs at the hips. "A very sad sight, but by far the saddest were those who had lost their vision."

A few days later, his father went to Johannesburg. This postponed Arthur's departure, because he needed to await his return so he and his parents could travel together. This, he was forced to accept, although chaffing at the bit to return and join those who had already enlisted, and were, as far as he knew, already in France.

On the twenty-eighth, he received a telegram from his father, indicating that he had heard from the board and was to return to the States immediately. And so Arthur booked cabins for the three of them, on the SS *City of New York*, which would be the next ship sailing direct to New York City, departing December 24.

* * *

CHRISTMAS DAY dawned bright, and warm, and the sun shone from a cloudless sky. The ship left the dock at seven o'clock, and immediately headed for the open sea. It did not take long for the Lion's Head to begin to recede from view as they steamed northward.

During the month-long voyage, Arthur noted that the *City of New York* was the steadiest ship he had ever sailed. Even in rough weather its roll and pitch were minimal. But on January 22, after having crossed the Atlantic, and less than a day out of Boston, they encountered a storm of such severity that they had to lay to in order to prevent being blown onto Nantucket Shoal. Seas were taken over the bow and some broke on the promenade deck. Arthur, on deck to "experience the storm," was caught by one of the larger seas, which drove him to the rail, where he grabbed a boom with both arms and hung on until the force of it was spent, when he scrambled to safety.

The City of New York, the ship Arthur and his parents took home to the States, December 1917.

The storm subsided in two days and they were able to resume their course. The ship steamed into Boston Harbor on January 23, and they passed through Customs and registered at a hotel. Although his parents now lived in Africa most of the year, America was home. For Arthur, this culminated a challenging twenty-five-month journey.

* * *

ARTHUR WROTE TO DARLOW AND FAMILY, in Oregon: "Again in the U.S.A. We are staying in the 'hub' for a few days, after which New York. I hope to go on to Washington, D.C., immediately thereafter, get a commission, or whatever they will give me, and perhaps take an examination for aerial service. I hope to visit you before leaving for France, if they will let me. If I can, I'll tell you all past happenings at that time."

He then departed for New York. The next three weeks, Arthur spent doing secretarial work, exploring New York City, attending the theater, and dining at restaurants or, on invitation, at the homes of friends. Sarah went to stay with the Cruses, church friends, in Chicago. All the while his father appeared at various places, in and out of the city, preaching, speaking of their mission work in Africa and their forthcoming Centennial Celebration.

His father arrived on the ninth, and, together, they called on General Logan, Adjutant General of the State of Iowa, and old friend of the Bishop, from the Spanish-American War days. He told Arthur that he should apply to the Ordnance Department, or Aviation Signal Corps, in Washington, D.C., for a commission, since it was too late to enter Officer's Candidate School. He immediately applied to both places, still hoping to get into the air service. The business of enlisting seemed rather cumbersome and involved another wait, which frustrated him, since he was eager to get into the fray. He decided, while waiting, to enroll in Morningside and use the time profitably.

Back in Sioux City on March 21, he registered for thirteen semester credit hours at Morningside: biology I, embryology, brain, drama history, and advanced ornithology, all of which could be squeezed into two months toward his B.A. degree. Meanwhile, his father brought with him the information that there were still vacancies in the Motorcycle Dispatch Service of the Tank Section. Although the mortality rate in this service was very high, Arthur immediately applied, and then returned to his studies. He soon received notification from Washington that his application for the Tank Corps had been accepted and that he was to report to the local Draft Board for transportation to Jefferson Barracks, Missouri, from whence he would later be sent to Gettysburg, Pennsylvania. His comment was, "At last I have obtained entrance to the army, in a branch where I will see much excitement and no little danger. For several reasons, I think it is where I belong."

In a letter written on May 8, he informed his brother of his induction into the army. He had, he wrote, all red tape notwithstanding, succeeded in getting transportation to Jefferson Barracks in St. Louis. Leaving Sioux City by train, in the late morning, he had a short stop in Omaha, continuing on to arrive in St. Louis the next morning. His contingent of about seventy-five men was met by a private, who lined them up, and marched them into a tent, at Jefferson Barracks.

* * *

JEFFERSON BARRACKS was an induction center. Arthur was berthed in a tent with eleven others. He had drill all morning the second day. A few of the fellows "fell out" because of the intense heat. He sent Darlow his diary and some personal effects to keep while he was gone, and said that he and Dorothea were free to read it and to use whatever they wished of his personal effects for he wouldn't need them for some time.

Tent village, induction center, Jefferson Barracks, St. Louis, Missouri, where Arthur was inducted into the Tank Corps, c. 1918.

One morning, all who had arrived in the previous two weeks—perhaps 2,000—were assembled in the barracks. The name of each was called, with his assigned division. Arthur was rejoiced to hear his name called, just before noon, his division being the Tank Corps. Being called early meant they would be traveling early. They boarded a train bound for Camp Colt in Gettysburg, Pennsylvania.

In Gettysburg, they were trucked to Camp Colt, where they had another roll call, and stuffed bed sacks with straw and took them to the barracks where they lay them on their spring cots. They arose at 5:30 the next morning, had roll call at 6 o'clock, washed in a horse trough—their barracks having originally been built as stables—and went to mess. After cleaning quarters, they were taken to headquarters where they were questioned and officially assigned to a division. Arthur was assigned as a motorcyclist in the Tank Corps, as expected. But it was not long before he began to realize there would be little opportunity for him to advance or to distinguish himself in the Tank Corps.

One lazy afternoon, Arthur picked up a *Cosmopolitan* magazine and was gripped by a thrilling story of an oceanic yacht race. The wind and sea kept increasing, and the race became more and more challenging. One skipper dared to add more sail than the others, and this led, not to dire consequences, but to the championship. Arthur's observation: "Any feat that takes nerve and daring surely thrills me, for it strikes an answering chord in my own nature. I would love to be able to do something that takes real backbone and sinew—to battle with the elements, or anything, where the odds are several against me. That makes real life—overcoming obstacles—that, coupled with a tender and absolutely understanding love."

Arthur was getting restless with the routine at Camp Colt and anxious to get to France. By the end of June, they had but one Indian motorcycle and one small French tank in camp. The two-man tank was only about ten feet long, but quite maneuverable. Without more equipment, it seemed obvious that there would be no operational training, which apparently would be done overseas. For Arthur, a young man who yearned for action, this became increasingly boring.

On July 30, Arthur was called to the office of Captain Whittingham, his commanding officer, and told that he had a telephone message from his father, who was about to leave for Africa and would first like to see his son. He was given a furlough, and traveled to New York, there meeting his sister Dorothea. Bound for Seattle, his parents were to board a ship for Cape Town, via Japan, a week hence. The direct route, via the Atlantic, was too hazardous.

Lieutenant Arthur Johnson, fresh from Officers Training School, Camp Cole, Gettysburg, Pennsylvania, 1918.

Upon his return to camp, there were many rumors that changes were in the offing. Some of the battalions had been moved to Camp Merritt, an embarkation camp near Hoboken. Arthur, having earlier been transferred to the 301st Depot Company, was dismayed to find that his company was not to be moving. He wrote: "I'm beginning to think that this new company, into which I have been foisted, is not going to go over with the first to embark. I'm going to try my best to find out what's what, and again attempt to transfer to a unit likely to go over soon."

On August 17, following the departure of yet another soldier, the office was reduced to the two of them, Arthur and Evans, plus two orderlies to run errands. They were then covering the work previously done by six, but were just as happy to be kept busy. Evans had been appointed Private First Class and Arthur was surprised, that day, to receive a warrant as Sergeant.

He was able to transfer into Company C and gain acceptance into Officer's Training School on August 21. In his writings, he went into great detail describing the intensity of the training, including a typical day's schedule, the martial discipline, and the intense physical fitness training. He completed the course and received his commission from Washington. He noted that the others in training with him were a convivial bunch, but not much more refined than the average. One Harvard graduate, and another graduate, of Cornell, had not passed the course because they were not rough enough with the company on the drill field. He was advised, by his commanding officer that, had he not passed, it would have been for the same reason and that he should get more "hard-boiled."

Chapter 6

Off to War

1918

A RTHUR'S NEXT LETTER was written "somewhere on the Atlantic" on October 25. Most of it had to do with the rigorous program in officer's training, but mention was made of a Spanish influenza epidemic, which had been widespread through the army camps and had a fairly high mortality. Arthur felt they would not be sent overseas until it subsided.

Presumably the epidemic was subsiding by the eighteenth, which, incidentally, was his twenty-second birthday. The battalion had boarded the train for New Jersey, then a ferry to Long Island, and another train to Camp Mills. Arthur spent the next two days as a supply officer, seeing that everyone was outfitted according to orders. On November 20, they returned by train and ferry to the docks in New York City and boarded their ship, the SS *Megantic*, to begin their trans-Atlantic voyage. The ship was in convoy with escort, but the number of ships was not to be divulged. Aboard were the ships' officers and crew, the army officers, the troops (numbers not divulged), YMCA women, and Red Cross nurses.

The officers were quartered in staterooms, the crew in bunks in the Tween-Decks, with their own mess. Arthur was one of three liaison officers, each spending an eight-hour daily shift below decks with the troops. He found the troop quarters comfortable. They had good bunks to sleep in, and good food. The officers served as temporary C.O.s, saw the troops turned out for occasional musters, and censored their mail.

One evening when censoring letters, Arthur came across one written by a young soldier to his sister, in which he told her this was the first birthday he had ever spent away from home. He was obviously homesick. Arthur sent the orderly to have the fellow report to him, and when he did he wished him a happy birthday, and asked about his home folks, his life in the army, etc., which cheered him up a bit. He wrote, "the men are human—as are we—and it is not going to aid an officer to drive his men too harshly. Although severity is needed at times, a lot more can be gained usually by kindness."

The SS Megantic, Canadian troop ship, Arthur's transportation to France and the front, via England, 1918.

The voyage was without mishap, except for a number of soldiers stricken with the Spanish flu. About two days out from England, they struck a real "danger zone" and were met by an English destroyer escort. They were ordered to "don your belts, with a canteen of water, loaded revolvers, and extra ammunition, and wear them with your lifebelts until the voyage was ended," including when they were sleeping.

When they arrived in Liverpool, one man had died from the flu during the voyage. The company was marched straight through the city on the way to Knotty Ash, a tent camp for American troops, about five miles from the dock. Along the streets were many little boys and girls welcoming the "Sammies" to England. The schools were closed because of the epidemic. Few men were seen but many women waved from their windows or ran out on the sidewalks. Some waved American flags and shouted, "God bless you all."

One sweet little girl, after shaking hands with Arthur, ran after him and grasped his hand, walking by his side. The little girl told him that her father and brother were in France, and that two other brothers had been killed in the war.

They were billeted there until arrangements were made for transportation to France. The next day they marched to the train station, where an English band played a few American songs, and a designee delivered good wishes from the King before they embarked. They stopped at Birmingham, long enough for the Red Cross canteen girls to feed the troops coffee and crackers, then continued on to Winchester. Once there, they marched to a camp where the officers were berthed in chilly, rambling dormitories, two to a room, warm water and a fire being provided in the evenings only because of a shortage of firewood.

In the afternoon, Arthur and Harris, one of his company, went to town to see the sights. They visited a plain stone hall, which held King Arthur's Round Table, with the names and coats of armor of the original knights painted at their places. They attended a service in the Winchester Cathedral, which was originally built in 1079, in the time of William the Conqueror. They viewed the tomb of the bishop, who founded Winchester College and the New College Oxford, and were given a bit of history and a tour of the Deanery by a woman of the community. The porter then proudly conducted them through the college, which was older then even Rugby or Eton, pointing out the stained glass windows, which were among the most notable in England.

They departed the next day by train for the Southampton docks. Their ship was the USS *Yale*, and she was loaded to the gunwales with troops, all cabins and even passageways occupied. They left in the evening, and all lights were extinguished when they retired.

✳ ✳ ✳

ARTHUR ROSE AT 4:30 the next morning, shaved, and shined his shoes in preparation for arrival in France. They docked in Le Havre, at the mouth of the Seine, at 7:30. They marched along cobblestone streets, through town, passing many stone buildings and nice residences, to Camp Sévigné, an English camp on a hill.

The next day at midnight, the troops were assembled and left Camp Sévigné, to take the train from Le Havre at 2 o'clock in the morning. Most troop movements in the theater of operations took place after dark. It was November 7. Their destination was unknown. The men were put in third class, ten to a train compartment, the officers, six each, in a second-class compartment. Crowded as they were, they were fortunate, since many troops were shipped in boxcars. The train was not heated and it was chilly. For the three days of their journey, they sat in high-backed, narrow seats, fully clothed, with little room for their feet.

The northern Brittany landscape they traversed was very hilly and they passed through many tunnels. "The whole countryside was a grand riot of autumnal beauty—the trees and foliage in all shades of browns and reds and yellows—really as beautiful as any fall scene I have ever witnessed. Instead of wire fences, scenic hedges and stone walls formed the division between fields. The towns, although in many respects like those in England, had a quaintness all their own, the houses being especially attractive."

For meals, they had a can of sardines and a loaf of bread between the six of them. Just west of Paris, they passed many scattered graves of French soldiers, who were victims of engagements in that region in 1914. Crosses, sometimes bounded by little log fences, stood in fertile fields, and farmers had plowed around them. They saw many camouflaged cars standing on the tracks, some carrying severely damaged military equipment. Red Cross trains passed them frequently, bearing wounded soldiers from the front. News came that the German Ambassador was on his way to the Eastern Front to sign the armistice, and the French soldiers on board were exuberant, and ran about crying, *"La guerre est finie! La guerre est finie!"*

With six in an unheated five-by-nine-foot compartment, with little rest, and little but sardines and bread to eat, they were ready to arrive somewhere . . . anywhere! They passed through General Pershing's headquarters in Chaumont, and stopped at Langres at two o'clock in the morning. At seven o'clock they moved four miles to their tank training site. A two-mile hike took them from there, through one typical French village to another, Cohons, where they would be staying.

The men were billeted in various stables around town, and the officers were installed in homes and chalets. Nestled among the hills, this was a typical French village with broader main streets and narrow side streets, some climbing up very steep grades to access chateaus on the hillsides. The village was picturesque, filled with ancient moss- or vine-covered stone-block houses and shops. Many structures housed cattle and chickens in addition to the peasant families, who farmed the surrounding land. Cattle and chickens roamed the streets, contributing to the setting and, to a certain extent, the aroma. Fresh water was piped from springs in the hills under the street, filling occasional cisterns that served as laundry facilities and domestic water.

Arthur and four other officers were billeted in a room in an old château about 300 yards up a steep hillside. A window in the rear looked up into fall foliage and evergreens, and one in front looked down upon many mossy, tiled roofs of the town, an ancient church, and the surrounding serene countryside. Some walls were crumbling, and it was very "rustic." Come evening, each spread their bedding—three wool blankets—on the stone floor, and retired.

An early spring morning in Cohons, France, 1919. Arthur takes advantage of the balmy weather to do his morning shave in the sun.

After *le déjeuner* the next morning, it being Sunday, bells in the tower of the neighboring *petite église* announced the morning service, and he and Harris decided to attend. The women of the village, dressed in their Sunday finery, "with hats, and bustles, and all," were converging on the ancient building, and they joined them as they passed through the ancient wooden doors. After crossing themselves with holy water, as those ahead of them did, they were shown to an old wooden pew by a wizened, white-haired old man. Here they knelt, entered, and took their seat, as others had done. The entire service was chanted in French, with many incantations, much kneeling and crossing. Occasionally, a little bell would ring, which was a signal for the congregation to bow. At a second tinkle, the bow was a little deeper, and, at a third, deeper still. The priest delivered a brief sermon, but his French was a little too much for Arthur, who gained only the gist of something about the brotherhood of man.

They learned that they were responsible for making arrangements for their furnishings and their care. They were allowed to purchase their own food at the commissary, and to find someone to cook for them, if they wished. In this regard, Arthur's smattering of the language certainly came in handy. The first evening, he negotiated with a neighbor, Mme. Nicard, to cook their meals for ten francs (two dollars) a day. Adding the cost of food, they found that the total cost for board, for each of them, would come to about 80 cents a day. If they wanted heat, they needed to purchase wood to burn in the fireplace, when it was available.

Monday evening, just after retreat, they heard an unusual amount of chattering in the streets, followed shortly by a loud ringing of the church bells. Going among the people, they found them loudly, and happily, proclaiming, *"La guerre est fini! La guerre est fini!"* And this time it was true, for an armistice had been signed, amounting to almost unconditional surrender. Arthur wrote, "Not knowing whether to be glad or sorry, and rather expecting this news, it left me exactly as it found me, except with a desire to get back to the business of my education."

The war ended before it began for the 304th Tank Corps Battalion. They adapted to life in the village of Cohons, and their routine became relatively comfortable. Arthur was busy managing camp supplies while the troops were drilled and kept in shape, but he chafed at wasting time when he could be pursuing his medical training. In early December, they learned from the newspapers that their unit was to be one of the first to go home. The officers were given the option of transferring to the Motor Transportation Corps and extending in France. Arthur was not pleased when he found that he was being chosen as one of two officers to remain with six men, as a skeleton crew of the Tank Corps.

On Sunday, December 15, Arthur wrote, "Christmas is nearly here— the glad season that heretofore I have always spent with Father and Mother—and I am many thousand miles away from them, or anyone with whom I have the least in common. Of course, my associates here are fine fellows, but they are used to an entirely different life than I. They care nothing for religion—never attend church; they swear and drink, and the room is often filled with obscene language which makes me absolutely heartsick. The only way I get along with them so well is by ignoring them, in a way. If there were but one human being who could be my friend and to whom I could talk, naturally, conditions would be improved 100 percent."

He took solace in beauty, and roamed about the château grounds, finding them enchanting. "Being on the mountainside, the grounds were laid out in terraces, resembling the seven hanging gardens of Babylon, to each successive one of which, old, moss-covered, partially hidden, stone steps led. Here and there, one would come upon cave-like openings, which might contain stone benches, and, occasionally, a stone stairway which, when followed, would lead to the next terrace. There, after following a labyrinthine path lined with dense shrubbery, one would suddenly come upon a miniature lake, in which goldfish could be seen, gaily swimming about. A little farther along, through the shrubbery, one could see a beautiful vista of gardens, and little waterfalls fed by a mountain stream, spilling from one terrace to another. Sometimes one would find, at the end of an almost obscured path, a cleared area surrounded by shrubbery, overhung by the branches of evergreen trees, where would be old stone benches facing marble statuary of great age."

Through December and January, members of the company had transferred to the Motor Transport Corps from time to time, slowly diminishing the numbers in Cohons. These were deployed elsewhere in France, involved in cleanup and occupation activities. One, Lieutenant MacLean, returned for a visit and told of having been through Verdun and Rheims with a train of trucks bound for the army of occupation. He reported that conditions there were worse than could be imagined. All buildings in Verdun were ruined. In Rheims, the great cathedral was virtually destroyed, and out of a population of 150,000, only 2,000 remained. Bob Kennedy, also a transfer, wrote from Amiens that he was in charge of a truck train that went to the old battle fields to pick up bodies, some of which had lain there for months, grim reminders of the fortunes of war."

Arthur soon received an order to get everything ready for "overseas." They boarded a train for the trip to Castillon, 50 kilometers from Bordeaux, the second largest city in France. At Castillon, an attractive city, late on Thursday afternoon, the whole trainload disembarked and lined up in a large public square. Billeting began with the troops, and it was dark by the time they came to the officers. By the time they reached B Company, they must have run out of accommodations in the city, for Arthur and four others were driven to a château at 5 kilometers distance. Viewed in the moonlight as they approached and illuminated as their headlights swung around, the buildings and grounds were mysterious and magnificent. They were welcomed at the door by the caretaker's wife, who greeted them politely, told them their rooms were ready, and escorted them down a long corridor. In flickering candlelight, they passed swords, paintings, and ornate portraits on the walls. He was shown into a large, candle-lit room with its canopied double bed, fireplace, and mirrors, which was to serve as his room for at least a month, when the owner would return from the war. He drifted off to sleep, enfolded in the fine feather bed.

Château de Fompeyres, where Arthur and three other officers were billeted for a month on their way home, Castillon, France, March 1917.

* * *

ARTHUR LEARNED that the American Expeditionary Forces were offering a few scholarships to both French and English universities, so he applied to Oxford University on the chance that he might be chosen. The same day, in the afternoon, he was offered the position of Personnel Officer of his company, the highest rank short of Commanding Officer. Concerned that this appointment would compromise his opportunity to be chosen for a scholarship, he declined.

A transfer came in for Arthur to Oxford University, where he had been accepted for one term. He was to be on detached service and to receive his current salary while there. Arthur spent a few days in Paris, visiting many sites, before he boarded a train at Navarre Station on March 4, bound for Le Havre.

Chapter 7

Oxford

1919

ARTHUR LANDED IN SOUTHAMPTON and boarded a special American student train, which arrived in Liverpool about 2 a.m. the following morning. He went to Knotty Ash Camp, where he had been before, where he spent the coldest night he had experienced since joining the army. He arose early, filled out cards expressing British school preferences, reasons, and personal qualifications. He spent ten days in Liverpool, and while there, he met two other fellows from Morningside, and was impressed that three from his own university would be spending a term at a British institution.

He checked the bulletin board daily, and on the seventeenth, was delighted to find himself, "on the first assignment to Oxford." He would be at Oxford from April until June. When he and his cohorts arrived by train, he was taken to temporary quarters in St. Edmund Hall. They were shown to their rooms, which were 600 years old. They had dinner in the dining hall, an edifice about the same age.

Arthur was advised to take chemistry, and this fit a premedical curriculum, so he was happy to do so. He found rooms in the heart of Oxford, at 34 St. John's Street, and moved in. He was granted permission to spend the month until the term began with his family at Sunderland. He then caught an evening train for Sunderland. Sunderland, on the North Sea in northern England, was the home of his father's brother William, his aunt Ethel, and their two daughters, his cousins. After changing at York and again at Newcastle, he reached Sunderland at about 7 a.m. and took a cab "home." This had become, in his mind, his home away from home. He was welcomed by the family, who were delighted to see him, and was soon enfolded into the household routine.

*Arthur's "digs," at 34 St. John's Street, Oxford University,
fifty miles north of London, England, March to June 1918.*

In a letter to Darlow, he wrote, "The girls, Irene and Winifred, have
to leave at 8:30 each morning for their schools, and do not return until
4 o'clock in the afternoon." Further, his schedule included studying or
writing letters during the day, and he had "gone through" some books
on evolution and was "taking up" anthropology, after which he intended
to "get through" some general chemistry before the term began on April
25. When the girls came home, it became playtime, and they would
play ping pong or go to a movie. On weekends, they often had picnics
on the shore. They had an "especially good time," one Saturday, when
they ate their picnic lunch in the sun, on a large rock, with the North
Sea lapping at its base, and spent the afternoon climbing along ledges
in the rocks, exploring caves, hunting for sea anemones, and looking at
various mollusks on the sea floor after the tide went out.

His month at Sunderland was very restful. His relatives were very
good to him. Aunt Ethel thought of him as a son that she never had,
and she and the girls were very fond of him. She confided in him that
she sometimes wished Will were a little more like Sam (Arthur's father),
who was a bit more impulsive and lovable and whom Arthur resembled.
The girls said they were most proud of Uncle Sam, who was the only
relative who had the courage to venture forth to America, and who had
achieved "one of the highest offices in the world" (the Bishopric).

This set Arthur to musing: "I think that Providence has provided wisely, because, if father had married someone like Ethel, or she, someone like him, neither couple would have amounted to so much. It really is a fact, although Father would not admit it, that Mother had a large share in shaping his destiny. She has always held him level, and spurred him on. In fact, I understand, perhaps with a great degree of truth, that it was she, originally, who made a preacher out of him—wisely, I think later events proved. However, Dad is the most lovable man in the world, with all of his impulsiveness and so forth, and I would not change him. They all tell me, here, that I am certainly a chip off the old block, considering fondness for the ladies and all."

He left Sunderland, and arrived in Oxford on April 25, and checked in at his "digs" on St. John's Street, looking forward to matriculation.

*** * ***

ARTHUR APPLIED TO OXFORD because the opportunity was afforded; because it was one of the most famous educational institutions in the world; and, probably more important, because it had been his father's school. The next day, he visited the censor, where he was asked many questions, filled out a number of forms, paid 15 pounds and 6 pence for university and delegacy charges, and was told that he would be matriculated the following Saturday and to "come in his best." He then called on his tutor, Mr. Whiston, from Jesus College, who gave him "a list of expensive books to purchase" and said that he would explain more when the lecture lists were out.

He learned that, with his college credits from America and his military service, he was exempt from preliminary examinations and passed "right to Final Honors School." Honors, he explained in a letter to his father, were considerably more difficult than a Pass Degree, and regarded of much higher value. The army was paying for one term but Arthur was toying with the idea of completing his undergraduate work there.

His tutor had suggested that he might investigate sports while waiting to be matriculated, and he was invited to St. Catherine's Sports Club that same afternoon. This was one club, of many, organized for those with common interests and available to him. He joined, and indicated that he was trying to get a little pep into the club, and get them to rejuvenate their barge and start athletics, and so forth. They thought that, just because they were crowded on account of post-service conditions, they could not begin the usual prewar sports all at once. "At any rate we have the tennis court started and I hope will get out the boats before long." His day for matriculation, he had a conference with Mr. Whiston in the morning, followed by matriculation at 2 p.m. Together, they outlined a schedule of chemistry classes. He was also urged to participate in sports in the afternoons.

He outlined his schedule: academic classes, mostly in the mornings; sports, mostly in the afternoons, and; study periods, mostly in the evenings. Recreation was listed only on Saturday afternoons, and Sundays were devoted to church, letter writing, and rest.

After lunch, he and nine other "non-colls," who had been accepted, were escorted by the delegacy clerks to the Divinity School. This school was built in 1460, and the hall, where matriculation was to occur, had been used for that purpose, from the Princes of Wales down to Arthur. Every student signed his name in the big Matriculation Volume, seated himself, and awaited the appearance of the Vice-Chancellor. When he arrived, he signed each of the student cards, calling each of them forward in turn to receive their card and a copy of the University Statutes. Then, following a very short speech in Latin, all were discharged, having been matriculated in "the greatest seat of conservative education in the world."

The Oxford Divinity School building (1919), where students had matriculated since it was built in 1460.

To his father, he wrote, "The morning after matriculation, I attended my first lecture by Mr. Chattaway at 9 o'clock. He chatted away on general chemistry, beginning with sodium and potassium, in a most breezy and humorous style. After lab and dinner, I kept an appointment I had made with the captain of our rowing club and appeared at the docks at 2 o'clock dressed, quite correctly, in "shorts," vest, and blazer, and took my first lesson in professional rowing. The captain complimented me on the way I 'got on' and I was told to be down at the same time each Monday, Wednesday, and Friday." Rowing, which had been discontinued during the war as had most sports, was just being re-instituted.

About Oxford, he said, "One never knows how many streets are going to enter a square, nor could one ever surmise where any of the streets were going after leaving it. A stranger in Oxford—this is true of any English town—often finds himself where he began, when he thought he was going elsewhere. Rather disconcerting, at least. I am told that the main streets of the town were originally laid out on existing cow paths. If this be so, all that I can say is that early Britain gave sustenance to some very disorganized cows."

Non-college student rooms in Oxford consisted of a "sitter," or sitting room, and a "bedder," or bedroom. His sitter was on the ground floor, with a front window facing on the cobblestone street. It was a medium-sized room with a carpet that had seen a number of years' wear. It had a fireplace, as did every sitting room in England since there was no central heating. For a shilling a day, the landlady would keep a fire going. There was a smattering of furniture, sufficient for a somewhat Spartan existence. Even so, in the evenings, with a fire going and the lamp emitting "a full 15 watts worth of light," it was quite cozy.

His bedder was two flights up at the back of the house. "It was plainly furnished with similar carpet and wall paper, but not so pretentious; a double bed with a rather pretty English quilt and bolster; a commode with a pitcher on top and a catcher inside. The pitcher was kept full of water, which was poured into the large porcelain washbowl for use. Each morning the landlady would bring up a smaller pitcher of hot water for the morning shave." It was an English (and family) custom to take a cold tub or shower every morning. "For your cold tub, you would put this wash basin on the floor and sponge cold water over yourself, trying to keep as much of it as possible in the bowl. Carried out each morning, the custom was more an ordeal for building character, in the winter, than a pleasure. One must admit, however, that the thrill that ensued, after a brisk rubdown, was worth the—sometimes hesitant—beginning.

"Thirty-four St. John's Place was owned by two spinster ladies of rather venerable age, who had inherited the place from their father, who had, doubtless, inherited it from his, and so on. A compliment would bring most excellent service, and the two sisters would outdo themselves to make their paying guest comfortable, if their efforts were appreciated. These estimable and chaste ladies (I am sure I speak the truth) were members and most regular attendants at the Church of England."

"Meals were served in the sitter, in front of the fireplace, provided the daily shilling had been afforded, and consisted of whatever was desired, provided this had been communicated in advance. In typical English fashion, breakfast would be served at seven o'clock, and would doubtless include eggs, probably soft-boiled, toast and marmalade, as well as tea. There could be a morning tea at eleven o'clock, if lectures allowed, and the next meal would be lunch, which usually included a chop or mutton cutlet, perhaps with a light broth, or soup, toast, and tea. Afternoon tea is an institution. One may desire to have a friend or two, male or female, in his digs, which is perfectly proper, or one may make arrangements to meet the friend in some popular or quiet tea room in town, or—and this is the very finest—one takes his friend for a delightful trip, by canoe, or punt, up the magic Charwell River, to any one of a number of quaint rural tea houses, nestled back in the shrubs along the river bank, where tea will be served on a delightful lawn, under a tree, or a canopy, over the river steep.

"In many places, there will be high tea at about six o'clock, where bread is sliced thin, buttered, and served on the table, which also contains cold meats, and any number of different kinds of cheeses, a relish, and tea, with sugar and cream. This is a delightfully relaxing affair, where one is supposed to dawdle with the food, sipping the tea slowly, and, engage in intellectual conversation." This left about two hours for study, or a friendly stroll, or just davenport conversation until the last meal, supper, which was about 9 o'clock, and consisted of some fine roast and all the accompaniments.

"Never ask for a cup of coffee in England. You wouldn't like it if you are used to real American coffee. But you will like the tea, as only the English can make it. It must be brewed in an earthenware pot—and the pot must have been prewarmed by pouring in some boiling hot water, letting it stand for a short time, then pouring it out again—putting in the tea leaves—then adding water which is not boiling but just freshly boiled. Then, let the pot stand a few minutes, pour out a cup and pour it back into the pot. This settles the leaves and, after another moment's standing, delicious, clear cups of tea will be the result, which you sip slowly and thoughtfully, in company with your friend or friends, meanwhile discussing any topic in the world in the most delightful and satisfying manner. This is true whether the tea is in one's digs, or in a tearoom in London. Tea is a wonderful institution and I am entirely won over to it without any mental reservation."

Students living within the college also had a bedder and a sitter. These were in a building at the college, approached by a winding stair with rooms at each landing. Each stairway was attended by a scout, who was an attendant for the student as well as a monitor, to see that their behavior conformed to the statutes. The scout was very helpful, always polite yet very firm. He awakened the student in the morning. Sufficient time was allowed, before attendance at chapel. Failure to attend chapel would be reported to the dean, and could result in gating—being restricted to campus—and perhaps fining, say, a shilling per day of confinement. After chapel, the student returned to his room for "brekker," which was served by the scout. If the student had attended roll call, scantily clad over his pajamas, and rolled back into bed, the scout would place his meal before the fireplace to keep warm.

A student could invite friends to his room for brekker and have the scout serve an extra course. The meal would be similar to that described for the man in digs served by his landlady. In the colleges, luncheon was usually light, consisting of bread and marmalade or other preserves, or cheese, and tea or beer. All students were back in their college by 4 o'clock for afternoon tea, which was held in their rooms, with as many as they wished to invite, or in a club, or in the common room. After tea, usually about 4 o'clock, until dinner at 7 o'clock, the student usually repaired to his room, where he could review his lekker notes of the day or, toward examination time, bone up for the exams.

Dinner was a formal event at all colleges. It was held in a great hall, possibly built several hundred years ago, with framed portraits of former college dons adorning oak-paneled walls containing artistic stained glass windows, all beneath a high, hand-wrought arched ceiling. Oak tables, extending the length of the hall, seated the students, whose main courses were served on oaken platters, while a shorter table on an elevated platform at one end seated the dons, who monitored the mealtime behavior. If any altercation arose during the meal among the undergraduates, it was settled by the dons who would, in appropriate cases, mete out punishment.

After dinner, students could go to the store for their wines and desserts. There, they might help themselves to cigars, cigarettes, varieties of fruits and sweets, all of which were recorded and for which they received a "battles" (bill) at the end of the month. Then to someone's room, the common room, or to a club meeting to enjoy dessert and a smoke before returning to their own room to study or, occasionally, going to town for the evening. There were a number of clubs in Oxford, each representing common interests of their members.

When going to town, students were required to wear a cap (mortar board) and gown (short version of that worn at graduation), except for the military, who wore their uniforms. They were not to be seen in the pubs and bars, which were monitored by two university proctors. They were required to pass through the gate before 9 o'clock, and return by 10 o'clock, to avoid a fine. After 10, the fine was thruppence; after 11, a pound or more. Often, after midnight, a student would stay out all night to avoid detection—apparently there was no bed check.

Attendance at lekkers was not mandatory. If, on a bright, sunny day in spring, a student preferred to spend his time in a punt, or a canoe, on the classic Isis, or the charming Charwell, he was at perfect liberty to do so. It was this liberty, as far as studies were concerned, that was the chief difference between undergraduate life in America and England. One could obtain a degree in his own time—could proceed as rapidly or as slowly as he wished. The tutor would informally quiz the student, from time to time, and advise how to supplement his study as needed. The purpose was the accumulation of knowledge toward the degree, not the isolated learning of the single subject. A comprehensive examination would not be administered until the tutor and the student thought he was ready.

Arthur had taken it upon himself to write an exhaustive history of Oxford, beginning in the first century A.D., and including all its colleges, as well as an explanation as to how the educational system worked. He wrote: "I found in St. Catherine's some very charming and intelligent gentlemen, not only Englishmen but also men from India, Persia, and China. Some of the most enjoyable tennis games I have ever played were with a Hindu, and the talks on world conditions and philosophy which we had of an evening about the fireplace, in St. Caths, will long be remembered as the most cultural of my educative period. Whether in college, or St. Catherine's, one meets real men—men who are thinkers and doers, educated men, well-read men, sporting men. One cannot find a better or a cleaner sportsman than an Oxford undergraduate."

The spring term, however, was not for serious study. Young men's fancies strayed, there, as in America, at this time of year. "Each afternoon, there was a general exodus to the streams. One attended his lekkers, taking copious notes, then ran to his canoe or punt to enjoy lazing in the shade of the magnificent and stately elms, or maples, that lined the banks of the graceful Char. Here he might sit and discuss philosophy with his student companion, or love, with a feminine companion, or just revise his notes and orient himself, mentally, with his courses, alone.

"There is nothing more lovely than an English spring, when the more or less constant rains let up. One can see why the poets of this right little, tight little isle cannot but burst into song at this season of the year. Whether one is punting or canoeing along the peaceful, winding streams with the fresh trees, opening flowers and warm, exhilarating air, or cycling along the equally winding and beautiful roads of the English countryside, one is filled with joyous song and utter, peaceful tranquility."

Elsmore, who originally taught Arthur the art of punting, was his frequent companion during his Oxford stay. He had introduced her in a letter to his parents: "My Oxford girlfriend is a leading jeweler's daughter, Alice Elsmore Atkin: she is a very good dancer, punts in true Oxford form, and is a very good companion, since she knows how to be serious when the occasion demands." Further, he explained, she was an intelligent and refined young lady, well read, and was conversant with many things, having spent two years in Haddon College.

Arthur described the punt as "a flat-bottom boat, about eighteen or twenty feet long and perhaps four feet wide, with the middle six or eight feet used for sitting or reclining. This is filled with cushions and rugs and has seat backs at either end so that one can sit or lie full-length among the cushions and enjoy perfect rest and relaxation. Behind the seat backs at either end of this section are some slots for about four feet, then a short deck to the ends of the punt. The punter stands on the slats and propels the boat by means of a long pole, which reaches to the bottom of the river, this being of somewhat uniform depth and one becomes very skillful at this form of propulsion. Of course, when learning, oftentimes one may give a mighty heave on the pole and find that it is stuck in the soft bottom. Not desiring to lose the pole, he may hang onto it, and lose the punt, and be left dangling in midair until he is rescued or wades ashore, dripping wet—rather embarrassed, particularly if his companion is a lady friend."

Arthur spent a modicum of time on his studies, later commenting that he had been given credit for the term in chemistry. He had not, however, really learned much about it. He spent many hours punting on the Thames, cycling along English country roads, and socializing, or simply enjoying the English springtime. Before the term ended in June, the record stops, and there is a gap until October 1919, at the University of Oregon in Portland.

Chapter 8

Medical School

1919–1923

ARTHUR ENTERED THE UNIVERSITY OF OREGON MEDICAL SCHOOL in Portland in October 1919, to start his pre-med studies. Up until this time, there had been only casual mention in his diary of his education. But the medical school experience would be different, for he would have to devote the great majority of his time to study.

Before he was even settled in his room in the YMCA, he encountered a catastrophe. An overnight guest had been put in the room with him, who was still sleeping when Arthur went to class, but who was gone when he returned. Gone, also, were many of his possessions. The manager of his father's emergency account gave him enough money to replace his lost belongings.

He received a letter from his father dated March 19, and was surprised to learn that both parents were upset at the story of his experiences in France. He responded: "I note that you got me entirely wrong concerning my experiences in France. I am sure after I tell you of them in person, you will change your mind, even to the imbibing of light wines at the times I mentioned." Suspecting that his mother was the source of the parental concern, he added, "You ought to know, dearest mother, that I could not do anything far wrong. I couldn't very well with the kind of training I have had."

He wrote to his brother, "Tomorrow is a holiday at school but I intend to put most of it on study. I flunked miserably in a quiz today in anatomy, so I've got to spend more time on it." And, in a letter to his father, nearly a month later, he outlined the courses he was taking and, interestingly, explained that, "A medical course, these days, is just a grind all year long—as much as the last week or two plugging for exams in a liberal arts school. That is, the first two years are that way. If those two years are ever completed, the next two should be very interesting."

He explained to his father that he was really concerned about anatomy. "In anatomy, we finish the head and neck entirely before the exam next week and, believe me, when one has to learn every branch of every cranial and cervical nerve, and every branch of those branches, as well as every artery and branches and subbranches, not to mention the dural sinuses, veins of brain and face, glands of all kinds, origin and insertion of muscles, contents and boundaries of triangles of the neck, all special sense organs, and many other things, one's brain becomes incapable of assimilating anything more."

Meanwhile, Darlow and Arthur had been shocked when they received a cable in November from their parents in Cape Town: "Our daughter is to be married Nov. 19." She was to become Mrs. Graham Botha. They were surprised because they thought Dorothea—then eighteen years of age—was wiser than to marry before she had completed her education. A letter from Dorothea to her mother, who apparently had some misgivings, was forwarded a few weeks after the cable, assuring Sarah how considerate her husband was and how happy she was. The letter mollified them all somewhat, but the marriage also meant that Dorothea would remain in South Africa and it would be long before her brothers saw her again.

His father apparently took Arthur to task about his spending habits, because on in a letter written on January 23, 1920, he responded: "You reprimand me for something that I am not doing at all. You say that you have neither money to give away nor money to lend, nor for the recipient thereof to spend on any member of the fair sex. First, let me say that I haven't spent five dollars on girls since I returned to the United States, and second, I am drawing just fifty dollars a month on your account. If you stop to consider the high cost of everything, you will be surprised that I am able to make such an amount do: eggs are 70 cents a dozen; butter, 80 cents a pound; flour $14 a barrel; sugar, $18 a sack; a former $25 suit now costs $60, and a former $4 pair of shoes $12. In addition, I have made a $25 payment on a microscope and have paid a similar amount to my fraternity. I am rooming at the YMCA where, although there are many features that are not enviable, I share a room with a roommate for $12 a month, which is less than any decent room in town. I board at an old-fashioned boarding house that provides as inexpensive and wholesome meals as can be found.

"I would like to impress upon you—if it be possible in the light of past events—that I do think seriously of my life work. I have not done nearly so well as I would like in my studies thus far but it is not from lack of trying. I had simply forgotten how to study and it took the first three months to get back into the swing of it. Although I received only 77 percent in my first chemistry examination, I received 88 percent in my last one, showing a definite improvement. I am also doing much better on the thorax in anatomy. Being out of school three years certainly does make a difference." Arthur also explained to his father that since coming west, he carried out several assignments that gave him credit toward a B.A. in liberal arts from Morningside. And coupled with the completion of the year at Oregon, this degree would be granted.

He went on: "My chief difficulty in chemistry came because of the fact that physiological chemistry is based quite largely on organic chemistry, and all the organic I ever received was in lectures at Oxford, not one of which I understood, although the folks here gave me credit. I, therefore, spent the first month reviewing and outlining organic chemistry for my own understanding. This review took a great deal of time, not only from my biochemistry but also from my other work, and that is probably one reason for my poor start. We finish chemistry the first of March and then jump right into bacteriology. Believe me, they surely crowd the first two years to overflowing. How glad I will be if I can finish them successfully, but I need your sympathy, instead of your lack of trust, to help me."

By April, Arthur was getting on much better with his schoolwork. In physiology, bacteriology, and embryology he was "up with perhaps the five best students in the class of fifty." On April 14, 1920, still mending fences, in a letter to his mother he wrote: "Schoolwork and girls never did go together successfully with me, and I have enough sense, now, to realize that fact. Of course I take an odd girl, now and again, to Saturday night parties that are scheduled so I can attend, but I haven't been with the same girl twice in succession since coming west. I feel I have come to realize that life is not frivolity—that the worthwhile things are those which take effort."

Arthur was quite a romantic, and had enjoyed the company of the ladies. An entry in his diary from September 2, 1920, addresses this: "Tonight I took my favorite stroll along the cliff overlooking the most majestic of all rivers, the mighty Columbia. I grew pensive—yes, and a little sad. Surely there is such a thing as love. There must be. I had seen those who seemed to be experiencing the true, lasting kind—even after years of married life—few, its true, but some. Love, in its best, the purest of all emotions. If it really is, what is it? It cannot be defined any more than hope—or faith. It is intangible, and, I almost said, 'unreal.' It seems real, to certain, more fortunate ones! But, I have never loved. I've always wanted to—even to the extent of thinking I did, but it is only that I was in love with love and, naturally, not lasting. I wonder if I will ever find a girl who will arouse this wonderful emotion in me—really—one that lasts. I hope so, but I feel more and more as though there is no one who will ever effect this glorious miracle. Had I been financially able to marry years ago, when I thought I loved with all the idealism of youth, I would probably have found it, but now, when heart is more and more subject to brain and when idealism has been all but blasted by contact with rough reality, I am skeptical. Reason and judgment are deadly enemies of love and romance. However, no man knoweth what the future may hold and it is the right of a mortal to possess immortal hope."

✳ ✳ ✳

THE NEXT RECORD was a long letter to his father dated November 7, 1921. It was written from Chicago after Arthur had transferred to Northwestern University for his continuing medical education. He had successfully completed the year at the University of Oregon and, taking into consideration his transferred credits, obtained his Bachelor of Science degree.

He filled a page-long paragraph on Chicago which dwelt with the sexual promiscuity of the members of his medical fraternity, the young women who were fully as "open" as the women in France, the predominance of saloons and gambling establishments in the city, the criminal element, which included the mayor and chief of police who condoned all of this. He felt, somewhat, like a fish out of water. "I want to get married and get a home of my own where I will be removed from temptation. Of course I will not fall, my ideals have been drilled into me in my early training, but I get so lonesome that I do desire human and feminine companionship—at times very keenly."

Northwestern University Medical School, in Chicago, 1923.

He told his father that schoolwork was going wonderfully well. "I am enjoying it intensely—it is so practical. And right here, I cannot help giving you an illustration of the standing of Northwestern University Medical School. There is a chap here, in the junior class, who transferred from Harvard, which is supposed to be one of the best schools in the country. When asked why he did not continue his work there, he responded that Northwestern was the better school—Harvard was too theoretical—Northwestern was practical. But, believe me, it keeps us working. The assignments are long and require much reading, but they are much more interesting than last year. I have had to spend my Sunday mornings and afternoons in study, but have always gone to Epworth League and church at night."

On the last page, he looked ahead, wondering where he might spend his medical internship. For this, he thought he might need his father's advice, perhaps his influence, so he could find himself in a position of learning to do things other than pass catheters and do blood counts, which was what he had heard some internships comprised.

With the arrival of spring 1922, he wrote to his brother. In this letter, we gain a nostalgic glimpse into the carefree Arthur of his earlier days. "During the five Easter vacation days, I went with a Hyde Park family to the Sand Dunes where they have a summer cottage. I gained a coat of tan and a very nice rest from studies. The days were spent in taking a morning dip in the lake (it was cold) and rambling through the wooded sand dunes observing the newly arrived birds as well as the emerging spring flowers." This location was on the shore of Lake Michigan and there was a "typical tamarack swamp, just as pictured in Gene Stratton Porter's books." There was canoeing, when the lake was calm, and stargazing in the evenings.

He mentioned that he sometimes attended Trinity Church, which was within a block of the house, and that the pastor seemed a good Christian but not much of a preacher, and people were, as most Episcopalians, very sufficient unto themselves. He illustrated this, by quoting what a longtime lady member of the church told him, after a sermon on missionaries. "I do not see why we have to be bothered with all the heathen in the world. We have enough to do to look after our own church." Having had a missionary experience, he felt this was quite a different attitude from most Methodists.

Six months later, in a letter to his parents, he was found deeply engaged in his studies, "intensely interested" in what he was doing and doing it well. This, most likely, was the reason for his infrequent correspondence. He went over most of his clinical services in some detail and then came to the important issue of his future: "And that brings me to the question that you have broached in two or three recent letters—that of my future work. I have rather wanted to feel that my work lay in Africa, because I somehow felt that would please you, and also, I wanted to be near you. I have not, however, been able to make myself feel that I can do the most for God and humanity in Africa, and I have prayed about it much before saying this. As you know, I have a personality that seems to appeal to people, among such as one dwells, in America. I do not say this boastingly, for it is not of my making. This is my honest feeling in the matter and is not a hasty or a selfish conclusion. It is not that I want to make money, at least for myself, although I hope I can make enough to put forward the very needy work that you have in Africa, for money is one of Africa's great needs. But I honestly think I can be of more benefit to God and humanity, here, in America."

Later, in the same letter, after he had attended and returned from class, he wrote: "During lunch, a cablegram came from you, reminding me that I am almost twenty-eight years of age. Dear Dad, not a birthday of mine have you ever missed. What a dear, precious father you are. I remember, once, thinking it was one time you wouldn't be able to reach me, on the train en route from Rhodesia to Cape Town, when, *lo and behold,* the conductor entered the dining car where I was at breakfast, called out my name, and handed me your greetings! I showed the card to the other fellows with great pride in the thoughtfulness of my very special father."

* * *

BY JULY 1923, Arthur had his medical degree from Northwestern, and was two weeks into the second surgical service at the Methodist Hospital of Brooklyn, New York. He wrote to his father: "The fellow interns here are fine fellows, three from Johns Hopkins, one from Harvard, two from Jefferson, and one from Montreal. Quarters are nice—billiard room, piano, and tennis court and golf links about twenty minutes car ride away. The hospital is large and, although old, very nice and up-to-date. A new maternity building of 100 beds is almost completed and will be the last word. There is a general spirit of good fellowship and helpfulness throughout the hospital, including the attending staff as well as the administrative officers and nurses and even the maids—just like a big family. I could desire no better situation for an internship, and work is sufficient.

"Services for interns the first year are pathology, first surgical, second surgical, and medicine, three months each, being a junior in these services. The second year we have obstetrics, pathology (one intern each), first and second surgery, first and second medicine. The senior intern has the entire responsibility for the service—makes his rounds before the staff physicians arrive in the morning, again at night after the night shift of nurses comes on. He visits critical patients as often as he thinks necessary, and makes prescriptions for any of them when indicated, private or ward patients alike. Of course, if there is anything he does not know, he calls the staff physician on the service (for advice), but his responsibility is great.

"Now, the reason for my being unable to write sooner. I am the junior house surgeon on second surgical service. However, the senior of the service is taking a three-week vacation and I am acting house surgeon with all the responsibilities such an office entails. I have had no more than five hours sleep a night on the average and have had no time during the day. I sat down several times to start a letter, but as I started, my ring would sound (two shorts), and answering the phone I would hear something like this: 'Dr. Johnson, this is Miss Kibboy, supervisor in halls three speaking. Mr. Williams is very uncomfortable and has a fever of 104. What shall we do with him?' Or, 'Dr. Johnson, there is a patient in the accident ward with a fractured skull, do you wish him admitted?' And I have to run to see Mr. Williams, or go to the Emergency and admit the patient if we can help him.

"As another example, I had just finished my last rounds the night before last, about midnight, when I was called to admit a boy, age eight, who had fallen off a garage on his head. On examining him, I found one pupil dilated more than the other and reflexes on one side more lively and the patient in a dazed state. I immediately had the nurse get the spinal puncture apparatus and prepare him for a puncture, which I did immediately and found greatly increased pressure in the spinal canal and much blood. After ascertaining all the facts, I called my attending physician on that service, gave him the facts, and suggested that we should operate. He immediately came to the hospital, went over the case with me, and agreed. I told the night supervisor to get the operating room ready, scheduled the operation for 1 a.m., then scrubbed up and assisted the doctor in doing a decompression, from which, I might say, the patient is recovering nicely.

"If you will pardon a few personal allusions in which I take some pleasure: Dr. Goodrich, my chief attending, told me, yesterday, 'Johnson, you've had a hard job jumping right into the house surgeon's job first thing, and I want to tell you that I am very pleased with your work.' And Miss Duryea, the night supervisor, told one of the men that she thought Dr. Johnson was a wonderfully fine young man and she could trust him anywhere.

"Second surgical operates Tuesdays, Thursdays, and Saturdays, first surgical on alternate days. On the days when the service does not operate, the junior rides the ambulance. I examine all patients admitted, ward and private, do the more particular dressings, prescribe narcotics as needed, make three daily rounds—one with the staff physician—sign patients out (none on our service can leave without my signature). I also need to talk to relatives of patients, which is the hardest thing of all, especially if the patient is dying. We had one skull fracture, on whom we did a decompression, who had such severe brain injury there wasn't a chance for him. I had to tell his mother."

* * *

IN A LONG LETTER TO DOROTHEA in December 1923, he said how much he enjoyed hearing from her and how much letters from sisters and family members meant to lonely bachelors. He told of the ambulance service, a few important people who had been patients of his, some of the shows on Broadway he had seen, a graduation speech he had heard given by a Dr. Cadman, who was a charismatic speaker and who knew their father, and then he philosophized about dancing and card playing. He and his sister had been rigorously indoctrinated in the evils of both, the former being an invitation to sexual behavior, the latter to gambling, both major sins.

"That brings us to the subject of dancing, for fear you might think mother would be distressed at our dancing. Mother has very high ideals but she is really of the old school. I am sure, myself, that there is no harm in dancing itself—on the other hand, it is a fine source of entertainment and physical exercise. Personally, if I ever find a wife, I would want her to be able to dance. Before, I was rather jealous of having my girl in some other fellow's arms for a dance, but since I have been dancing and seen the freedom in the dance, I will want my wife to be able to dance well with other fellows, gentlemen, as I am. I am glad you enjoy dancing. I would just as soon have mother dance, if I thought she could relax sufficiently to get about the floor gracefully with a partner." He also talked about cards and other games. Dorothea had mentioned a card party that she had attended (or given), and he felt obliged to justify card playing to assuage any guilt feelings she might have been harboring about this.

In another letter to Dorothea, he mentioned that in his last letter from their parents, they had said they were leaving Cape Town in January and expected to arrive in New York in April. It had been several years since he had seen them. He wrote, "I am surely anxious to see them.

How I wish you and Graham and the boy could come with them! I shall have to wait longer to see you."

On first surgical service at Methodist, Arthur had plenty to do and not enough hours in the day to do it. The hospital provided room and board for its house staff, but internships paid little or nothing, feeling the training they were providing was remuneration enough. Therefore, Arthur still had to depend on his father for spending money. This had been so, except for his short stint in the National Guard on the Mexican border and his service with the tank corps, and employment during a few summer vacations.

Chapter 9

The Romance

1923–1924

IN DECEMBER 1923, a few months after Arthur began his two-year surgical internship at the Methodist Hospital, he met a young woman in nurse's training, Fostina Bishop, who was friendly, attractive, and one of the brighter nursing students. He was extremely busy on surgical service and there were no entries in his diary for most of this period, so what eventually became a courtship was documented mostly by her.

Fostina Bishop, student nurse, Methodist Hospital, Brooklyn, New York, 1924.

Her diary begins as follows: "This little book is to contain memories, thoughts, and snatches from conversations that I hold dear."

On January 6, she wrote, "I haven't seen Dr. Johnson to speak with at all lately. I would like to, as I want to tell him a few things." And on January 9, "I haven't talked with Dr. Johnson in an age. I hope to some day, in the distant future, however."

On January 11, quoting from a letter from Eunice, a friend, "The value of a kiss, lies in the anticipation and the afterthought. The kiss, itself, is merely a collusion of lips, which means nothing." Fostina's thought, however, was that "the kiss of the person I love, *does* mean something. It would mean, to me, the seal of love. I'll not rave, as I'm not in love yet, and I suppose I'll be an old maid."

She continued: "Dr. Johnson walked over to the house with me today. I wonder if he cares for me—but he is a lady's man." Next, after returning from a visit home in Patchogue, Long Island, New York, she wrote, "Had a long talk with Dr. Johnson this afternoon. I am sorry I don't care more about him, but such is life." And a week later, "I went to church with Dr. Johnson and have concluded that he is very nice, as a friend, but I am not in love with anyone."

She wrote, on Lincoln's birthday, "Last Thursday evening, I went to the dance, and had a very nice time. I confess I enjoyed my dances with A.J. exceedingly. I think I cared more for him that night, than I ever have. I was thrilled, again, for a change. I wonder how things are going to work out."

On March 1: "Dr. Johnson came up to the East Wing this morning to see me, so he said. He is intending to have his tonsils out Monday. I may sneak up to see him. I'll write him a letter while he is there."

March 21: "Arthur is all better. That is, he has recovered from his tonsillectomy. Last week, Thursday, we went to New York, to the Capitol, in the afternoon, and saw *The Great White Way*. Went to dinner at Enrico's, a darling little Italian restaurant on 11th Avenue in Greenwich Village, then we taxied over to the Cast Theater and viewed *The Swan*. A wonderful evening—and I kissed him good night, for the first time. Sunday afternoon we went down to Mrs. Taylor's, and had tea, spent a wonderful evening listening to the radio—a very wonderful evening, indeed. Last night, we had the St. Patrick's dance, and he danced almost all of the time with me, another wonderful evening. I surely do like to dance with him, better than anyone I have ever danced with. He came to the ward around dinnertime, tonight, and we fooled a bit. I am going to try to love him. If he really loves me, I ought to be able to love him. I think I do."

And on March 25: "We had the dedication service in the new building (Maternity Wing) and I took Arthur through—also received a letter from him today."

On June 26: "Having searched everywhere for the key to my diary, I finally broke the lock. It is long ago that I wrote in here. Since that time, I have been on night duty on Mat-Three (maternity wing, third floor), which I am not likely to forget. While there, Arthur visited me several times, and gave me his picture. I went on my vacation (early) this month, had a wonderful time, and Arthur came out to see me. I am convinced that I really love him. It is not necessary to record everything that happened in here, except that I accepted his fraternity pin June 7, which means that we are now engaged. How funny it seems."

Budding romance, Fostina Bishop and Dr. Johnson,
Brooklyn Methodist Hospital, New York City, 1925.

June 28: "I met his Dad and like him very much. There isn't anything about him I would change. We saw Douglas Fairbanks in *The Thief of Baghdad.* The following Wednesday, we went to the Strand Theater and saw *The White Moth.* I like Arthur the most when he doesn't know it— isn't that peculiar? When he is thinking of something else, I like him the best—women are the limit."

Arthur wrote to his father on July 16: "I had a very good vacation. I did much ocean bathing, and some sailing and motor boating, with friends of the Bishops, having spent one week in Patchogue with them, although Fostina was on duty in the hospital. While away for nearly two weeks, I came more and more to the realization that Fostina is the one, and only, girl for me. I missed her terribly. She does not have every qualification, nor would anyone, but she does have those that are most worthwhile and lasting. She is a true, unassuming, modest Christian girl and, with it, very sweet, bright, efficient, healthy, and several other things that you know for yourself, having seen her."

July days were filled with dining at restaurants, movies, a dinner cruise up the Hudson River, walks in the park, all courting behavior, and, finally, on the twenty-first, Fostina announced, "Arthur has given me my ring. How happy I am, and after it is known, I wonder how I will feel about it." On the twenty-third, "I wrote to Arthur's daddy today. I do love Arthur, so much, and I'm glad!"

On August 10, 1924, Arthur wrote: "Much has happened since I last wrote—much of very great importance for my future. I have found a young lady whom I have learned to love better than myself—a thing that many, perhaps, would have thought improbable. She is a nurse in training in this hospital whom I met several months ago and whose real underlying and evident worth became better known to me as the months rolled by, until my admiration and respect grew into a very deep and abiding love, and we were engaged last month.

Arthur felt that Fostina, whom he affectionately called Frostie, fulfilled his ideal in almost every way: "She gives me the sympathy and understanding that comes with an unselfish love, and I trust her absolutely and implicitly. And I love her so purely, and yet so strongly."

We come to an entry on October 10 from Frostie's diary: "It is ages since I have scribbled in here and we have had many happy times together. Arthur is on obstetrics, now, and I miss him so much. I have my black band now, and am in charge of the women's ward. I hope I make good, for mother's sake. I want to be a success, so the family will be glad to own me. How I love Arthur. I will be glad when we will be able to be alone."

New Year's Day, 1925: "I have been glancing over the last few pages of my diary. How silly they seem, since I have found out what love really is.

I cannot thank God enough, for giving me the love of a man like Arthur. I can hardly breathe when I think that, in two months, I will be his wife. We have had so many wonderful times together. His folks have been in New York for the past two months and we have enjoyed being with them once or twice, every week, as circumstances have permitted."

Arthur, surgical intern, in the lab at the Brooklyn Methodist Hospital, New York, 1925.

A final note from Fostina's diary on April 5: "I finished training March 1, and Miss Hinckley told me I had done excellently all the way through. I could not come home directly, because Hewlett [her brother] had scarlet fever. I boarded at Mrs. Conklin's, and spent my days serving and running errands. On March 12, we were married. Daddy Johnson married us, in the living room, at home. It was a very simple wedding, but, oh, so sincere! I am now Arthur's wife. There never was a more wonderful man then he. He is so wonderfully kind, and considerate. I am in a trance most of the time. I cannot write how much I love him. We had four wonderful days at the beach after the wedding. It is wonderful to be a woman. It is more wonderful to have the love of a Christian man make you into a woman. Dear God, grant that I may ever be a good woman, equipped to be Arthur's helpmate and worthy to be the mother of his children. Dear Father, I want a dear little baby of our very own, something which will prove to Arthur the depth of my love for him. I long to feel baby hands in mine and to see baby's eyes look into mine with confidence and love. It must be glorious when we realize that it is a part of us both."

Fostina, the bride, soon after the wedding on March 12, 1925.

Arthur, wrote sometime after the honeymoon: "Our wedding day! How much is contained in that phrase, no one can understand, who has not been through the experience of marrying for absolute and unadulterated love. It is a glorious thing—being married to one who means so much. It is a culmination of the blessed courtship. While the courtship was a joy, and being together seemed heaven, there was an incompleteness about it that prevented perfect satisfaction and contentment. Marriage makes this complete. It *does* make of the two, one: with one united love; with one united aim; with one manner of living; with the same desires and aspirations; with a realization that we *are* everything to each other.

"The ceremony, itself, is very serious to the chief participants—and, may I say, somewhat of an ordeal. Realizing the solemnity of the step, I was more tense than at any time in the past. I saw scarcely anything, except the face, especially the eyes, of my bride. When I made my vows at the altar, I was so intensely serious that I got the order of some phrases wrong, but, at that, they were the most sincere of my life. It was only at the conclusion (amid) congratulations and illogical tears, that I began to realize I was breathing."

Arthur had arrived from the hospital at 4:30, and in the living room of Fostina's Patchogue home, the momentous event unfolded and was over by 5 o'clock. They were taken in Fostina's grandfather's launch to the Bishop's summer cabin on the beach at Fire Island, where they were left with four days' provisions and a sailboat. Arthur had taken his homemade crystal radio set, which provided orchestral music from Chicago as background for the first meal of their new life together.

The honeymoon cottage, Fire Island, "four wonderful days,"
Long Island, New York, March 1925

Chapter 10

A New Life Begins

1925–1929

WHILE STILL AT BROOKLYN METHODIST HOSPITAL, Arthur received a proposal to practice with a Dr. Ross of St. Helens, Oregon, near Portland. The practice would involve sharing office space, doing Dr. Ross's surgery, and supplementing this with general practice. If he took the offer, and the population of St. Helens did not grow enough to support a general surgeon in four or five years, he was concerned that he would have to look to Portland. But he decided to accept the offer.

In December 12, 1925, Arthur wrote: "I ended my internship on June 9, against the wishes of the Intern Committee, because I had to get to Oregon in time to take the State Board Exams. Fostina and I started west together, and were really by ourselves for the first time. We spent one evening in Chicago before continuing our westward journey on the Canadian Pacific Railroad. The beauties of this Canadian Rockies route, although seen once before, were enhanced considerably when shared with my beloved wife."

Darlow met them in Portland, and drove them to St. Helens, where they enjoyed a delightful visit with him, his wife, Alta, and their three children. They were invited to stay with them while awaiting the readiness of their home. After taking the State Boards and while waiting for the results, Arthur showed Fostina some highlights of the beautiful Northwest. They saw Portland's Rose Garden and the Columbia River Highway's beautiful vistas. They drove through the virgin forests to nearby Vernonia in their new Ford coupe, and spent a week camping at Cannon Beach, where they enjoyed a daily dip in the Pacific Ocean. When they finally moved into the house they were renting, Arthur said he "could not describe the satisfaction and pleasure of at last getting into our own delightful five-room bungalow and having a home of our own."

His practice nearly paid their expenses from the start. His first operations were tonsillectomies and adenoidectomies. He did several surgeries, several deliveries including one set of twins, and considerable general practice. He hoped, finally, to confine himself to surgery, but at the time, he was doing everything. He and Fostina enjoyed their radio, which he had made into a four-tube radio frequency regenerative set that could bring them programs from stations in California, Washington, Utah, Montana, Canada, and sometimes even two Chicago stations.

Fostina was pregnant, and on December 24, she reached the end of her pregnancy and started mild labor pains, which held off until the next day, when she and Arthur had their first Christmas tree with its ornaments and tinsel, and exchanged gifts in their new home. A few hours later, I arrived, weighing 8 pounds 12 ounces. Thus, the Johnson family was increased to a threesome, at 11:05 a.m. on Christmas Day, 1925.

Arthur as a new dad, St. Helens, Oregon, 1925.

Over the next several days, as Dad watched my gargoyle-like features disappear and the real me begin to appear, he felt better. He wrote: "I watched the little fellow, who received the name of Robert Holmes, nursing at his mother's breast, and I must admit that I felt a glow at my heart. I am going to become quite fond of him in time, I'm sure."

On December 29, Dad was languishing at home, alone: "What a difference a beloved woman's presence makes in a home; in fact, it *makes* the home. I spend as little time in our house as possible with her gone. It seems cold, and gray, and cheerless. I am only awaiting the time when the house can again be transformed into a home: when the sunshine of love will be present within, even though the day be cloudy without; when there will be a warmth, and comfort, in the atmosphere; when the music, from the radio, will again be delightful; when Fostina leaves the hospital and returns, to weave her magic, and make the house a home, once more."

Dad wrote a letter to his mother on May 9, 1926, Mother's Day. "I am only now beginning to realize the thousands of little trials, anxieties, fears, disappointments, ambitions, and so forth, that a child causes its mother. Only the mother fully realizes them. The place you occupy in my heart, Mother mine, if anything, grows larger as the years go by, and I gain an added appreciation of your early love and training. It is Sunday morning here. Fostina has gone to church to hear her first Mother's Day sermon. I am sitting in our living room, thinking of you and listening to Dr. Bowman of the First Presbyterian Church, in Portland, preaching a sermon on 'Mothers.' Bobby is on the front porch, sleeping in the sunshine. I have the dinner ready to put on the stove, at the proper time—and that is the present picture." He and Fostina were looking forward eagerly to a visit from his father in another two weeks. They were sorry she could not come, but they were hoping for a *long* visit from both of them, in 1928, which would be, presumably, their next leave.

Mother wrote a newsy letter to "Daddy," the Bishop, in August, about how I had progressed since his visit: "He now says 'Da-Da, Da-Da.' He also creeps and sits up. He has five teeth. He is beginning to have a will of his own." She said Dad was doing more surgery, and they had a little balance in the bank, after paying the month's bills, which "lets one breathe a little more easily." She mentioned that they had taken Darlow, Alta, and the three children sailing that afternoon and had a picnic on the river, a pleasant outing, returning in the twilight. (Dad had bought a nineteen-foot, open-cockpit sloop not long after their arrival in St. Helens, and this became an inexpensive means of recreation, and social entertainment, particularly in summertime.) Since the Bishop was returning to Africa, she said, "We shall miss you, Daddy. Having you in

America seems so much closer than Africa. We wish you a happy trip, and will welcome any or all of you in our home, at any time."

To his father, in October, Dad wrote: "Darlow has returned to St. Helens for another year at a $200 increase in salary. This is his seventh year. I think the church is going to get behind him in building up our membership, first of all. As recreational director, I have planned socials for the church every third Friday during the winter, for the Epworth League every second Friday, and the other two Fridays are reserved for Sunday school class activities. Wednesday is the senior, and young folks, prayer meetings. Other nights are filled with gymnasium classes, especially volley ball and basket ball, so you see it looks like a full winter. I was elected chairman of the finance committee, and we have had a dinner where we raised nearly half of our required pledges. We are allowing them until next Sunday to get in their pledges, and after that we will canvas each one who has not pledged. I hope we will be able to get about $3,800 subscribed for the budget.

"Some time ago I took dinner with Dr. Pease, one of Portland's leading surgeons, and played golf with him at one of his clubs. He also invited me to be his guest at the University Club, when Dr. William Mayo was the speaker and guest of honor. Last week Dr. J. W. Thompson invited us to his house to meet Dr. MacCollum, another Portland surgeon, and his wife. Dr. Dalton, whom you met when here, is still a very good friend. He said he would put up my name for membership in the University Club. I told him in another five years, when I could afford to pay dues, I would be glad to consider his kind offer.

"We are already looking forward to 1928, when we can see our beloved Africans again. We talk about you much, and have so many things to show you. Of course, chief among these, is Bobby." His grandfather, who had seen him during a short visit, "wouldn't know him by now. He has progressed in every way. Dentally, he has eight teeth; muscularly, he is perfectly developed; he is almost walking—stands alone and walks about the furniture, especially our new davenport and chair that we want him to keep away from; intellectually, he is a wonder, of course— look at his family connections; emotionally, he is stable but has a mind of his own which we do not pamper, and he is the sweetest baby in the world. So much for Daddy's description of his son. You will love him."

In a letter to his father in July 1927, he said he had been busier in his work, and his earnings had improved, and he was pleased to report that, unlike the previous year, he would not have to borrow from him. Further, he hoped that in the next year he could begin to pay back their cumulative debt to him. Their social life was frugal, in view of their need to conserve in this early stage of their marriage, but was all that they needed it to be. He wrote that, "His Grandmother Bishop thinks Bobby is just about right. Yes, she is visiting us this summer—has been here over two weeks, now, and is expecting to stay until September. You can imagine Frostie's delight at having her with us. She seems quite well after her illness this spring and is, I hope, enjoying her visit to the West Coast. She told us of your visit to them, while you were in New York, and how much they, and Hew, appreciated it. Next Saturday, we are expecting to drive her around the Mount Hood loop, via Hood River. In another week or two, we expect to leave early Friday morning and go to the beach, until Monday morning, and give her a view of and perhaps a dip in the Pacific Ocean."

✳ ✳ ✳

THE ONLY WAY Dad could make himself known and build his practice, since he was new to the community, was through his social and community contacts. He was elected president of the local Chamber of Commerce in late 1927, and in that capacity occasionally gave the town newspaper an interview regarding community issues in which he was involved. One such was their industrial committee, which was formed to assist any prospective business considering a location in St. Helens. Another was the consideration of instituting civic planning for the community. He also helped plan a midsummer festival, which was attended by nearly 200 local folks and visitors. He was also involved with the Masons and the Kiwanis, rose to positions of leadership in each, and his practice grew fairly rapidly. On May 1, he rejuvenated his diary, which had been pretty much ignored ever since he enrolled in medical school. He reported his gross income in 1928 at $6,100, the first year he did not need a loan from his father.

He found that local citizens who needed surgery and could afford it often chose to go to the "experts" in nearby Portland. His training was in surgery and obstetrics, and he intended to specialize in surgery. In early 1929, he began to make contacts with Portland surgeons, and this led, eventually, to his membership on the medical staff at the Emmanuel and Good Samaritan Hospitals, where he performed occasional surgery. He also joined the surgical teaching staff of the Multnomah County Hospital, and became clinical instructor of surgery at the University of Oregon Medical School. He became known among his peers as a young surgeon of considerable talent, so when Dr. Kirby, a well-known Portland surgeon died, his partner, Dr. Cable, invited Dad to use Kirby's office space, in return for performing surgery on Dr. Cable's patients.

Dad and the author on our front porch, St. Helens, Oregon, August 1928.

After this arrangement was in place several months, Dad and Mother decided to consider moving to Portland. They found apartment rentals in Portland ranged from $75 to $100 a month, which was too expensive for their budget, so they decided—sort of as a lark—to look around at houses on the off chance that they might find something more affordable. In mid-June, they found a charming house built by an excellent builder at 1125 Wisteria Avenue, and purchased it for $9,500, with $500 down, $60 a month for a year, and then $75 a month.

In the next few days, whenever he did surgery or saw patients in Portland, he spent some nights there on an army cot, tending to minor tasks in preparation for their move, until he was called to reserve duty—now in the Army Medical Corps. He completed reserve duty the end of July 1929, and he and mother made the move to their new home in Portland, keeping the office open in St. Helens, where dad intended to hold office hours three days a week, hoping to supplement his new practice.

Our first home, 1125 Wisteria Avenue, Portland, Oregon, 1930.

Chapter 11

The Great Depression

1929–1937

THE YEAR 1929 proved not to be a propitious time to begin a new practice, since it was the year of the Crash and the onset of the Great Depression that was to last a decade. Dad moved into Dr. Kirby's offices, in joint practice with Dr. Cable, who was nearing retirement. The last half of that year, in spite of commuting to St. Helens to see patients three days a week, his income dropped greatly.

In a letter to his mother in late January 1930, he noted that his charges for the first half of 1929 had increased $600 over the equivalent time in the previous year, but after the move to Portland they had decreased so that by year's end the total charges were $300 less than in 1928. This was a rather bleak outlook, although he was being referred surgical cases and was becoming known as a capable surgeon. He could make contacts through social and service organizations, so he determined that he would attend every meeting that came along and accept all social functions to which they were invited. "Work has been encouraging this year, so far, at least during the first two months. It has been very slow this month again, but we are always hoping it will pick up. I am bound to get ahead sometime, because every one of my operative cases—and I have had nearly eighty majors—have gotten along extremely well. One reason, I think, is because I do not operate unless there is something that can definitely be remedied by surgery, and, secondly, because I use a definite and careful technique, know what I want to do, and do it with the least possible trauma to tissues. I have no fear of the future."

And Mother wrote, "We are getting a few patients in Portland. The patients we have had pay their bills, so that's encouraging. Considering that A. Holmes has only been in town three days a week, and that there are over a thousand doctors in Portland, I think we have progressed very well, having lived in town only six months. I like Portland very much, and am very glad to be away from St. Helens. My chief objection there was that someone was always telling me what Mrs. So-and-So said, and enlarging on it." Mother had begun to refer to Dad as "A. Holmes," because he had found himself directly across the hall from an Arthur H. Johnson M.D. in the Medical Arts Building in Portland, and knew he would have to differentiate himself from him and from other Arthur Johnsons, so he changed his name.

Dad spoke of having joined the City Club, a group of leading business and professional men in the community, and he had been appointed chairman of the Physical Education Committee of the YMCA. "I am busy every night of the week and, of course, on my afternoons off, I go to St. Helens and hold office hours. I am doing considerable surgery but no one seems to have any money. The Depression is affecting us in Portland, much as it seems to be in the rest of the country. I am working very hard. I ought get ahead."

A good share of his financial problems was the result of his arrangement with Dr. Cable. He wrote: "I have been doing considerable surgery this year, but most of it is for Dr. Cables' patients, for which I receive nothing but name recognition, which is a good thing, but, it does not pay the bills. My private patients haven't had any money, so there you are—or rather, there I am—and where am I?" His arrangement provided rent-free office space, but nothing more. Add the $1,400 worth of surgery performed, in one month, for Dr. Cable, and this was definitely not a good deal.

Dad remained busy, professionally and socially, but the family continued on the verge of poverty. He was independent, not accustomed to asking for help from anyone, and was loathe to ask his father for more money. He had, however, no alternative, and Mother assured him that his father would rather carry his debt than a stranger, so he asked for help again. The following letter reveals that he was under considerable strain: "My sweetheart. It is twelve thirty a.m. and, having one of my jerky times, which I get with too much on my mind, I had difficulty sleeping although I went to bed early. I got my book, thinking I would read a few chapters as a soporific. I am glad I did, because I came upon your very sweet note, which sounded like the Frostie I married. I will be very thankful when collections pick up because it will doubtless bring normalcy again. I realize I'm an old bear most of the time. I didn't really mean that you are selfish and inconsiderate. It is I that am that. If I were as sweet and lovable as you are, when you are yourself—most of the time—we would have little trouble. It was good to read, in spite of this, that I mean more to you than anyone in the world. You mean more to me than anyone, or anything, and someday, maybe, I'll be able to act toward you in a manner to demonstrate it. If we can weather this testing time, I am sure we will have a very happy life together, forgetting the mean and small things and putting stress on the things that count. Your loving husband, Arthur."

Mother expressed her concern about Dad in a letter: "He started having infections (boils) when Alta was here with the mumps, and has had one after another for the last two months. He had ten on his legs, two on his neck, three on his hands, and two on his nose. He has been very miserable with them. He was unable to work for ten days, while he had the hand infections. He has finally had some serum made, and I do believe it is stopping them. I shall be so glad when he won't have to travel back and forth to St. Helens—he's so tired at night, he can hardly rest."

In early August, Mother wrote: "We read in the *Christian Science Monitor* that Daddy had been taken ill. It worried us considerably because we know Daddy very seldom gives up, unless he is very sick. We are hoping for a letter soon. We haven't had a line for over two months."

There had been no response to Dad's loan request, now explained by a letter from Sarah a few weeks later: "I do not know whether you have heard from Dorothea about Daddy's illness. This is the first time in a ministry, of over forty years, that he has had to leave a conference. He was not well when he came back from Madeira and Liberia, and was only home three weeks before starting on his itinerary. It being Pentecostal year, he was anxious to get to all the charges, where we have a white missionary in the field, to help them in their evangelistic efforts. Dorothea writes that he has been very near to death's door. They feel that the only thing that saved him was the wonderful nursing care he was given and the prayers of the people. Miss Hansson, a trained nurse of the W.F.M.S., has been with him day and night, except between lunch and supper when Dorothea relieved her, and she slept. Daddy was in bed in Old Umtali a month, but is now sitting up and gaining." This letter probably didn't reach him until July. In a later letter, the Bishop described the onset of his illness, with a fever of 105 degrees, and the nurse treated him with enemas and quinine, indicating that he likely had malaria.

Sarah had sent a check for $1,000. Dad wrote: "I am breathing again for the first time in some weeks, because your check has saved me from losing my credit. It arrived just before two of my notes at the bank, totaling $600, came due, and I was able to pay them. I had been sending the department stores a few dollars each month, to let them know I had not forgotten them, but this permitted me to pay them up. I was also able to pay my Medical Society dues, which were due last January, and finish paying for a set of surgical instruments. To you I will owe interest on $600 from March 8, 1930, and the $1,000."

The Shrew, our sailboat, with Mom, Dad, and me, and a little friend. It was the first sailboat at the Portland Yacht Club, 1930.

Dad brought his 19-foot open-cockpit sloop, the *Shrew*, to Portland and moored her at the Portland Yacht Club. The club was predominantly for motorboats, and he introduced sailing to the group. Within a year, the number of sailboats at the club had grown to the point that they began to have weekend races on the river. The yacht club provided opportunities for Dad to meet people and build his practice, as well as the major family social recreation. There were evening picnics, with other yacht club folks and their families and friends, and their children became friends of mine. Sometimes we took weekend cruises upriver to Rooster Rock, where there were games and races.

Meanwhile, Dad and Mother did their best to trim expenses to a minimum, but their income was a pittance, sometimes less than $20 a month. They worried, they borrowed what they could, they apologized for belaboring the issue of their poverty, to Darlow and to their parents, from whom they borrowed from time to time when they fell too far behind. Dad concentrated on perfecting his surgical technique and expanding his repertoire, which he did very well. He was complimented by patients and was considered exceptional by doctors, which made his poverty all the more ill-deserved. They took in a boarder, a twenty-year-old young lady, who occupied their spare bedroom for $30 a month and babysitting when they went out for an evening.

* * *

IN LATE 1932, Dad's father bought a home for them at 3113 N.E. Klickitat Street, to relieve some financial pressure. The family moved from the Wisteria house, terminating monthly payments of $75, to the new house, for which the rental payment to the Bishop was $50.

In an October letter to his father, Dad announced that he had completed his 100 case write-ups for the American College of Surgeons, and they were approved by the Board of Regents. He had been accepted as a Fellow, and the honor was to have been conferred upon him at the St. Louis meeting of the college on October 17. This, however, required the payment of a membership fee of $100, which he did not have, and which, if he did, was needed to pay overdue bills. That letter was written on the fourteenth, and prompted a check from his father, for which he wrote expressing his thanks and noting that this allowed him to pay a number of pressing bills.

Then came some relief! He immediately wrote his father: "Now—some good news for a change! I am delighted to be able to write this to you, after sending little but bad news. In a time when hundreds of women and girls were going from office to office, looking for work, my resourceful little wife went out and got a job! She is working for Acme Fast Freight, a transfer company, at $80 a month. This lets us see the way through the winter for the first time. She will work from 8:30 in the morning until 5 in the afternoon, with Saturday afternoons off."

In the same letter, he noted that Darlow and the whole family had been up for Thanksgiving dinner in their new home. They enjoyed a wonderful turkey dinner together, the bird having been part payment on a surgical bill. They managed to stow the family here and there, and all enjoyed a three-day visit. Plans were made for our family to visit their family over Christmas. These family visits were warm and friendly times together.

With Mother's salary, and now no more rental payments either, they were less destitute, but they never reached a point in the 1930s when their expenses could be ignored. The medical profession in those days was still considered a human service, not unlike religion, and was not operated as a business. To refuse treatment because someone could not afford to pay was unheard of, and it would never have occurred to Dad, raised in a missionary family, to refuse treatment or to badger anyone for payment.

As the '30s progressed, economic improvement was noticed in the business community well before it was in the professions. This was illustrated by the freight business. As more goods were shipped into Portland, Acme Fast Freight became busier and busier, until Mother often had to work overtime to keep up. At that time, another girl was hired as her assistant to alleviate some of the workload. Others were hired, over two or three years, until five girls were employed, Mother becoming the office manager.

In November 1934, Dad's father developed prostatism and, as was characteristic, he did not let it interfere with his work until it became serious. At the time, he mentioned it to Dad and they exchanged a few letters before he was convinced he should see a doctor, and a few more before he saw a specialist and had surgery. He was unable to return to work for months. Not long after he did return to work—traveling throughout the continent, holding conferences and giving sermons—he had a recurrence of malaria that set him back considerably. Apparently he had had occasional recurrences following the first episode. In another year or so, he became unable to continue the level of intensity required for his calling, and had to retire.

In a letter to his father in August 1935, Dad wrote about his activities at the Portland Yacht Club. They had just held an annual sailing regatta in which thirty boats competed, and well over a hundred members and guests had tea on the veranda, watching the races, many attending a formal banquet in the evening, at which Dad was master of ceremonies. He said it had been a most successful season. He was asked to accept the role of commodore which he, at first, declined, but when several of them said they would be proud to host him as commodore, providing the prestigious vessel required to fly the commodore's flag on occasions where needed, he agreed.

The folks continued to host evening picnic cruises to fulfill their social obligations, and we went on occasional weekend cruises for fun. My parents, although optimistic, still had financial disaster hanging over their heads by a thread, which, with the illness of the Bishop, was becoming somewhat frayed. Always hoping for an unexpected opportunity or a financial miracle, they continued a very busy life, while eking out a living from month to month, until in early 1937 Dad received an unexpected letter.

The letter was written to him as director of Internship Training at the Good Samaritan Hospital. It was from the superintendent of a cannery in Bristol Bay, Alaska, on the Bering Sea, asking if one of the interns might be interested in serving as company physician for the summer salmon season, a period of about three months starting in June. The contract was for $3,000, more than Dad's total annual income. After conferring briefly with Mother, he wrote immediately to accept the job for himself. He notified the hospital that he would be taking a leave of absence during the summer, and, greatly encouraged, looked forward to an Alaskan adventure.

Chapter 12

A Summer Up North

1937

THE SS *OTSEGO* DEPARTED SEATTLE at 2 o'clock in the afternoon in early May, with Dad and several hundred fishermen and cannery men on board. The ship was a 4,640-ton, 315-foot vessel, which had been a German raider during the war. It belonged to Libby, McNeill & Libby, a canned food company, which owned the fish cannery. The cannery workers were Asians, chiefly Filipinos, and Swedes predominated among the fishermen. Dad had the doctor's stateroom, and had free access to the bridge and chartroom at all times, which helped to fill many an hour of the eight-day passage. The third mate gave him instructions in navigation, until his noon sights, taken with his sextant, came within two miles of that of the other officers.

On the first day out, they encountered increasing breezes in the afternoon, which became high winds with heavy seas that night. "About 3 o'clock the next morning I was awakened with a great crash and clatter of dishes in the firemen's dining room, opposite my stateroom, and the main dining room overhead. I heard benches falling down, pots and pans crashing about, doors banging. The ship would roll to one side, then back, and when my side was down, great waves would crash into the side and my porthole with the sound of thunder. Throughout its entire length, the ship would creak and groan like it was in mortal agony. The turmoil continued, subsiding somewhat, to the point that I became used to it, and slept fairly soundly. The next morning revealed that the cabins on the windward side were flooded with water.

"The wind moderated somewhat the next day, and although rain squalls continued, the sun peeped through at short intervals. The fishermen began getting their nets unwound from the manufacturer's rolls. Thereafter, one day continued much like another. Besides handing out Epsom salts and painting a few scratches with iodine, I would walk the decks, visit the bridge, set back my watch about half an hour every day, sleep a great deal, and read some old *Redbook* and *Cosmopolitan* magazines that made up the ship's library.

"The seas became gentle swells, the sun began shining at longer intervals, and it continued pleasant sailing. I got caught up on my sleep, and found much interest in talking with the various officers and fishermen. The first machinist at Koggiung had been to Russia a few years ago to install salmon canning equipment for the Soviets, and many were the tales he told about the deplorable economic and moral situations there.

The first land, sighted on Friday, May 14, was islands south of the Alaska Peninsula. The ship ran west and south along the Alaska Peninsula to reach Unimak Pass the next morning, through which they passed north into the Bering Sea. There they steamed, east and north, back along the Peninsula, beneath its towering, snow-covered mountains, for the rest of Saturday. Sunday dawned clear and warm, and proved to be the most ideal day of the trip. They passed Ugashik Bay, Egigik Bay, where Libby had a cannery, and Naknek River, and anchored off Libbyville. Four Libby barges with tugs approached from the Kvichak River, and made fast to the ship. There, 200 fishermen, cannery men, beach men, and Asians got into one barge bound for Koggiung with their complete bedding, mattresses, and personal articles. Other barges had to be loaded with groceries, meats, canned goods, and coal from the hold and upper decks. After an early supper, Dad and the officers sent their baggage aboard a barge, and boarded the tugs for the two-hour run to Libby's cannery at Koggiung, near the head of Kvichak Bay.

On June 10, 1937, Dad wrote, "No mail has reached me, although I have been here nearly a month." There was very little correspondence during this period, due to the isolation of Bristol Bay. The mail service was dependent on infrequent visits of company supply ships, which stopped at every little nook and cranny, so it took weeks each way. There was a mail plane, which came to Koggiung every few weeks, but it had to await delivery, via one of the Libby tugs, to Nushagak River, where Dad was stationed at Ekuk.

Koggiung, Alaska, where Dad spent four months as company physician in the summer of 1937 at a cannery owned by Libby, McNeill & Libby. Family postcard, 1937.

Dad continued, "There are no good charts of the rivers and bays in this out-of-the-way region, and as the sands shift every year, navigation is more or less by intuition. The channel was tortuous and full of shoals, and our tug ran onto a sandbar. We had visions of spending the night there, with all the cannery help on the barge facing the cold wind, and those of us on the tug sitting on an uncomfortable bench in the galley. Luckily, a few toots on the tug's whistle brought the *Wooden Shoe*, a tiny extra tug, from the cannery, which hooked onto the other side of the barge and took us to the dock, where we soon found our various locations and we were ready for bed.

"The canneries in Bristol Bay can be approached only at high tide, there being a twenty-foot tide in this region and nothing but mud flats for a hundred yards at low tide, and by that I really mean mud. It is much like the South Dakota gumbo, and it is not uncommon for those wading through it to lose a boot in the muck and to sit down plop in it. Hip boots are really one of the first essentials for folks up here, because one cannot always make a landing at high tide and must do some wading, so my first purchase from the company store was a pair of these.

"I remained in Koggiung until Wednesday and set up the hospital. With the male nurse doing the work, I treated about forty patients a day for minor ailments and colds, sent the net boss by plane to the Anchorage Hospital with a bad heart [the net boss was in charge of the net loft, where the fishermen's nets were hung, dried, and mended], and explored the cannery thoroughly. I was relieved by Dr. Messiar from Seattle, on the twenty-sixth, when the Libby ship *Gorgas* came over from the Nushagak River to unload and return to her base, just off Ekuk Point."

Dad was able to travel widely about Bristol Bay and became familiar with its various communities and canneries. He spent a week in Koggiung, and became familiar with the Kvichak River and its communities, and learned of the country inland from there. Then he went to the Ekuk cannery, his main place of operation, which was in the bay fed by the Nushagak, the other main river into Bristol Bay. During the season, he went three times to Kanakanak and Dillingham, farther up the river, and to Snag Point, the largest town on the river. "Towns in this country consist chiefly of scattered Indian huts, and perhaps a store, which is run by a white trader. There are two post offices: Dillingham post office, at Snag Point, and one at Clark's Point, which is three miles from Ekuk. I am going to walk over, when I get time, to meet the doctor at the Alaska Packers cannery."

East of the site, looking inland from the river, stretched miles of rolling tundra, consisting of reindeer moss, grass that grew about two inches a day at that time of year, various berries growing close to the ground, and other short vegetation. There were no trees or shrubs. When the grass reached its height, winds skittering across the surface revealed eccentric patterns and created a constant sea of motion into the distance.

Looking across the river to the west, he could see a distant shoreline of rugged mountains, covered with snow, beautiful under the changing patterns of cloud and sun, and the moon. "They were a never-ending delight to the eye, and an inspiration to the soul." The peaks extended to the north, and behind them the sun sank in a blaze of glory about 10 o'clock in the evening, took a short trip beneath the horizon, revealing its nether course by a persistent pink blush in the sky until it rose again, about 2 o'clock, not far from where it had set. In fact, during the longest days of the summer, you could read a newspaper at midnight without artificial light. In another week and a half, the days would begin to get shorter again, so that by mid-August, darkness would begin to come earlier, and last longer.

"Three miles upriver is Clark's Point Cannery, four miles farther, Nushagak, another few miles, the Creek Cannery, and at the bend of the river, where the Wood River and the Nushagak meet—really forming Nushagak Bay—is another Alaska Packers cannery. Across the bay on which we are situated is Egegik River, where Libby's has a fishing ground and a tally truck [related to counting the number of fish delivered by boats to the cannery]. Then comes Snake River, and about fifteen miles up is Kanakanak, where the Government Hospital is situated, and there is a radio station operated by the Army Signal Corps. Near this is Dillingham, which contains some local houses and huts and a jail. Six miles farther is Snag Point, the largest settlement, where two company canneries are operating, and around which many Natives live. The government game warden lives there, as well as about ten other whites, not counting what they refer to as the 'squaw men'—whites who have married local Natives." The Natives in Bristol Bay country were more or less supported by the canneries. Some of them did some trapping during the winter, but most of them earned enough in the short fishing season to last them until the next season.

He was based at the clinic in Ekuk, and traveled to other locations as needed to provide medical care. He was flown to a few other communities, to deliver babies, one in Nome, the first child of Dr. Louis Salazar, who eventually became the resident surgeon in Ketchikan.

Dad's exciting summer at Bristol Bay was over before he knew it, and he headed home to Portland from the Bering Sea. When the ship stopped at the village of Kodiak, on Kodiak Island, on that fateful day in late August 1937, he had fallen in love with the place.

Kodiak Village, c. 1930 from Near Island.

The village of Kodiak, which was settled by the Russians in 1792, was named St. Paul after the Czar. It was the first permanent caucasian settlement in Alaska.

Siberian hunters had come upon the remote land to the east of Russia in the 1740s, when they sailed in search of fur-bearing animals because sable had become scarce in Siberia. They found beaver and fox aplenty, and more important, they discovered the sea otter, whose dense, soft fur brought a fortune in China. The Russian-American Company was formed to develop the fur trade in the new land, and they pressed the Native hunters of the Aleutian Chain and the Kodiak archipelago into service.

Three Natives in a baidarka off a cannery dock, 1930s.
The baidarka, an ocean-going craft made of marine animal skins
with a wood skeletal frame, was a traditional mode of travel rarely seen after 1930.

The Natives of the new land, believed to be of distant Asian origin, probably had migrated across the Bering Sea land bridge at least 7,500 years before. The Kodiak Natives were indigenous to the island as well as to the adjacent coastal areas of the mainland. They had their own language, and had survived well in this often harsh environment, with a complex hunting and gathering culture that was supremely adapted to the sea. As colonization progressed, the Natives became largely acculturated and most were members of the Russian Orthodox Church.

When the United states purchased Alaska from Russia in 1867, the great majority of the people in Kodiak were of mixed Russian and Native heritage, Thereafter, it remained a small, quite fishing village well into the twentieth century.

A Native family beach seining for subsistence at Karluk, a village on the west coast of Kodiak. Kodiak Historical Society.

Chapter 13

The Move to Alaska
1938

I CLEARLY REMEMBER the early September Saturday when Dad arrived home in Portland from his four months in Alaska. He brought three Sunday papers with him, which was striking, in the face of his frugality during the past few years. The next day, I was up early and jumped into bed with my parents, to read the funnies, and to listen to stories of Dad's summer up North, and of the captivating island called Kodiak that would become our home.

Dad left Portland for Alaska on Friday, January 28, 1938. In Seattle, he boarded the SS *Baranof* to travel north through the Inside Passage, so named because it had little exposure to the open sea. He then sailed across the Gulf of Alaska, reaching Kodiak in a little over a week.

That same afternoon, from her office in downtown Portland, Mother wrote to him: "Dearest, It is difficult at times like this to express what is in one's heart, but you know my thoughts are with you constantly. Bob and I will be very lonely without you, but we will keep our chins up, and so must you. It will certainly be a happy day when we hear from you again. If necessary, send a telegram collect. Be sure to let me know what kind of radio to bring, or maybe you are planning to get one from Sears in Seattle later.

"It is time to go home now, but I wanted to wish you bon voyage and all the success in the world, and assure you I love you very much. Affectionately, Frostie."

From the wharf, on board the *Baranof* in Seattle, the next day, Dad wrote: "Dearest Family, The YMCA fellows are down to see me off, so I shall have them mail this last-minute message to you. I love my family very much, and am going to make a new home for them. I shall live for the day when I can meet you in Kodiak and our family will be together again.

"Love to you, my wife and son, and to Father, Mother, and Darlow, et al. Most lovingly, Arthur."

There followed daily letters from Dad, often written on ships' menus, telling of events, of people he met, and of their course and ports of call. He had met about half of the seventy-five passengers by the evening of the first day, his intent being to become acquainted with as many Alaskans as possible and to become a part of his new community. He wrote of the dance he attended on Saturday night, where, although there were about three men to every woman, he had no trouble circulating.

Sunday morning table seats were assigned and he got in line early and was assigned first table, where his tablemates were: "Lieutenant Wright, Naval Radio man, to Dutch Harbor; Mr. Robinson and Mr. Alvenstad, lumbermen, Ketchikan; Mr. Anderson, Bristol Bay, stopping at Kodiak; Mr. Johnson, Ketchikan; Mrs. Hansen, Seattle, visiting Juneau; Mrs. Williams, returning to husband at Ketchikan."

His letters were mailed at each port, so Mother received them fairly frequently, while hers would not reach him for weeks, since the post went by ship. He listed the names and occupations of everyone he met. "They are from all over Alaska and are really interesting folks. I am learning much and all reports about Kodiak are excellent—especially the climate. We are going to like it!"

Among others he met "Mrs. Parks, wife of ex-Governor George Alexander Parks (1925–33); Mr. Sullivan, Collector of Internal Revenue; Dr. Evelyn Butler, Commissioner of Education; Miss Pentz, in charge of new Child Welfare Department; all of whom will be visiting Kodiak sometime during the year and some of whom are very influential in the government. Mr. Sullivan knows Dr. Manlove (Portland physician) very well and is going to speak to the chief of the Bureau of Indian Affairs for me.

"There is very little difference between the people one meets in Alaska and those Outside. 'Outside' is the term we *Alaskans* use for those who come from elsewhere. There is little difference in the small towns we have seen so far: Ketchikan, Petersburg, and Wrangell. Juneau, the territorial capital, will be next."

Dad had written to Dr. Council, Commissioner of the Department of Health, who, he hoped, would meet him when the ship docked in Juneau. Dr. Council had encouraged him to relocate to Kodiak that summer when he passed through on his way home from Bristol Bay. The boat arrived at midnight, and the doctor met him in his new Buick. "We visited the Department of Health building, had dinner, and talked a while. He had nothing to add to what he had said in a letter. The hospital, when built, will be under territorial government, not the Bureau of Indian Affairs. I will be in a private office, practicing on a temporary license, until I pass the Alaska territorial license examination, there being no reciprocity with Oregon. After the hospital is built, my office will be there. The hospital—at least a $25,000 first unit—will be built this spring and the government will add $10,000 worth of equipment."

Dad learned, from talking to Dr. Council and to folks on board from Kodiak, that the town was split into two fractions: those who supported W. J. Erskine, owner of a general merchandise store and community activist, and those who supported Ben Kraft, owner of a competing store. The two did not cooperate well on community issues, with the Kraft faction generally opposing issues supported by the Erskine faction. Dr. Council felt these folks needed to get together to support funding for the hospital. Dad wrote, "It seems that healing this schism and merging these divergent factions will be my first job!

The ship entered the Gulf of Alaska at Cape Spencer, skirted the shore of the mainland, in view of several gigantic glaciers, to enter Prince William Sound and stop at Cordova. Then, under way on Saturday, February 5, Dad wrote: "We dock at Seward this morning, so I am getting this last note off before breakfast. You probably will not get another letter from me for five weeks."

The *Starr* was waiting at Seward, and departed for Kodiak, as soon as they boarded the passengers from the *Baranof.* She arrived in Kodiak the next day, and Dad, a stranger in town, booked into a room at the Sunbeam Hotel. Before getting unpacked, he sent us a wire: "Kodiak is the prettiest spot I've seen. Sun shining. Usual people, some very nice. No place to live or for office except hotel at about $100 a month and board at $50. Collections [income] not expected until fishing season ends or salaries are paid, but future exceptional. Missing you both terribly, Holmes."

There is no mention of a reception committee, and it is presumed that he arrived unannounced on a winter day. Alone in a village community he knew only by casual visit and hearsay—one chosen under the influence of his financial need and the compulsion of his missionary spirit—he found himself starting from nothing, to build a system of health care and earn a living for his family.

Chapter 14

A New Practice

1938

THE DAY AFTER HIS ARRIVAL on February 6, Dad wrote to Mother: "After I sent the wireless to you yesterday, I came back to my room at the hotel and started a letter to you, twice, only to get so choked up with lonesomeness that I couldn't continue without breaking down, which I didn't want to do. It might have been good for me if I had, however, because I am still all pent up inside, until I do not want to do anything but be with my own family again—and, of course, this is impossible. Believe me, I have had hours when I could hardly restrain myself from chucking the whole thing and returning to you. Then my reason would gain the ascendancy and, remembering that we would just be going in the hole deeper there every month, I knew that it would be no kindness to you. Then, too, the folks have been so magnificent that it would be impossible to let them down, and here I am, having probably the biggest fight with myself I have ever had in my life. If I just knew I would have you with me in the next few months, I could endure it until that time. But with money so scarce here until the close of the fishing season, I am not going to be able to save any at this end for your tickets until fall, especially with having to pay such high rent here for office, room, and board."

He went on to talk about the hotel and its owner, Charley Madsen. Charley was a Dane and a member of the Explorers' Club, an international organization. He had traded with the Chukchi Natives of Northern Siberia before coming to Kodiak (and he would document these experiences in his book *The Arctic Trader*, which would be published in 1957). He and his family came to Kodiak in the late 1920s, he began guiding in 1929 and became, according to Dad, "a real big game guide, who knows all about the business," whose fame was evidenced by letters Dad was shown from senators, Lords, Supreme Court judges, princes, and the like, who came to hunt the famous Kodiak brown bear. Kodiak was known for the huge and fearsome bear long before it was known for its fisheries. It was the largest carnivore in the world, and it made Kodiak a favored destination for the big-game hunter. After telling us about Charley, as he began to describe the beauty and serenity of Kodiak, revealed and photographed during his explorations the day before, his mood improved.

An elderly Dr. Jones had arrived in Kodiak for the first time on the same ship as Dad. Dad noted that he was fairly nice to talk with but seemed like an old-timer who hadn't kept up, and who hadn't stayed in any one place more than two or three years, so Dad was not expecting much professional competition from him. Dad was told that the Territory intended to build a hospital in Kodiak in the spring. The head of the Navy Department had asked for sixteen houses for families to start building a naval air station, also in the spring, which would eventually accommodate thousands of military and civil servants. With this, and the anticipated growth for Kodiak, his natural optimism began to return.

He called on the principal of the school the next morning and found that they were working toward having an accredited high school within two years. This meant that I would be able to get everything needed except Latin and foreign languages, but Dad thought he could tutor me in French. He was looking forward to meeting the rest of the teachers at a party the following Saturday night.

Everyone in town was very cordial, and he wondered whether there were some with whom he and Mother could form friendships. From what he had heard, the Erskines would likely be among them. Mr. Erskine visited him at the hotel one afternoon and invited him to his home for the evening. He went, and found a most delightful home, "a living room with many books and other necessities of life," and a man whom he could like, and with whom he felt at home. They spent a very pleasant evening, and he was told he should drop in anytime, day or night. Mr. Erskine explained that his wife was in California, visiting her daughter at Stanford, and was expected back in March. He apologized for not being able to entertain him, but assured him that would be taken care of when his wife returned. That invitation lifted Dad's spirits considerably.

He had been informed by Dr. Council that, once he was licensed, he would be paid for services rendered to Native patients. He had learned from Dr. Bannister, whom he had met in Seward, that this was accomplished by simply wiring Juneau with the patient's name and the need, and the necessary care or surgery would be authorized and paid for. Dr. Council also indicated that he would likely have some salary as Acting Assistant Base Surgeon after the naval station was in operation. These sources of income would not be immediate, though, so it was still necessary to build a practice from scratch with little more than his own office equipment and instruments, and the supply of drugs that he brought with him.

He had seen a few patients, and performed one minor surgery without ether, since he had not yet unpacked. The day of arrival, he saw a man with edema of the legs that he feared was due to cancer, but would require the diagnostic services of a hospital to confirm. He removed a splinter from a man's head. He went on an emergency call to Woody Island, in a little outboard skiff at the insistence of the orphanage nurse. There, he found a boy who had strangulation of the head of the penis from a tight foreskin, which he had had for three days and the part was becoming gangrenous. He had been crying with pain all that time. Dad had no ether, so "gave him a good shot of morphine and had them hold him while he operated and relieved the situation." If he had not been there, and the boy had had to wait for a ship to take him to Seward, he would have lost his penis. "That shows the need here, and the opportunity for service," Dad wrote.

The next day, he saw a man with a possible cancer of the stomach, who was "just about gone," and an Oscar Bostrum, with a bad cardiac condition that he would "try to digitalize," as soon as his drugs were unpacked, and a middle-aged lady with a "cystic tumor of the ovary, which would need excision, probably before the hospital is built." The next morning, he was taken to see Mrs. W, a little old lady who lived on the beach four miles from town. She had a cardio-renal condition that was rather hopeless, but he was determined to do what he could for her.

By this time, Dad became aware that he would not have enough time to see all those who needed to be seen, since the houses were strung out along the shoreline in both directions and it would take too long to access them on foot. It had taken four hours to walk to Mrs. W's house that morning, and when making several such calls in a day, he would spend most of the time walking, leaving little time to actually care for folks. So he told Mother that there were suitable roads, and she would need to bring a car when we came up.

At the end of one letter, he wrote, "I must write to Dr. Council, the Bureau of Indian Affairs, the Standard Oil Company, and six canneries. I forgot to mention the canneries as possible sources of income, but they are, and Mr. Erskine is going to help me secure them, as well as Standard Oil employees, who may be doing some digging not far from Kodiak."

On February 10, Mother wrote: "We received your night letter this morning, and it relieved our minds to know that you were not out in the cold. It looks as though we will have to build, so I will put the house on the market right away. I am sending you the FHA circular. Perhaps it will give you some ideas. The thing that concerns me is that we may not be able to come up for some time, or would it be practical for us to live at the hotel and leave our furniture here until we build?

"It isn't practical to wire you money, as it costs $5.50 per hundred to get it there. Advise me the best way of handling it—I expect money order, or a bank transfer.

"Is the food good? Oh, there are a million questions I want to ask you. We are very anxious to get up there. We don't feel as if this is our home any longer. We have itchy feet. We really would like to come in May.

"This is Scout week and Bob is wearing his uniform all week. We are going out to the folks' to dinner tonight to talk the situation over, so they will see him in his uniform. He is very proud of it.

"Well, darling, give them service and plenty of it. Be sure to take their pulse, as it makes a good impression. Be very interested in everyone's aches and pains.

"Claude went with Bob to the Father and Son banquet. The skit turned out to be a riot. The boys got to laughing on the first number and got all off, all but Bob who kept on playing his trombone. Claude said he believed Bob would have finished if it killed him. The second number was OK."

The next day: "The folks are interested in getting us up there as soon as possible—also your mother certainly is a sweet thing. She told me she wouldn't let you pay back what you borrowed. All she asks is that you make a living, and at least get a roof over our heads. She sure is a grand person, when it comes right down to it." Mother went on to talk about what she should send, and what she should bring with her when she went north, what furniture she should sell, what realtor she thought of using, and other such things before closing but, of course, Dad didn't get her letter for two or three weeks.

Mr. Erskine informed Dad that it was likely he could rent the house next to his, which had been occupied by his son, Wilson. If this materialized, it would mean that we could join Dad as soon as Mother finalized things in Portland. This would minimize expenses: payments on the Portland home would cease, and the rental for the three of us would be less than for Dad at the hotel. He wrote Mother to sell the house as soon as possible and, if it didn't move quickly, to look for reliable renters, so she and I could join him. It would take weeks for her to get this message.

After four days in the hotel, even without an office, he was making about four daily calls which, if paid for, would have amounted to $16 a day. He had made a couple of calls that day and found his first patient much improved (to his surprise) and the old gentleman Bostrum, whom he had evidently digitalized, almost entirely well. The latter paid the $10.50 he was charged for the service. The fact that his first patients, although old chronics that he knew little about, were better, made him feel more confident. Also, having been paid enough to feed himself for a few days definitely lifted his spirits.

One day when Dad was standing on the street talking with someone, a Native whom he had seen in the home of one of his patients, came up to him and gave him a sack of "cherries" he had just purchased. The cherries were delicious white grapes, fresh from the States, "but the act was a delightful one of appreciation for the new doctor."

Another day, a patient of Dr. Jones was brought to see Dad by his mother, who wanted him to care for the young fellow, stating that Dr. Jones had told them to apply hot packs to his sprained knee and it was no better. Dad told her that hot packs were probably the best thing to do and that such an injury could not be expected to get better in just a few days and that she should return and tell Dr. Jones about it. "I told them nicely, and they appreciated it." Dad said that actually he would probably benefit from Dr. Jones's presence, since other doctors would not likely consider settling in a small community served by two doctors.

Wilson Erskine arrived within days, and started moving out of the house. He emptied the living room, and asked Louise Coon, wife of the Standard Oil agent, to hire two men to pack some of his possessions and some women to clean the house, since he wouldn't be there long enough to do it by himself. Dad went over and cleared out the workshop at the back of the house, and had his office furniture and equipment delivered. He had the heavy items—desk, bookcase, examining table—deposited on the front porch, and he moved them right into the living room. He unpacked the smaller items in the shop, removing the nails from all the crating lumber and setting them aside as he went. This took the better part of the day and, having not had much exercise in the previous two weeks, he found himself "tired in all his muscles."

Dad helped Wilson's workers pack while he unpacked. By Thursday, the transfer was complete, and Dad was settled in our partially furnished new office-home. He described it all to Mother and me, including the fact that his office would be in what had been the dining room, which was in the back corner of the house and could be closed off from the rest of the house. He was a bit concerned that patients would have to pass through the living room to the office, but noted that this would not be for long, since he would transfer his office to the hospital as soon as it was built.

Then, he wrote to Mother, describing the house in considerable detail, and telling her how nice it looked and what furnishings and equipment it contained. The only thing lacking was silverware, and he was going to purchase a couple of cheap knives and forks. He said, "I slept at home for the first time last night. It was lucky you insisted on my bringing bedding. I made my bed nicely, got out my flannel pajamas, and got into bed and had a fairly good night's sleep—except that the other twin bed was awfully empty and wouldn't respond when I talked to it. Also, I didn't have a chance to kiss Bob goodnight."

Now that the quarters were ready and there was nothing in Kodiak standing in the way of a family reunion, Dad was anxious to get on with it. "I thought of some things to tell you before you start up here, and perhaps this will be the last letter that reaches you before that happy event. You better bring a ping-pong table with you, as there is no place to get one here and lumber is quite expensive. It might also be a good idea to bring a couple of cases of Pard dog food, as it sells for 15 cents a can here. Meat, however, is quite good and not much more expensive than it is in the States.

"As soon as you know when you can come, send me a wire. The passenger lists are going to be full almost any week now with returning Alaskans." He reminded her that Captain Ramsauer of the *Baranof* said that if she came to the Seattle office, they would find a place for us. But there were still many matters Mother needed to settle in Portland: they needed enough money to pay our fare and the freight on all the belongings and a car, before booking passage.

On February 28, she wrote: "Time is beginning to drag, although I am very busy. I am putting the house on the market this week. It is practically ready except I have some junk to be cleaned out of the basement. You said in one of your letters it might be two years before you would make any money, and I am wondering if it will be that long before we can come up. I think I'll just curl up my toes and die if that's it. Couldn't we all get along on the $150 you are paying at the hotel if we all had a roof over our heads? Of course, your first letter will have the answers to my questions if it ever gets here."

On the same day, Dad wrote: "I seem to be becoming an extraction specialist. My two patients yesterday, I understand, are singing my praises today. The Lord was with me. The chap with a third molar that I was so fearful of, because it was so far back in his mouth and so decayed and my ignorance was so abysmal, returned today to let me look at it, and told me he had had three teeth pulled and this hurt him less and was quicker than all the others and hadn't hurt since I pulled it.

"Concerning a storage place for our furniture, Mr. Erskine said it could be put in his warehouse where it would be absolutely dry.

"Another rather fortunate thing happened to me today! My last OB patient is the daughter-in-law of the Russian priest of the village [Father King], and today her husband asked me to come over and see him, who was paralyzed. I saw the old gentlemen and told him what he must do and what he mustn't do, and he told me how glad they were I was here, and they hoped I would like it and would stay for a long time. Dr. Jones had gotten himself in trouble by condemning midwives in general since coming to town, so I told him how fortunate the town was to have his wife to care for the women during the dearth of doctors. I said I had heard how good she was and how much confidence people had in her.

"I am sure that Mr. Erskine is behind me, and the owner of Kraft's store is also quite friendly to me, as I have dropped into his store for a chat several times and made some purchases there. I am trying to keep the town from splitting on me. His bookkeeper had me to dinner and has repeatedly asked me to drop in anytime, and I sat in church with him last Sunday morning. Erskine's bookkeeper has consulted me as a patient. The town's lawyer has been in for a complete overhaul, and Erskine says he is 100 percent for me. The folks I met on the boat, the postmistress and others, have been boosting my stock, so it looks as if I am going to be able to do some real service for these needy people."

The next day, in another letter: "The *Starr* is in and I have read the letters from you and Bob with keen delight. I find that I have already answered almost all of your questions but I am going to try to get this brief note down to the dock before the *Starr* pulls out. Everything is going along nicely. We have a place all set for the family to live, and we can live a lot cheaper than in Portland, so the sooner you close everything down there and come up to take care of me and let me take care of you, the better.

"Put the money from the house in the United States National Bank, in a checking account. Then we can draw on it as we need it for building. But I think it will be best to use as little of that as necessary, and get a loan from FHA for the remainder, and pay it off by the month, keeping the rest of what we get from the house for a nest egg. Of course you will have to use some of it to pay the freight and other expenses, which will probably take about $1,500 dollars, depending on what it costs you for a new second-hand car and what the freight will be."

"You speak of coming up in May, but if you can make it in April, so much the better. In fact, you might be on the same boat bringing Mrs. Erskine home. She is a Christian Scientist. I understand she is one of the sweetest and most unselfish women, so you will probably like her—and I know she will like you."

On March 2, Mother received the first of the Kodiak letters, and she was "deliriously happy." It had been over a month since Dad left Portland and three weeks since he had arrived in Kodiak. They had received only those letters written during the passage. She had been anxious to hear something to reassure herself that he was all right and that he would be accepted; that people would want to see him; that he would find a suitable place to stay, and that they would be soon reunited.

On March 4, she wrote: "The picture has changed a little. The folks have made the house over to us and given me a free hand. I have listed it at $5,250 with the Stevens Mortgage Company. I am wiring you tonight asking that you send me your power of attorney so that I can sign the sale papers for you, and I hope you will do so at once so that I can close the deal as soon as I get a buyer. Of course, the folks want us to save all we can to keep a roof over our heads and I will do the best I can. I didn't ask that they give me a free hand, but Dad [the Bishop] just went and signed the house over and then told me. He wants me to make my own decisions and not have to consult with him, and it will be a relief as I have felt my hands were tied.

"I shall take your advice; sell, pay freight and ticket costs, bring or send you $1,000 and put the rest in the bank. I think I will offer the folks some of it, but they probably will refuse.

"I have made up my mind to bring our bedroom set, the twin beds and the two fir chests. I have packed the chests with draperies and towels, linens (etc.), as they will be crated and these things are not heavy and might as well go that way as to be boxed. I am selling the dining room set and leaving all our wicker stuff with Mother until later. She can use it in the den. I will bring the sewing machine and mangle. Elinor will buy the washer and Grace Butler, the stove. There won't be much else to dispose of. I will see about trading in the radio; we can't sell it, as it finally gave up the ghost and I can't afford to have it fixed. Perhaps I could turn it in to Sears Roebuck here and have them ship one from Seattle.

"I talked to Alaska Lines again yesterday. It will cost $6.35 to get Simba [our German shepherd] up there plus a $1.50 tip for the steward who cares for the animals. He doesn't have to be muzzled, just a strong collar and leash. Mother didn't think that was at all bad.

"I will send you a certified check for $50, which is every extra cent I have at present. I had to spend $27 on the paint job, $5 on plumbing and fixing that mirror, and then the rest on bills. I am keeping up the checking account, as I didn't like carrying my money around with me. If I should lose it, I'd be out of luck, so it is worth a dollar a month for insurance. The $50 should pay your license fee and perhaps you can get by on your collections until I can sell the car. The gas bill, for the last month you were here, was $16.41 and is paid, and I am on a cash basis. It costs me about 84 cents a week for gas. Mr. Armstrong thinks I should stall on the car for a month or so, since the market is low. If I wait until the sun shines again, people will be more in the mood. I have two people mildly interested. I would like to trade it in on a roadster with rumble, or a coach, then I could drive to Seattle thus being able to transport my baggage and the dog and bring a new car up. Will await your advice on this.

"Mr. Bates called me on the phone and told me when I came to Seattle to make his place my headquarters. He will take care of the dog, Bob, and me too. You must write and tell him all about the news.

"By the way, I balanced with the bank perfectly on the March statement. I'm getting to be a better mathematician. I have cut expenses to a minimum—have a four-party telephone line and am burning wood in the furnace or not using it at all. I will not buy any more sawdust. We are getting along fine.

"I have not paid anything on the davenport and chair, will pay if we sell, if not put it on contract. I am glad we have it as there is no point in paying freight on that old relic that we bought for $6.

"Dr. Cable just called and read me the letter he wrote, which was strong and to the point—very good, in fact—he said you had been associated with him for ten years and had done his surgery. He said you were 'efficiency personified, doing your work neatly and quickly, and he was sure any surgery you did in any hospital would be a credit to that institution' or words to this effect." Drs. Manlove and Leitch also wrote letters of recommendation in support of Dad's application for an Alaska license.

After all of that, she wrote, "Must go home now and am I tired. Haven't gotten to sleep until 2 o'clock for two nights now—brain too active. Love from us both, Frostie and Bob."

Then Dad wrote, "I appreciate your letters, my darling. You are doing everything just right, with your natural efficiency, and I am sure I could do no better, if as well. My only hope is that you will be able to shortly accomplish your business there and start north. I need you, terribly."

Mother followed with a letter, on March 9, letting Dad know that she had everything lined up so that if the house didn't sell by the fifteenth she would start negotiating for a loan. She would not wire her departure information until she had something definite and knew she had the money for the trip. She closed with, "I'm quitting my job the fifteenth—hulla! All my love to you, Frostie." And a postscript: "Bob's OK—wants to work hard and finish the eighth grade this year."

* * *

ON MARCH 10, a wire arrived for Dad: "*Sailing April second will wire if plans change cheerio.*" This buoyed his spirits greatly. Mother had her last day at the office on March 15, which she greeted with "three cheers and a war hoop." She was given a farewell luncheon by the staff at work, and another by the women of the yacht club. She sold the car and the boat, but had no good offers on the house. On March 22 she wrote that she had the transfer company pick up and ship her household goods so they would make the *Cordova*'s direct trip to Kodiak.

In Kodiak, on April 1, Dad received another wire: "*Sailing delayed account labor troubles stop will have to wait first available ship stop will bring car house unsold goods in warehouse have shipped you radio all charges prepaid Bob and I anxious to be with you.*"

Expecting the family in a week, Dad was devastated by the news. He had not written since the March 10 telegram, since he expected we would be en route before the letter arrived. He replied the same day in a two-page letter, his last before the reunion: "Just received your wire and am still hoping it is an April Fool's joke, but I'm afraid it is not. My hopes, built up in anticipation of your arrival in about a week, were dashed to the ground. Just another of those disappointments that will fade into nothing when the real event occurs, but a month or more without my family is hard to take."

He spoke of "feverishly drawing house plans and getting estimates from log men, excavators, etc.," and talked of ways to finance their home. He could buy property at $25 an acre and thought that "ten acres should be enough for our cow and horse and garden." He had to spend $17 for oil for the stoves, $10 for a raincoat, and some for a pair of rubbers, which depleted his reserve. Cash payments had dwindled, and he had received none in three days. The strike gave him something else to worry about. He felt that if it lasted too long, it would quash the fishing season—presumably because fishing gear, cannery supplies, and workers could not be transported—and that would mean none of his fees would get paid at the end of the season. "However," he said, "the man worthwhile is the man who can smile when everything goes dead wrong. We must just live by faith from day to day. I will set the new goal and hope you will be here soon."

Chapter 15

The Transition

1938–1940

B Y LATE APRIL 1938, Mother had arranged for the sale of the house, paid all the bills, and bid goodbye to friends of eight years, and we, with our dog Simba, drove to Seattle in a recently purchased 1936 Chevrolet sedan. There, in a few days, we boarded the SS *Yukon* and began the voyage to our new Alaskan home.

The *Yukon* was a traveling community of its own—a new world, with new folks to meet, new surroundings, a different routine, meals prepared and served, fascinating and changing scenery, new activities, and time to do whatever one pleased. The route north from Seattle to Alaska was through the Inside Passage, the same route traveled by Dad on the *Baranof* three months earlier.

The ship cruised through the islands in Canada and Southeast Alaska, some channels so narrow a rock could be thrown to the shore. In the narrowest, strong currents created whirlpools and tide rips, which swung the big ship back and forth and kept the helmsman busy. Evergreen forests blanketed every island, from their shores to their very tops.

We stopped at Ketchikan, Wrangell, Petersburg, and Juneau, the state capital, and then continued north to Cape Spencer, where the brave ship entered the Gulf of Alaska. We cruised along the southern coast of the continent, stopping at Cordova, Prince William Sound, then Seward in Resurrection Bay, where passengers for Kodiak were transferred to the *Starr*, the same ship Dad took to Kodiak.

Captain Tronsen of the *Starr* was particularly nice to us, probably because he took a shine to Mother. We met two Kodiak passengers, one being Mrs. Edna Kraft, a nice, white-haired lady who was married to the owner of Kraft's, one of the two general merchandise stores in Kodiak. The other was Tim Gilmore, who was part owner of a bar. Both were on their way home.

This portion of the voyage took a little over a day, the arrival being presaged by an abrupt and welcome calming of fairly heavy seas, as we entered the lee of Woody Island, across from the village of Kodiak. Soon we could see houses scattered along the beach on our right. Two long, deep blasts of the whistle vibrated the entire ship, announcing our impending arrival, as we entered a narrow channel. Everyone crowded the railing, as the old ship neared the dock. It was Saturday, April 30, 1938.

The Erskine Company dock was crowded with people and dogs. Most of the town had come to meet the ship that carried relatives, friends, groceries, fresh fruit and vegetables, supplies, and a few newcomers. As we came nearer, folks began to wave at friends and relatives, and then shouted greetings. "How was the crossing?" "Did you see George?" "Is Mother with you?" A babble of voices. As the ship's engines growled in reverse, swashing water alongside from the stern, we spotted Dad and started waving vigorously. He waved in return and was smiling broadly, like Mother and I.

Center Street, the stone steps, and the path through the Erskine's rockery to our new home, which is hidden in this photo.

In the midst all of the cheerful tumult, while the ship was being tied to the pier, I went down to get Simba. Our bags were ready, and we were among the first down the gangway, where Dad met us. We hugged each other for a minute or two, while Simba barked and jumped up on Dad. He introduced Allen Heitman, a polite young Native boy who had come to help with the bags. We pushed our way through crowds of people and dogs. Big, friendly Chesapeake Bay retrievers, feisty with newcomers, kept us busy as we moved forward through the throng, trying to keep our equally feisty German shepherd in hand. We reached a gate to the Erskine property, on the shore side of the dock. Passing through, leaving the crowd behind, we climbed a curving stone stairway, through a rock garden, then past the Erskine house—formerly a Russian storehouse—to our house, just beyond.

The next day Mother and I unpacked, and moved in the bedding, the clothing, and a few small pieces of furniture. It took several days to choose what furniture we would use and what would be stored. We began to feel more at home. Being reunited, after a separation of three months, we were beginning the transition to this our new, and very possibly permanent, home.

Russian Orthodox church in Kodiak Village, c. 1940.
KIodiak Historical Society.

The next week, office hours began, and from time to time, patients came traipsing through the living room to see the doctor. This became the norm, and would last until the hospital was built and Dad could move into an office there.

*Kodiak Village was our home for the next four years, overlooking the warehouses
and dock, April 30, 1938
Kodiak Historical Society.*

Our house had a covered veranda across the front, and a roof, with
a generous overhang, at each end. The back yard and the garden were
fenced in, and contained a gate in front and in back. Our Chevrolet
had no garage, and was kept alongside the house. In the center of the
veranda, the front door opened into an entryway that was open to the
living room on the left, which occupied the front two-thirds of the
house; the back third, on that side, was a den, which became the doctor's
office. To the right, a door led to my parents' bedroom and, in the space
behind the entryway, its walk-in closet, in which a ladder led to my
room in the attic. On its back wall were two doors, the right leading to
the bathroom and the left to the kitchen, which had a narrow pantry
extending behind the bathroom. The remaining space was divided
between a breakfast nook, next to the office, and a large back entry on
the right corner, which also served as the workshop.

The house was one of several in the village that had running water and
electricity. Most folks carried their water from a well, and illumination
was provided by candles, kerosene lamps, and Coleman lanterns. The
Erskine Company and Kraft's store each had a generator that furnished
electricity to a few houses. Erskine's had water piped across town from
a dam below Pillar Mountain, which supplied the Erskine house and a

few others. The house, like most other dwellings in town, was heated by the kitchen's oil stove, which kept us quite warm.

The electricity supplied by the Erskine Company generator was not the service to which the family was accustomed in Portland. It came on at 6 o'clock in the morning and was shut off at 9 o'clock at night. We became familiar with the alternative lighting, common to most folks in town, in the off hours and during unannounced power outages that were heralded by a dimming of the lights and then complete darkness. After the first loss of power, we knew exactly where auxiliary light sources were, and with the first flicker of the lights, we would light a lamp.

There were seven hand-crank telephones in town, all on a party-line system. Each had its own ring, so anyone within earshot would know who was being called. Those on the circuit, curious about what was being discussed, could tap in. With a little experience, though, it was not difficult to detect the *click* when another person tapped in.

Most radios were battery operated, the most common being a portable Zenith Trans-Oceanic model. It contained twenty-four D batteries that lasted many months. It could reach many foreign and some domestic stations, usually with considerable atmospheric interference. So communication with the outside world was limited. This contributed to the insular character of Kodiak that many enjoyed. Kodiak was special, and as most folks said, "Who cares what is going on Outside?"

In addition to the two stores, Kodiak had two taverns, a Russian Orthodox church, Blinn's Pool Hall, Louie Thompson's Transfer Company, whose flatbed truck, with our Chevrolet, made up two of the four vehicles in town, the Baptist Mission, in the process of moving over from Woody Island, the Standard Oil Company tanks and dock, McConaghy's salmon cannery, a post office, the Alaska Steamship Company office, a federal jail run by Karl Armstrong, a U.S. Marshal, the office of Gil Bubendorf, a U.S. Commissioner, and a federal court, presided over by Judge Naughton. Warren A. Taylor was the town lawyer, and Drs. Johnson and Jones were the town doctors.

The downtown school, 1942. High school enrollment was about forty students. Kodiak Historical Society.

Long, balmy summer days stretched before us as we began to get acquainted with our town. Dad worked at his medical practice daily and on occasional weekends when emergencies occurred, the most common being inebriates whose problems always seemed urgent. In his spare time, he was busy trying to hold the state to its promise of a hospital, as well as studying for his medical license examination. Mother was developing friends among the women of the town, and soon became involved in raising funds for the hospital.

Letters written late in 1938 revealed that the Bishop had not been doing well. He and Sarah had retired to an attractive Tudor home on an acre of land in rural Portland. He had developed a urinary problem, which early in 1939 proved to be cancer of the prostate and became widespread. He died on December 9, 1939.

Dad did not show a response to his father's death that I remember, except one morning at breakfast, much later, when it was mentioned, and I was startled to see tears in his eyes. I had never seen him cry, and I guess I didn't think he could. I later found the following letter that he had written to Darlow, two days after their father had died: "As I just wrote Mother, I am sure Father wished to go. He has not really been happy and contented since retiring. He could no longer give of himself, unstintingly, as he did through the years. He felt that his work was finished, and he was ready to relinquish his hold on this life. He had told me this on several occasions. Therefore we should not feel sorry on account of Dad. However, I do grieve when I think of how lonely mother may be when she returns home and misses the mate with whom she has lived for over half a century. I am so glad that she has such strong faith in God and his Heaven so that she knows beyond a doubt that this is just a temporary separation for the two of them—that father is happy where he is and waiting—without his earthly impatience—for her to join him when God is willing it be so. With that sublime faith, she will probably be able to go about the house and do her regular work and worship just as she did during his frequent, prolonged absences from her during his stay on Earth. She waited for his return then—she awaits her going to him now."

When Nellie Erskine arrived back in town, the Erskines became fast friends of my parents. We also began to know Louise and Merrill Coon, Louise being the lady who helped clean the house when Wilson moved out, and Merrill being manager of the Standard Oil Company; Frank McConaghy, manager of the only fish-packing plant in town, and his wife; and Mr. Watkinson, the bookkeeper at Erskine's, a gruff old Scotsman who was not particularly sociable.

Within a year or two, several other folks arrived and joined their circle of friends. Avery Roberts, the first town dentist, arrived with his wife, Maxine. This relieved dad of the onerous task of tooth extractions. Oscar "Torgy" Torgerson had arrived in 1939 and built the Bank of Kodiak, thereby relieving the stores of the need to serve as depositories for fishermen's funds. With him came his wife, Ruth, who became one of Mother's best friends. Then came Mr. Clifton, the new school superintendent and his wife, and Frank Lahtonen, bookkeeper at Kraft's store, and his wife, Elsie.

In 1939, Dad became a member of the first board of directors of the bank, a position he held until 1960. He became a Fellow of the American College of Chest Physicians in 1939, and governor of the college in 1940. He had been a Fellow of the American College of Surgeons before coming to Kodiak. He continued to be very busy with his practice, trying to get the hospital built, and coping with a population that began to expand as construction workers arrived to build a naval station on Women's Bay, five miles southwest of the village.

Dad, c. 1940.

In February 1940, Dad began to keep a diary again. On the last day of the month, he noted that Mr. and Mrs. Sharp, the city manager and his wife, were dinner guests, and they had discussed the plans for their new log home. The original plans were grandiose, and the estimate for construction was $75,000. So Dad began new plans, which he hoped would not exceed $9,000. The next day, he showed the plans to Bill Sharp, who was also an architect, who said, "That extra four feet and that outside fireplace will each cost a thousand dollars," so it was back to the drawing board a third time. On March 2, he wrote, "New plans still have to be abbreviated." And so, the practical world continued to abbreviate his dreams, which would, eventually, reach an achievable form.

By the end of 1940, the naval station was completed and military families had begun to arrive. The Bank of Kodiak was in full swing. Pacific Northern Airlines (PNA) had begun scheduled flights to Kodiak. The *Kodiak Daily Mirror*, a weekly newspaper, was started.

On Saturday, the second weekend in March, the family took Torgy, the founder and manager of the new bank, his wife, Ruth, and their ten-year-old daughter, Theron, for a drive to Mill Bay and then to Sprucehaven, the name they had given to the property where they were going to build the family's log cabin. It was at the end of the road, just beyond the new mission. With eight acres of spruce forest, Sprucehaven was a virtual wilderness located between what became known as Mission Lake and the ocean. They looked at the site of the proposed cabin, and then hiked around Mission Lake before returning to town, the Torgersons to their home in an apartment above the new bank.

In mid-March, Dad wrote that the weather was becoming cold and that maybe they were going to have a little winter after all. The next few days heralded clear skies and colder weather, and finally, "fair skating on Sprucehaven Lake [a.k.a. Mission Lake]—fine going with the wind, but very cold when facing it—thermometer 6 degrees above zero—coldest in years." The next day, Sunday, there was skating on Big Lake [later known as Lilly Lake] on Mill Bay Road, and the sun, bright and warm, reminded him that this surely was beautiful country.

Sunday morning, Avery Roberts, the dentist, and his wife, Maxine, came for breakfast, after which Mother and Maxine went to church, and the men went to work, Avery to his office and Dad on a house call. The call was to a Native woman whose ascites (fluid in the abdomen) had ruptured through her umbilicus, releasing gallons of fluid. Examination then revealed a "knobby" liver and an enlarged spleen, which led him to make a clinical diagnosis of advanced cancer. Nothing could be done to change the course of her disease.

On March 31, he called on a woman, whose labor was starting at six months gestation. He had delivered her first child in December 1938, after she had been married five months or so. A divorce had followed. In a few months, she had married a cousin, and this pregnancy followed. At her first office visit, it came out that the cousin was really the father of the first child. "Thus goes life in Kodiak," Dad commented. Her labor could not be stopped, and she produced a premature infant who lived ten minutes. The placenta would not deliver by the usual means, so, since she was not bleeding, he decided to wait until morning. By then it was clear that it would not deliver by external pressure, so the mother was put to sleep at home with Evipal for a very difficult manual removal of an adherent placenta. He returned to the office, worried of the possibility that she would develop a fatal infection.

At the office he found a father and his fourteen-year-old son who had been brought from Afognak village, on Afognak Island, part of the Kodiak archipelago to the northwest of Kodiak, by cannery tender. The boy had developed pain in the abdomen the previous morning, which the schoolteacher thought might be appendicitis, but there was heavy surf and no harbor there so they couldn't launch a skiff. Before dawn that morning, worried that they should wait no longer, they carried the boy two miles around the point to a beach sheltered enough to launch a skiff, which they then rowed, for two hours, against wind and heavy seas, to get to the cannery at Port Bailey, where a tender brought them to Kodiak. Dad wrote, "Another wait of two hours to get word to the naval hospital and receive permission, and I took the two of them in my car over six miles of terrible road to the only hospital yet in this region, and operated, finding a red hot appendix which, luckily, had not yet ruptured."

The woman who had manual removal of her placenta three days before had survived with no sign of infection. Dad concluded that she was out of danger and commented, with relief, "Nature was good to me!" A little girl, two years old, was brought in with generalized swelling. A urinalysis showed severe kidney infection and she was begun on treatment. The young fellow who had an appendectomy was feeling fine and had a normal temperature.

Sunday, the Roberts, Lahtonens, and the Cliftons went with the folks on a hike to Sprucehaven. They visited the proposed site of the log cabin, then followed the cow path along the cliff edge several miles beyond the property and the lake. The early afternoon quiet was disturbed only by wisps of conversation, the sporadic chatter of ground squirrels, early spring bird song, and the gentle swishing of waves on the beach. There were no signs of human habitation in this neck of the woods. It was a paradise, and reminded them how peaceful it could be on this beautiful island.

Dad later wrote, "Called furtively to Sally's Dress Shop where a local lady was in hiding from her husband. She had a badly broken ankle from jumping from her window when he tried to kill her. Again, my lack of X-ray facilities becomes apparent, but Dr. Roberts took a fair picture with his dental machine and I reduced the fractures under Evipal anesthesia and applied a cast. Another picture showed excellent setting, so I'm letting her stay here instead of sending her to the Seward hospital, as I first told her. Her husband is now in jail so she is safe, temporarily."

* * *

ON JULY 19, the steamer *North Coast* arrived in Kodiak bearing Dad's mother, who had come for a visit. She had a very pleasant voyage and Dad observed that "she gets about in good shape, looks no older than before, and is still as firm a believer in the grace and the power of prayer." During her several-week visit, I recall that we all went to church every Sunday.

On July 23, a Native man was sent in from a cannery with a ruptured appendix, which had perforated and spilled infection into the abdominal cavity, causing peritonitis, a life-threatening problem. The treatment required hospitalization. The base hospital was filled to capacity and refused admission, so Dad called a plane to transport the patient to Seward. He spent until 1 a.m. with the patient, when he learned that the plane would not be available until daylight. He gave him a "hypo" [morphine] for pain, went to bed, and returned early in the morning to get him safely on the plane. He was criticized severely by the cannery superintendent for not operating in Kodiak, which would have been extremely hazardous. Dad felt that, most likely, the criticism was prompted by the cost of sending the patient to Seward, which probably amounted to $2,000 or $3,000.

The remainder of the summer was rife with cases of "fish poisoning" (a common name for any infection occurring among folks who work with fish) among fishermen and cannery workers, injuries mostly among fishermen, and the usual run-of-the-mill problems, as well as a more or less steady stream of births that mostly occurred at night.

On a beautiful Saturday night in mid-August, the family had a picnic supper at Sprucehaven to which Gene Dawson, the editor of the *Kodiak Daily Mirror*, was invited. Gene was my boss at the paper, and I (now 14 years old) was working as the "printer's devil," responsible for mimeographing a twelve-to-sixteen-page issue every week. Grandma Sarah was attacked by bugs during the picnic. Returning from the picnic, Dad was met by an accident case from Karluk, on the west side of the island and eleven hours away by boat. He had to amputate the man's right index finger, "improving on the job done by the drive chain and sprocket on his boat."

The next day being Sunday, Grandma Sarah spoke at the morning service in the Community Baptist church and, according to Dad, did a very creditable job. The congregation did not seem distracted by the swelling of her right forehead from her picnic encounter, probably with "no-see-ums," bugs in Alaska that are tinier and more vicious than mosquitoes. Mother and I were founding members of this church, and Dad, though he never joined, was active in support of the church and attended on special occasions.

Dad had some thoughts on the conduct of one aspect of medical practice. Following the mention of having done a myringotomy (lancing an eardrum), he mused on the obscurity of Latin terminology when speaking to patients. "I wonder if, on the one hand, we should speak common English so the public could understand, or on the other, technical terms and Latin so doctors could understand, and the patient wouldn't. At any rate, Latin terminology comes in very handy when one has his back against the wall on a diagnosis or prognosis, for instance. Something must be said. The relatives want facts. One has no facts for them yet, but may have in a day or two. They won't have confidence if they are told we don't know, but will in a day or two. One doesn't want to say something he must contradict tomorrow—thus the recourse to Latin."

Another observation was prompted by a middle-aged woman who came to the office requesting that he "paint her throat." (Painting the throat is an old-fashioned technique thought to help people with sore throats. It was done with cotton on an applicator stick, dipped in mercurochrome, initially, and later replaced by iodine, thought to be more effective.) He did so, using a weak solution of iodine. "I don't think painting throats is of much value physically, but those who expect this are helped mentally, so I daresay it is good treatment." The next day she returned, much improved, requesting another painting, to which Dad obliged, using metaphen, a topical antibacterial liquid similar to iodine, this time. This was an example of the power of faith, or belief, relied on by physicians and referred to as the "art" of medicine in the old days.

The place of treatment varied as a practical matter in many instances. For example, when a drunken engineer fell down a companionway ladder and suffered a scalp laceration, Dad made a house call—in this case, a "ship call"—with bag in hand, and took six stitches right there on deck to put things back together.

The two weeks bridging the end of August and the first of September 1940 represented Dad's busy practice. On a Saturday, Dad and I were excavating a partial basement at Sprucehaven after office hours (the construction of the log cabin was soon to begin), when he was called to see a thirteen-year-old girl with a serious problem. She had a fever, abdominal distension, and pain in the entire right abdomen. She was breathing shallowly to avoid the agonizing pain caused by deeper respiration. Her lungs were clear but she had exquisite tenderness throughout the right side of the abdomen that indicated a peritonitis or inflammation of the abdominal cavity. The source of the infection was not clear, in spite of examination and microscopic smear of a vaginal discharge, so she was begun on sulfanilamide, the only available antibiotic, and watched closely.

The next morning, re-examination revealed tenderness a little more in the right lower quadrant. The vaginal smear had shown many bacteria but none in the cells, which would have indicated gonorrhea. At this point, the source of the problem could have been either a ruptured appendix or rupture of an infection in the ovarian tube.

"Besides a busy day of opening infected hands, incising a large left inguinal abscess in a boy sent from Larsen Bay, calling on a man with pain in the abdomen, which (I hope) will not become acute, I gave the thirteen-year-old 1,000 ml glucose in normal saline." A pregnant woman was in labor and tiring, so was given morphine, which quieted the contractions and allowed her to sleep a few hours. This was done twice during the day, and she delivered a ten-pound baby boy at 10:30 p.m., causing a laceration that was repaired, all of which would have been so much easier in a hospital."

Monday morning the young girl had developed fecal vomiting, which was a sign of intestinal obstruction. The vomiting would have been very serious were it not for the fact that she had begun to indicate some return of bowel function. Dad had instituted hot "stupes" to the abdomen, and he attributed the resumption of intestinal function to this, so it was continued.

On Tuesday, he observed that there had been no vomiting since the previous night, abdominal distention had subsided, and a mass was forming in the right lower quadrant. That morning he performed fifty-seven school examinations "in the clinic room of the health center, fitted for the purpose."

On Wednesday morning, the young girl had no nausea, no vomiting, no fever, and a normal bowel movement, indicating definite improvement.

Sixty-five school examinations were performed that afternoon. The next day, the girl had an appetite, but he felt that the mass, now apparent in the right lower abdomen, was an abscess that would have to be opened and drained. He elected to wait a little longer, until her strength increased, before operating. On Friday she continued to improve and the mass became well defined. Dad was still very busy in the office, leading him to quote the old adage, "It never rains but it pours!"

On the following Monday, she began running a low-grade fever once more, and Dad felt it necessary to perform an examination to determine if the abscess could be drained through the vagina. This was done under intravenous Evipal, which he preferred for brief procedures requiring an anesthetic. The exam determined that it could not be drained from below.

Her temperature rose to 102 degrees the next morning, although she continued to feel well. It was another busy day, "between visits to her, removing splinters, painting throats, draining a bursitis of the knee, fish poisoning, and a circumcision."

The following day, the twelfth day of her illness, her temperature was 102.4 degrees and she had slightly more pain. "If I had a hospital I would have operated about three days ago," he said. "As it is, I'm going to have to operate, so am arranging to have all prepared for tomorrow morning."

The next day: "Miss Spencer, Territorial health nurse, spread newspaper over the kitchen floor and prepared the room. A washbasin table (with no running water or drain) pushed to the end of the kitchen table made a table long enough for the patient. Frostie had drapes, towels, sponges, gloves, and the instruments I had chosen the day before, sterilized, by boiling or in a pressure cooker. The operation from start to finish took four minutes and quantities of pus were obtained from a well-localized abscess low in the right lower quadrant. The patient was awake five minutes after her return to bed and asking what she could have to eat." Over the next week or two the drainage from the abscess diminished and eventually subsided. She had a complete recovery, which was remarkable under the circumstances.

Chapter 16

Hospital Practice

1941–1942

THE QUEST FOR THE NEW HOSPITAL had continued throughout 1940, with it being necessary to finance its completion locally since Territorial funding did not cover the equipment needed. Dad had contributed to the hospital design, in particular a widening of the central hallway to allow a gurney to be maneuvered easily. The building was completed, at last—and partially furnished—by mid-November, and Dad moved all of his office equipment out of the house and into his suite, to be ready for opening day, November 15, 1941, and the exciting open house ceremony.

Griffin Memorial Hospital, November 15, 1941, Kodiak.

Christened the Griffin Memorial Hospital, it was named for a lady who had lived in Kodiak before there was a hospital, and who died en route by ship to the Seward hospital. Her husband, Edward W. Griffin, later became acting governor of Alaska, and was diligent in pursuing state funding for the hospital. It was therefore thought of as a dual memorial.

The building was concrete, two stories, on the high bank near the Johnson and Erskine residences. Built on the slope, its entrance to the second floor was three steps up from ground level, and its first floor on the backside was level with the ground. The front entrance opened onto a small landing, and steps went up to the patient floor, and a stairway went down to the ground floor staff quarters, utility, and furnace rooms. The administrator's office opened from a small foyer accessed from the front stairway. The wide central corridor, in addition to overhead lighting, admitted daylight via windows and a glass door at each end, and opened into the hospital rooms and the X-ray and surgical suites on the sides. A small pantry, accessed from the hall, was located to the right of the stairwell, and was connected to the kitchen on the first floor by a Lazy Susan for the transport of patient's meals. It was a compact, efficient, and durable building, and everyone who visited that day was impressed.

The next day, Dad transported a patient, whose Pott's fracture (a complicated ankle fracture involving both the tibia and fibula as well as disruption of the joint because of ligament injury) he had reduced and casted previously, from the Base Hospital, "so we would have at least one patient in the building." The first operation was an appendectomy on a seventeen-year-old girl from Afognak, on December 2. The new hospital was christened.

There were few diary entries during the remainder of the year and none until September 1942. But events of terrible consequence happened during that period.

* * *

ON SUNDAY, DECEMBER 7, 1941, the Japanese attacked Pearl Harbor, and the United States immediately declared war on Japan. Alaska became part of the Pacific theater of the war, which meant at least potential violence for Kodiak. Some of us began to suspect that there may have been some advance knowledge of the need for a naval station in Kodiak. The Naval Operating Base (NOB) in Kodiak had been completed in 1940 and soon had its full complement of naval personnel, support staff and families, and the kids from the base joined us in the town school.

Kodiak was to become the joint operations center for the Alaska military in 1942—1943, and functioned as a naval base with submarines and ships, an army base (Fort Greely) with coast artillery and infantry, and a communications station. There were admirals, generals, officers, and other servicemen billeted in Kodiak. Alaska was put under military rule as soon as the generals of the U.S. Air Force, Army, and the Marine Corps, and the Navy admiral were in place. In addition to Fort Greely at the naval station, there were several army encampments on the island: Fort Abercrombe, on a peninsula at the northern entrance to St. Paul Harbor; Fort Tidball, on an outer island; and Fort Smith, at the southern entrance to the harbor. New roads were built to accommodate all the activity.

Because of the wartime activity, everyone prepared inside covering for their windows, to make Kodiak virtually invisible every night. A decoy village was established well beyond the naval base on the other side of town, an emergency plan was devised, supplies and a field hospital were made available. Travel to Alaska was restricted and ships were escorted in convoy; nonessential items and people were turned back in Seattle. The military assumed control over who and what entered the Territory. We were encouraged to stock up on canned goods, in case we were cut off from supply. Other than that, life seemed to go on as usual.

Mother and the military commanders in Kodiak for a conference,
planning the recapture of Attu and Kiska, late 1942.
Left to right: Major General Butler, Air Force;
Admiral Kincaid, Commandant, NOB;
General Pete Corlett, Army; General Simon Bolivar Buckner, Alaska Command.

We were alarmed when Dutch Harbor was bombed by the Japanese on June 7, 1942, and we learned that Kiska and Attu in the Aleutian Islands had been occupied. But that was 1,000 miles away, and seemed distant to us. Kodiak was the headquarters for the Aleutian Campaign, and this meant that the admiral and generals of the campaign met in Kodiak to plan the expulsion of the Japanese, which resulted in a nasty, prolonged battle, later depicted in *The Thousand-Mile War: World War II in Alaska and the Aleutians* (1969) by Brian Garfield. With the community "blacked out" at night during that time, with not a crack of light showing, the nights were long and very dark in the wintertime at Kodiak's latitude.

* * *

ON MAY 13, 1942, I had graduated from Kodiak High School, in a class of eleven, the largest class to have graduated from the school. In the fall, I was planning to go to Willamette University in Salem, Oregon, a private school that allowed Alaska students to pay in-state resident fees, which was a financial break. That summer, Dad and I selected my first year's liberal arts classes. Mother and I left on the *Cordova* on July 30, for her long-awaited journey back east to visit her family. This left Dad the sole occupant of the nest. The plan was that we would spend a month with Mother's parents in Patchogue and, on the way home, get me settled at Willamette. Our departure heralded a new era for the folks, with me absent except for summers.

For the time being, Dad continued alone, busy with practice, now housed in the hospital, working to complete our new log home at Sprucehaven when he could squeeze in the time. He resumed the historical record via correspondence once again, beginning with his farewell note, that day: "Dearest Family: After the ship finally got away from the dock, I went down one of the side streets to the bay and watched, but the sun was shining so brightly I could not discern anyone, so went to the office and worked until 5 o'clock. I then gathered up the Torgersons, who had invited me to their shack for dinner, and took them to Sprucehaven, where we had a picnic of lamb chops that I grilled at the picnic spot, afterward washing the dishes, which Ruth dried. [The picnic spot was alongside the lake, where the folks held a picnic every Fourth of July and on other occasions. Torgerson's "shack" was built on a small portion of land they leased, and served as their retreat from "urban" Kodiak on weekends and holidays. They and the Johnsons occasionally shared dinners at each other's shacks.]

"Home at 9:30 but could not settle down, so took a walk through town, stopping at Wodlinger's Drug Store for a chat and to buy a couple of Pocket Book editions to keep my mind occupied until I went to sleep. In the morning, after a good night's sleep, had bacon and eggs for breakfast including the grapefruit left in the refrigerator, and went to the office, where I was busy until noon. Met Ward Beecher as I was walking downtown at noon and invited him to lunch with me. We had a couple of butterhorns, a piece of apple pie, and a cup of coffee, and a little chitchat, then I returned to the office until 4. On the way to making a call on Brooklyn Avenue, I stopped in to ask Avery to come over and help eat those left-over hamburgers, and I found him already at the house after I made my call.

"Beecher was next door at Erskine's for dinner, still awaiting his plane, and Ken, who was also there, was sent over to invite us to see pictures Ward had taken, so Ave and I went over for a half-hour of some fair pictures. Then we went to the show at 8:30, a mediocre film the name of which I have already forgotten. Ave hates to miss a show—just like a small boy—so I sacrificed my time and fifty-five cents and accompanied him." [Ward Beecher was the son of a Seattle engineer, a friend of the folks, who had been involved in design of the hangars at the naval station. Ken was a young sailor, who the family had befriended and made welcome while he served at the navy communication station at Spruce Cape, located three miles beyond Sprucehaven.]

"This morning, after arising at 7, I mowed the lawn, back and front, dry-mopped and carpet-swept the entire house, set the table and put on the coffee, took a bath and got dressed, got breakfast, and was eating by 8 o'clock, after having been interrupted by the hospital to tell me that an OB was in. After eating a leisurely breakfast, doing the dishes, cleaning sink and stove, etc., making the bed and dusting the house, I got to the office by nine o'clock.

"This letter, being sent by air mail, should be waiting for you in New York when you arrive. I want to be there, by proxy, to tell you that I love you both very sincerely. I am keeping very busy so that I do not miss you too much, but I will say that I don't care about going home, except to sleep."

"Ward Beecher may call you, or be at home when you call his mother in Seattle—that is, if he ever gets off in the plane. Wodlinger is also going out by plane to make sure he gets a druggist to help him. He is realizing that he cannot stand the pace by himself."

The next day, I wrote: "Dear Dad: This is our second day at sea and the swells are pretty big, but none of us is seasick. I got up at 5 this morning and ran around the deck fifteen times in six minutes and twenty-five seconds. There are a lot of nice people on board, and last night seven of us got together and played pit. The weather, then, was swell, but today it is so foggy that we can't even see the accompanying ships [American ships traveled in convoys during the war for safety]. Kay has behaved swell and Mother and she are getting along fine." [Kay was the attractive daughter of a rather brazen, but attractive, nurse. She was going Outside and would also be attending college.]

The *Cordova* arrived in Seattle on the evening of August 5, and Mother and I checked into the Benjamin Franklin Hotel downtown. The next day we were picked up after lunch at Frederick & Nelson's department store by Ward Beecher who, in company with his sister and Mother, drove us to their home. We spent five days in Seattle visiting with the Beechers and other friends, before boarding the train to New York and arriving in Patchogue on August 14. We spent a month with family, swimming and having fun, before returning to enroll me at Willamette.

Dad wrote about progress on the Sprucehaven cabin: "Knut had put on three more rafters which progress, if continued, would mean that all the rafters would be on by Saturday night, and the roof next week. I will keep you informed of the progress on the house."

The logs for our home had been selected, cut, and limbed by Louis Thompson, owner of the only flatbed truck in town, and founder of Thompson Transfer, which delivered fuel to residents for the next seventy years. The logs were cut at Monashka Bay in 1939, rafted, and towed around Spruce Cape to the property, where they were hauled out, stacked, stripped of bark, and allowed to weather. Knut Solberg, a vigorous Norwegian bachelor who lived with his brother, Fred, in a log cabin they had built on Mill Bay, three miles northeast of downtown, contracted to build the Johnson log home. What appeared to be a daunting task, he approached with confidence and zeal. He built it by himself, with the use of a crosscut saw, an axe, an adze, a peavey, and

Fred's sawmill, where spruce and cedar boards were made for doors, windows, trim, and inner walls, so that the entire cabin, except the maple flooring, was made from wood obtained in Kodiak. The cedar came from logs washed up on the beaches. Spruce boards were cut, planed, and used for interior walls. Rock for the fireplace was greywacke, containing white quartz, from a singular supply hauled from a secluded beach. Knut had a little Fordson tractor, which he used to snake logs from the pile, pull up to the site, and, with appropriate engineering expertise, pull into position, including, remarkably, the thirty-four-foot long log rafters.

Knut Solberg, local Norwegian builder, works on our log home at Sprucehaven, Kodiak, 1941.

When working on the log home, Dad spent time in the "shack" on our property. The shack was a ramshackle shed about twenty yards from the building site at Sprucehaven. It was built using discarded outer slabs of spruce logs when they were made into boards for the interior of the cabin, and was located in the woods. It was furnished with rudimentary chairs, camp cots, and a woodstove. After working a bit on the log house, Dad would build a fire in the shack, turn on the radio and cook dinner, then read a little, and, at about 8 o'clock, he crawled into a sleeping bag to sleep.

Friends helped Dad survive his time without us, as portrayed in an August 4 letter: "Mrs. Erskine told me that she was bringing my dinner to me Saturday evening. She didn't ask me if I would like her to do so, but told me that she would do so each Saturday. Anyway, she came out about 4 with a great veal roast and other things to go with it, and she had invited Ken to our shack for dinner. Billy [Mr. Erskine] couldn't get away, so the three of us ate dinner. She said she was leaving the roast for my Sunday dinner. I tried to refuse it because, as I pointed out, there was enough left to feed eight people, but she said they never ate anything on Sunday and I must keep it.

"Consequently, having been to Torgerson's for Sunday breakfast, I invited them to our shack for veal dinner. The Red Cross girls were using their shack that weekend, and they were simply lost without a place to go on Sunday, so they really appreciated the invitation. We had a pleasant dinner, and then returned to town early to see Deanna Durbin and Charles Laughton in *It Started with Eve,* which proved to be a very entertaining show. But, at its most interesting part, a note flashed on the screen: *Dr. Johnson is wanted immediately.* So I went back and found Mrs. Thomas [the nurse] who hurried me out of the theater to the Alaska Steamship station wagon where the agent was hunched over the wheel.

"We hurried to his house, where we found his wife shot through the abdomen [presumably by accident] with an army rifle. A hole about two inches in diameter was in her anterior abdominal wall through which omentum and colon were protruding. Pieces of flesh were splattered on the wall. She was almost unconscious and could just weakly moan that she was in pain. We took her immediately to the hospital and operated, debriding the anterior abdominal wall—skin, fascia, and muscles—of powder burn, then enlarging the opening for exploration. The transverse colon had an area where its serous coat was shot off, which we repaired. The descending colon was intact. The small intestines were examined through their entirety and one portion was found to be literally exploded to such an extent that about three feet were resected [removed] doing an end-to-end anastamosis [connection]. Two other holes were found, which we closed. Bleeding was controlled. Muscle and fascia of the back wall were closed—then the anterior wall was closed, as well as possible, the bullet having gone through the iliac bone and exited behind. We put in all the sulfanilamide we dared before closure and gave her 250 ml of plasma and 1,000 ml of 5-percent glucose in saline before sending her back to bed.

"The nurses thought she would not last out the operation, but we sent her from the operating room with a better pulse than when she entered. The next morning, she was improved, if one could believe her general condition, and the following morning, more so." With special nursing care day and night, five plasma infusions, one whole blood transfusion (from her husband), and numerous glucose and saline infusions, she finally began to resume normal intestinal function (six days post-op) and—miracle of miracles—survived. Dad said he was going to church that day to show his gratitude and appreciation for such a miraculous recovery. In a city hospital, where precious moments would have been required to follow procedure, both in the emergency room and surgical suites, she probably would not have survived. He heard that the nurses said this was the neatest and quickest emergency surgery they had ever seen.

* * *

The "shack," a retreat during the construction of the Sprucehaven cabin, and a storage shed after that, 1942–1955.

MORE NEWS ABOUT THE CABIN: "Did I tell you that Knut had all the rafters on by Tuesday—then did nothing all week? He says that he is going to build a bridge, next, and a strong gate—the bridge, so that he can bring over the remaining stones for the fireplace. He is expecting to build the fireplace next. As soon as the bridge is finished, I will have

Wolff get the lumber and plane it. Then Leo Sears will be ready to go ahead with the roof. Meanwhile, before starting the fireplace, I will have Knut put in the other piers for supporting the floor joists, then the subfloor can be laid. The finished floor will be the last thing put in place, and Leo will probably do that when he builds the cabinets."

One weekend, he decided to try to take a little time off. He told the nurses he would be at Sprucehaven and they were to call him only for emergencies. He needed a rest, and wanted to work on the log house, so he was going to live at the shack. "I awoke when it was still dark, lit a couple of candles, and built a good fire. By that time, it was light enough to clearly see the path to the lake, so I went down in the nude for a swim. The water was cold, so I did not swim very long, but it was certainly glorious in the lovely dawn, swimming in unrestricted freedom, followed by a brisk rubdown, and a return to the warmth of the shack to dress. Then, after a breakfast of bacon and eggs, I washed the dishes, and cleaned up the place, before going to work on the cabin."

He worked without pause that day, slicking the logs in the den and entryway, and applied the first coat of linseed oil and turpentine to all the logs, including the living room. He wrote, "I haven't been out there since, but I believe Knut has a good start on the fireplace by this time. He had laid the hearth and the firebrick, and had started on the rock sides the previous weekend. I think I told you he had finished the roof. We may be living there by Christmas if all goes well."

While Knut was building their log home, Dad functioned as contractor to see that things were done according to plan. This required problem solving from time to time. One Saturday morning, for instance, after he had cleaned the house, Knut and Wolff appeared at his front door. Wolff was the fellow who was in charge of cutting and planing the spruce and cedar boards for use in interior walls, ceilings, trim, and cabinets. They had spent all week planing the lumber for the ceilings because the motor did not have the power to run the planer at full speed. Dad told them to find a gasoline engine with enough power. They did this, and were able to finish all the boards needed by that evening. Little by little, our new home was taking shape.

✳ ✳ ✳

THE HOSPITAL WAS PRIVATELY OPERATED for the first few years. The head nurse, Mrs. Thomas, had been replaced by Mrs. Flood who, according to Dad, "gets things done without fussing and fuming and seems to have excellent cooperation from the entire staff." Her daughter, Kay, had been on the *Cordova* when Mother and I went Outside. The hospital not only expedited caring for patients who were seriously ill or needed surgery, but also, when patients needed to be closely watched, it was far easier when they were all in one place. And the delivery and surgery suites were equipped with the instruments needed, so they didn't need to be taken here and there.

"Very busy office hours Thursday morning after writing to you and, in the afternoon, Mr. Erskine and I went out to interview General Corlett, regarding two things. The first was to ask why the authorities refused to let our laboratory girl—who was badly needed, and had come all the way from Sheboygan, Wisconsin—get on the ship or plane at Seattle to join our staff. Torgy had the same trouble with a needed employee, Mona Long, who had given up her job and was now stranded in Seattle. The general said they were not letting anyone who had relatives at the base come to Kodiak. He showed me a wire he had sent in Torgy's case, which said that the authorities had said there would be no change in present policies at this time. The second thing was a request to use one of their Quonset huts to store the Red Cross Emergency Hospital Unit in the trees on Signal Hill, as well as to set up the twenty emergency beds.

"I was called to see Mrs. Erskine around midnight on September 11. She had been to an army dance and had been happy and joking on the bus coming home, but as she got out of the bus at her own door, she said, "Oh, I feel sick." She then vomited, and they got her into the house and onto her bed, where Dad found her restless, talking with difficulty, and probably unconscious. He gave her morphine to quiet her, and then had to return to the hospital to care for a woman in labor. "Mr. Erskine came over, rather stricken, at about 4:30 a.m. and said, 'She's gone!' "

Dad continued, "I had him taken to the kitchen for a cup of coffee while I delivered the baby—then I went back home with him, stopping at Mr. Whalley's [the undertaker] to ask him to care for the body. Mrs. Erskine looked very sweet and peaceful in death. As I told Billy, she had lived and died just exactly as she had wanted to—that if she had lived through the stroke she would have been paralyzed just like her father, which was the one thing she dreaded. I told him I was sorry for him, but I was happy for her. He said he could bear up under it, but it was hard.

"I stayed with Billy until they took Nellie out to the army hospital and until all business arrangements had been made. Mrs. Flood came over (she is one of the most sympathetic nurses I have ever seen—and the hardest worker) to help get him over to the hospital for breakfast, so about 9:30, we got him to a good bacon-and-egg breakfast, then put him to bed, giving him sedatives. He did not sleep much, but relaxed well, saw a number of army and navy officers who called, then had more sedatives and a good night's sleep, last night. His son, Wilson, returned from Cordova and was rather drunk and hysterical. I had told his father that he would not be of much help, but we got him to sleep, too. Billy awoke about 1 o'clock, and I saw that he had a good dinner—filled out the death certificate—and am now going over to tell Torgerson that I will bring him there for dinner tonight. He is rather depending on me to tell him what to do. He appreciates it." And thus departed a remarkable woman who meant a great deal to so many in Kodiak.

The next day Dad wrote to Mother, saying, "Up until last night, I had not been to bed for thirty-six hours but I got a good night's sleep last night, and, after cleaning the house, taking a shampoo and a bath, and eating breakfast this morning, I am, now, at 9 a.m., sitting in my office, writing to you, and feeling much better."

On September 15, he wrote that Mrs. Erskine was to have a military service, in the Baptist Church, and was to be interred in a plot chosen by Billy and Wilson on a hill, overlooking the bay. "Erskines asked me to act as one of the pallbearers—you know how I feel about that—and I couldn't refuse, of course. Mr. Watkinson, Colonel Madsen, Torgerson, and I are the pallbearers. We'll have our hands full, won't we [she was a big woman]. I'll be glad when the service is over, and hope it is not too long, drawn out. You know I don't believe in funerals, and neither did Nellie."

"Billy is getting better control of himself, now, so that I do not need to lead him around, and think for him. Carolyn [their daughter] is going to fly up, as soon as possible, which will be a great comfort to him. They probably will both go Outside, and Billy will take about six months for a vacation, during which he will do the buying for the store." In those days, folks were encouraged to take a vacation to assuage their grief, something now felt not advisable.

Dad seemed to be getting busier all the time. He spoke of his attendance at a banquet in honor of visiting senators who had come to inspect the military facilities, keeping track of progress on the log cabin, and being fed by the Torgersons, the Sutliffs (Norm Sutliff owned the lumber supply business), and others, who were intent on taking care of him in Mother's absence. At one point, when Theron came to invite him to the Torgersons' for dinner—the third day in a row—he protested that he couldn't board with them without paying for his food. Her response was, 'Why not? Frostie told us to look out for you, didn't she?' "

The roof was completed on Sprucehaven Lodge (the title becoming more grand as the structure grew), and, "no rain penetrates our cozy little cabin except through the open windows and doors." The big iron Heatilator was in place on its concrete base, and the massive one-piece slate hearthstone was laid. [A Heatilator is an air-tight sheet-metal box that surrounds the firebox, with an intake vent just above the floor on each side, with a fan, and outlet vents near the top. Heated hair circulates through the room, blown by the fans, and can warm a sizeable space.] The fireplace would next be built around the Heatilator. Dad had completed most of the slicking and oiling of the logs. Needed supplies had been ordered and arrived before Alaska went under military rule. Knut was able to improvise the few things they didn't anticipate. "Old Knut is certainly versatile, and independent of markets and all else—a good man to have, especially in these days where almost anything can hold up the program."

The last paragraph in that letter contained a sober note. Earl Douglas, a young doctor who had just completed his internship, had been in touch with Dad while he was yet in training, and had expressed an interest in joining him in practice. He was the only real immediate prospect for an assistant to join him in Kodiak. Waiting to learn his selective service status before making a decision, he—and Dad—had just learned that he was being drafted. This was a great disappointment and meant that Dad would most likely be on his own until the war was over.

Meanwhile, Mother and I had returned from the East, via Los Angeles, to Portland, and then to Salem, where I got settled in a rooming house where my cousin Wendell stayed, less than a block from the Willamette campus. Mother then went to Portland, to stay with Grandma Sarah in her suburban retirement home. She visited folks, including Darlow and his family, who had recently been transferred to the Fremont Methodist Church in Portland, which, interestingly, was just three blocks from our Klickitat Street house in Portland.

Dad wrote to Mother on October 12, saying that folks were asking when she was coming back, and saying that they missed her, and needed her so much. He admitted he would be very happy to see her, though he was capable of getting along, perfectly well, on his own.

Of the two factions that existed in town, one being the folks who supported the Erskines; the other, the Krafts. Each shopped in the respective stores. Because he had been initially sponsored by the Erskines, Dad was deemed a part of that faction. Dr. Jones, then, became a part of the Kraft fraction, which included the judge and his family as well. This led to an episode that he spoke of in a letter to me: "Do you remember, a couple of years ago, when Judge Naughton's boy had appendicitis, and was cared for by Dr. Jones? It had ruptured and the boy was very sick. Someone suggested they call Dr. Johnson, but the old judge—it was reported—said he would see his son dead first. Dr. Jones finally got a doctor off a navy ship, to come in, and they operated at the house (it was before the hospital was finished) and found a bunch of pus but couldn't find the appendix. The boy was so sick it took a few months before he recovered.

"About three weeks ago, they brought the same boy to my office, with pain in the right lower abdomen. He had an acute appendicitis, and I told them this, and that he should be operated on immediately. The mother said she would have to ask the Judge and, to my surprise, the Judge said to go ahead, which we did. To make a long story short, although the operation was difficult because of many old adhesions, and the fact that the appendix lay behind the cecum—accounting for the fact that the other doctor couldn't find it—we removed the largest inflamed appendix I had ever seen in about half an hour, and sent the boy back to bed. In five days, his stitches were taken out, and, on the sixth day, we sent him home, all well." By making a friend of a community leader who was of the other faction, Dad hoped to begin to improve relationships in the community.

On the afternoon of October 19, Dad was served a subpoena to go to Anchorage to testify in court on two murder cases. The next day, he got a travel permit, as required for everyone traveling to or within

Alaska during the war, and wired Judge Hellenthal to ask that he be allowed to testify early so he could return to Kodiak. General Corlett indicated that Dr. Gray, an army surgeon, would be available to cover his practice while he was gone. Two days later, having indoctrinated Dr. Gray, he boarded the *Denali* at the naval station dock at 9 o'clock. When he arrived in Anchorage, he spent the day in the U.S. Attorney's office, learning little about when court would convene, and finally getting to the Anchorage Hotel.

Since the wheels of the legal system turn slowly, Dad had a lot of waiting to do. It took two weeks before the trial actually began. Meanwhile, Dad visited friends and met with Judge Hellenthal in his office, becoming acquainted with his staff. The next week, the attorneys started calling up jurors. That afternoon, Dad called General Buckner, to say hello and request permission to visit the hospital at Fort Richardson. There he attended surgical rounds. He met Drs. Albrecht and Center, and, after rounds, had a long chat with Dr. Albrecht, who, after his retirement, became head of the State Public Health Service. The next day, the trial began. The judge had received a wire from General Corlett, stating that he needed Dr. Johnson back to free his own surgeon, so Dad was called first for testimony, allowing him to return to Kodiak by plane the following day.

Our Sprucehaven log home, completed, December 1942.

Arriving home, he found a "real situation" at the hospital. Dr. Gray was fine, but there were "no cooks, maids, or nurses." Mrs. Flood had been on a drunk, according to reports and, in effect, Dad was, once more, on his own, except for the fact that he had his office in the same building where his surgery and his recovery rooms were located.

Two weeks later, four months after Mother and I had left for the East Coast, Mother returned. Dad wrote, "Mother returned Sunday and docked at the Base. She had two ladies, who bunked with her, that were going to work at the bank, so they all piled into the car. We stopped at General Corlett's to leave a present that Captain Kraft's wife had sent him, and he insisted that everyone stay for supper." After supper, they negotiated the bumpy drive to town, dropped the girls at Torgersons', and returned to their own cozy home above the dock, together again, to begin another chapter in the life of the Johnson family, now just two in number.

Dad was, in spite of how independent he professed to be, quite happy to have his house become a "home" once more. Mother was pleased to find that considerable progress had been made on their new log home. She had brought back with her some antique fixtures for the log cabin. Ornamental ironwork, however, for front and back Dutch doors, had to wait until shipping became less restricted. Temporary doors had been hung to close in the building. Enough maple flooring, which had been ordered in advance in conjunction with the newly constructed Montmartre Inn in Kodiak, was available to floor the entire house. Still to be installed were built-ins and some frame partitions, but they anticipated that the house would be completed enough to move in by the New Year.

Sprucehaven, cabin interior (left to right): the kitchen, the den, and the living room, 1943.

Chapter 17

Difficult Years

1943–1945

KODIAK WAS FOREVER CHANGED with the advent of the war in the Pacific, which was presaged by the construction of the naval station and the influx of the military. The civilian population expanded quickly, at first, with the construction crews, and later, with civil service employees who provided basic services when the base was completed. This greatly increased the population requiring medical care. At the same time, Mother and Dad, along with a few other newcomers, became involved as hosts to those in command of all military units. They regarded the military as guests of the community, and wanted to make them feel at home. In addition to Mother's role as hostess to officers at numerous dinner parties, she served as a chaperon for frequent dances and other social events for enlisted men.

Ever since the hospital had opened, finding a knowledgeable administrator had been a problem, and nurses were scarce, since many were serving in the military. Even when staff could be found, the hospital never seemed to earn quite enough to pay them, and the community found it difficult to continue supplemental funding, so it was touch and go. Added to this were the ordinary problems of maintenance and repair.

During the first half of 1943, Dad's diary addressed mostly his multiple surgeries and deliveries. Included also were many who visited the office with the myriad problems often encountered in general practice. It appears that there wasn't time or energy to write in detail: "January 4—Car overturned many times when going over a cliff. Five passengers brought in and the most severe injury was a small laceration of the scalp. Lucky group!

"January 31—Several pneumonia cases, from a 6-week-old baby to elderly men, have recovered quickly on sulfapyridine, a wonderful drug (one of the first antibiotics available). Sulfathiazine for the gonorrheal cases cures most, too. They are increasing in number." On another occasion, gonorrhea was found in an eight-year-old girl. No age seemed too young.

"February 10—Al Lacrosse had put a case of Coca Cola in the oven, which was forgotten when a fire was built, until a terrific explosion gave multiple lacerations to two persons standing in front of the stove.

"March 28—Young boy from Ouzinkie brought in a very drowsy condition. My diagnosis—tuberculous meningitis—100 percent fatal. Spinal fluid chemistry bore this out.

"April 22—Dr. Jones, from Base Hospital, operated on J. O. Johnson for chronic dislocation of right shoulder. I assisted, at my request, he being an orthopedic surgeon. Some uncertainty regarding anatomy, but end-results presumed good.

"Sunday, May 2—Stayed in all day. Frostie had slight fever with her flu and I had a cold, so remained at home and got all meals and took care of my wife for a change. We heard some delightful programs on the air." This is a reminder that Armed Forces Radio had become available to local residents, a fringe benefit of the war.

"May 30 (Saturday)—Leveled ground in front of house by hand, with plenty blisters to show from spading and raking. More plants for victory garden, which Torgy is planting and caring for.

"June 1—Another cannery worker with severely cut finger. Summer rush coming on."

The rest of the summer was a busy time with few diary entries. I was home for the summer, so there is no word until October and November, when letters resumed after I left for my second year at Willamette. The first letter was written the night before my departure, and was one that must be similar to letters written by other fathers to their sons: "Tired as I am tonight, I am so full of thoughts of my beloved son that I cannot sleep. You are leaving home this time, probably for the last time, except to return for a visit. Whatever I have not said to you, or whatever failure I have had in my own character and life, that has been an example to you, cannot be ratified. I feel I have not been able to get across in your training some very fundamental truths—such as the basic reasons for idealism, honor, religion, and other truly worthwhile things in life—really, the only truly important things, not only for one's own happiness, but for all future real contentment. You know I do not mean this in a sentimental way but from the standpoint of basic foundations—I was going to say 'cold logic,' but these things, such as love, transcend logic.

"I am sorry we couldn't have become close while you were home. I have so many things I wanted to tell you, and I so wanted to be pals with my only male loved one since my father left me, but every time I tried you seemed to build a wall which said, 'Keep out. This is my life and you have no business in it.' So, I desisted. My heart was often lonely, but like you I do not show my feelings and, instead of exhibiting my hurt, I would become gruff. I felt particularly broken when you seemed to be absolutely indifferent, or even openly hostile at times—as if you resented my being. I know you didn't hate me, however, because, last night, you sort of let down the bars, as our little family sat together on the davenport, enough to show that you, underneath, still loved us.

"It reminded me of an incident, in my own youth, and for the first time made me realize my own father's feelings when he showed so much joy over a situation which I did not consider exceptional. We were driving in his car, when he almost overran our turning place on an Iowa country road, and, when his attention was suddenly called to it, he made such a short turn that the car turned over. I jumped clear, but he went down under the car. I'll never forget my grief, when, running frantically around the car, I found him unconscious, with his dear head smeared in the dust of the road. I sat down in the dust and put his head on my lap, calling to him very tenderly until he regained consciousness. Then I carried him to the side of the road and told him to lie quietly and I would take care of everything.

"I then took charge, and did things for him, whom I had always let and expected to do everything for me: hailed a passing car; got him to a hotel in the next town, and was so solicitous about his welfare that his face beamed as he said, 'This is the happiest accident, and I am glad for it, because I realize you love me after all, don't you, son?' Of course I loved him!

"I know you love me, son, even as I love you, but being of English stock, instead of the more volatile and sentimental romance peoples of Italy and Spain, we become reserved when we feel sentiment arising within us, and cover the sentiment with gruffness, often akin to rudeness. Consequently, we are often misunderstood—our behavior often interpreted as dislike. Now you are leaving us. I know, son, and I am proud and happy in the knowledge, that you are good, and honest, and that you do have high ideals, and that people who appeal most to you are those with high ideals. I do not believe college life or military life can alter you in this respect. God go with you and keep you safe, and, more important, keep you honorable. Goodnight, my beloved son."

The next letter, late in October 1943, told of the sanders coming in to finish the floor in the house. Then Dad and Mother cleaned house, with particular attention to the floor, so it would be ready for varnishing. The cabinets had been completed, in the laundry, kitchen, and bedroom, and Dad wrote, that, "The house is getting ever nearer to completion."

The log cabin was located at the town end of the property, somewhat back from the cliff edge on a forested point of land. The design was in the form of a T, the broad base of which faced southwest and contained a ten-by-thirty-foot sun porch, surrounded by multipaned windows, through which we could see the small islands in Chiniak Bay and the mountains surrounding it. A log wall separated the porch from a twenty-by-thirty-foot living room, which contained a ten-foot Heatilator fireplace in its center. A French door accessed this from one end of the porch, which was balanced by a window in the other end. Beyond the living room were two bedrooms, a bath, a kitchen, laundry room, and a den. There was a flat stone front terrace, and the woodshed and the garage-workshop were out back.

In December, the folks had moved in. The maple flooring and the cabinets were completed, and, although a few finishing touches remained, they had wanted to be in their wilderness home before Christmas. I was able to come home from Willamette mid-month. Happy to be home, I was soon comfortably settled in my own room at Sprucehaven.

＊ ＊ ＊

THEN CAME THE DAWN OF 1944, Dad's most difficult year. It was to challenge his pride in his ability to cope with adversity, effectively, and without rancor. It was a year of multi-tasking, and, since I was at home and he no longer had copies of letters to me for his record, he began to focus on his diary again.

"Saturday, January 1: I had to see the old year out with a temperature of 102.8 degrees and a real head. I was beginning to feel better by 1944, and fairly enjoyed the friends who dropped in for a word and a sip of good cheer. We are surely enjoying our 'lodge.' Sprucehaven seems to have just what we want, as well as being pleasant for our friends.

"January 3: Flu epidemic is past its peak, and practice has settled down to a pleasant tempo. Bob's being home certainly made it much better while I was bedfast for three days—there are always things to see to on an estate." The "things to do on the estate" fully replaced the task of supervising construction of the house. The separate garage with its second floor apartment needed completion, gasoline had to be pumped into the tank in the garage periodically to feed the generator, the generator needed care, the pump house on the lake, with its well and chlorinator, needed tending, wood for the fireplace needed to be sawed and split, the house needed caulking, and many minor things remained to be done that a new house needs when the owners can wait no longer to move in.

On January 9, we attended a midday Sunday dinner with Colonels Robinson, MacCawley, Boise, and Schaeffer, as guests of Colonel Schaeffer at the 201st officer's mess. I remember this as a cozily appointed Quonset hut in a forested encampment—known as Fort Greely—where we enjoyed a fine meal. That afternoon, Captain McDade and Commander Rice, commandant and executive officer of the Naval Air Station, came to tea at Sprucehaven.

On January 11, Mother had a meeting of the Girl's Service Club at Sprucehaven, so Dad and I went to town. We visited two pool halls and the ice cream parlor before stopping at the Red Cross Service Club, where we had a few games of ping-pong, and I played the piano for Nancy, the new Red Cross hostess. We chatted and danced, and arrived home at 11:30 p.m.

The next day, the generator wouldn't start. Dad needed to start it every day because it supplied our power for the fan in the oil stove, the toaster, the sewing machine, the iron, the mangle, and the Heatilator fans. The light plant, or generator, proved a cantankerous machine and, in spite of a great deal of tender, loving care, we would often be without power for several days while we found someone to get it going. That evening, Mother chaperoned an enlisted men's dance, so Dad and I spent the evening reading and talking. This interval at home was an important time for us, for I was now eighteen and would soon enlist in the service and would be leaving for an indefinite period.

January 13 was a very busy day in the office. Dad commented that, "We have three hospital patients who are dying: one with advanced pulmonary tuberculosis, another with terminal gastric cancer, a third with an old fibrinous pericarditis, with a heart filling half of his chest. In general practice, one must take the bad with the good." Patients who were beyond help were a heavy burden for the physician in those days, and, indeed, there were more then than now, with serious medical or surgical conditions that could not be wrested from the jaws of death, so to speak.

Friday night, January 21, saw us playing ping-pong on the sun porch after dinner. This was a common event, which we both enjoyed. We each won two games that night, which was the way it usually went, for we were evenly matched.

Saturday, Dad completed the hospital medical report for 1943. Then he finished workbenches for the lathe and the jigsaw in the garage-workshop, which was a two-story log structure about thirty yards from the house. There was a rustic apartment over the garage. That evening, we had dinner with Torgersons in their apartment above the bank, and after returning home, since the temperature was below freezing, lit a lantern in the pump house to keep the water supply from freezing.

Sunday morning found the temperature at 20 degrees and no running water in the house. Fifteen minutes after lighting the little kerosene stove in the pump house, however, we had water again. A very cold wind accompanied the low temperatures and it blew through spaces here and there between the logs, because the house had not yet been caulked. Dad caulked half of the living room that afternoon. (The logs were caulked with oakum, a jute fiber heavily impregnataed with tar or grease, also used to caulk ships and plumbing joints.)

There was a significant entry on March 4, which simply said, "Moved office from hospital to old residence, which had been all repainted and varnished until it shone. With my equipment in place, it made a fine suite." This comment failed to mention that there had been (reasonable) complaints about his having an office in the hospital, since Dr. Jones was still in town. Moving into new quarters was actually an improvement for Dad, since it allowed him to become less directly involved with hospital maintenance and management.

I finally made a decision regarding military service after having reviewed the options. I didn't want to be a little cog in a big machine, so it became a choice between the Coast Guard and the Merchant Marine. The latter finally won out, because it seemed like more of an adventure, and I liked everything that had to do with the sea. This involved a federal appointment, such as one needed to West Point or the Naval Academy, so Dad spoke to Judge Anthony J. Dimond, a federally appointed district judge whom he knew, and the judge obtained an appointment for me to the United States Merchant Marine Academy at Kings Point. On April 12, Dad reopened his diary and made the first entry since mid-January: "6:30 a.m., arose to get Bob to an 8 o'clock departure on the *Cordova*—to San Francisco and the Merchant Marine Cadet Corps Basic Training School."

The same day, he wrote: "Hospital dressings—busy at office—some school examinations—several calls—new front spring (car)—three new patients from Unga, two from Chignik, another from Port Bailey. Home to dinner by 7 o'clock. To hospital, again, for histories on new patients."

The next day: "Started light plant. Filled all wood baskets. Did not set table. To hospital by 8:30 and cleaned up patients. Old man OK. Boy doing well—eating now. Forty-five student exams in the morning. Very busy afternoon in office until after 5 o'clock. Hospital visits and home to pump up drum of gasoline for light plant—about 550 pumps. Split some small wood before late dinner, and played three games of ping-pong with Frostie in the evening.

"Sun appeared in the morning, at least long enough to say hello. School exams. Busy in office until 4:30. Cy to dinner, talked continuously. Mother drove him home. Lantern in pump house. Light plant off again." Cy was Cyril Crawford, a childless fellow, tall and friendly, who had come from Seattle to ply his trade as a painter and "sign-writer" in Kodiak—he befriended me and the family, did a lot of painting and varnishing in the house, and was an occasional guest at Sprucehaven. Not having a son, he often befriended boys who would have been about as old as his own, if he had one. Dad wasn't enthusiastic about him, but was always hospitable.

Saturday, the fifteenth of April: "Hospital and office hours and home at 1:30. Lunch. Chopped wood. Built fire. Found hole in stove. Coil burned out. Got Vinnie Root, who installed a new one. Cleaned stove."

The next day, "Usual chores—hair wash, breakfast, church. Tea with Russian Easter Bread which Heitmans had brought. Sergeant Dressel visited in the afternoon and stayed for dinner, which he helped make while I read *Charley Chan Carries On*. Captain Michaelson dropped in to say good-bye. He, Colonel Bill, and other hospital doctors are leaving—four new ones are here, Major Smaha in charge. Ice cream, before going to bed, made me lonesome for Bob."

"Logs heavy to lift onto sawbuck. School exams. Rotary features second-grade rhythm band." Rotary met every Tuesday and he never missed. There were sixty-two members, and he was president that year. He took the Rotary motto, "Service Above Self," seriously, and it symbolized for him the practical application of religion.

On this April Wednesday, he performed the last of the high-school student exams. He observed that those, whom he had first examined as little girls in elementary school, were now fully developed. This, of course, reminded him that he had been in Kodiak for some time, and was beginning to put down roots. It was the start of an interesting process, a subtle, growing familiarization that leads doctors, who remain in one place, to develop a sense of belonging to the larger community family.

That day, they ran out of oil at the office. Fortunately, there was a reserve tank and, borrowing his own gas pump at lunch, he returned to pump enough to sustain them until the oil truck came to refill the tank. "Mission after dinner—scarlet fever—oh, dear! Called to hospital for a child who said—and whose little playmate said—she had swallowed a safety pin. Parents rather frantic. Experience has taught me that three-year-olds are quite imaginative. Flouroscopy showed no pin. All calmed. Lonesome evening without Bob."

Thursday: "Left office at 3:15 p.m., to have tea with Lt. General Buckner, General Robinson, and Colonel Schick at Sprucehaven. General Buckner much interested in cruising, and we had a pleasant chat. Chamber of Commerce at night, and a church party Mother insisted on attending."

Another Saturday: "Emma King had her baby at 11:10 Friday night. Bed at midnight. Called at 2:10 AM for Ruth Fry, who was having contractions. She was carrying twins, so nurses a little nervous. Called again at 4:15 a.m. to hospital. Not in labor. Back at hospital at 5 a.m. Up again at 8 o'clock, after dozing a little. She still was not in good labor. After office hours, and shopping, delivered Ruth's boy at 1:20 p.m. and a girl ten minutes later. Home at 4 o'clock for lunch. Rested to the Basin Street music of Paul Laval and his orchestra—really hot—never heard better. Guild Benefit Dance at night—Mother sold 76 of the 225 tickets. The old bunch of girls were there—Val and all. I was up to my old form—danced every dance and made much mileage." In the three months before Mother and I had joined Dad, in 1938, the local girls said he never missed a dance and never failed to dance with every girl present—he loved to dance and also liked to make sure no one was left out.

The light plant continued to be cantankerous. May 11: "The light plant is acting perverse. It kept me busy all day between office hours. Finally started, but not running smoothly." The next morning, it wouldn't start, and Dad called Basil Clark, the auto mechanic and owner of Clark's Garage, who worked on it all afternoon but was unable to get it going, and Dad had to put it together again after he left. It wasn't functional the next morning, and they were without electricity all that day. This did not preclude a scheduled dinner party, for which Dad broiled steaks over the fireplace. The next morning, Sunday, it was "delicious" coffee and bacon and eggs, prepared over the fireplace, before Mother went to church, and because of no hot water, Dad went to Torgerson's for a bath.

That evening, Art Larkin, Red Cross director, and Nancy, canteen manager, came to dinner and brought a soldier (electrician) who managed to get the plant started by 10 o'clock in the evening. It was left on during the night, for fear that it wouldn't start in the morning, but with uncanny perversity, at breakfast, it stopped just as mother pushed down the toaster.

Dad's routine at this time went something like this: Up at 6 o'clock, followed by a swim in the ocean and a brisk rubdown, and perhaps a few chores while awaiting breakfast. Breakfast—most often soft-boiled eggs, English style. Then off to the hospital, for rounds, often for elective surgery, followed frequently by house calls, before seeing patients who were well enough to come to the office. Lunch, scheduled for two hours but, more often than not, hastily taken, returning in the afternoon to see patients again for two hours which usually extended beyond that, and occasionally into the supper hour. The evenings often involved social events that Dad and Mother enthusiastically hosted or attended, together or separately. Dad's solo extra-medical activities, in the 1940s, were mostly civic organizations, while mother's were the Hospital Auxiliary and the Grey Ladies, who chaperoned dances for the service men two, three, or more times a week.

On the weekends, Dad rested, or read, after tending to Sprucehaven, which involved completing unfinished jobs in the house, the garage apartment, and the pump house; pumping gas into the tank which fed the light plant; keeping the cantankerous plant going; cutting spruce and beach logs with a crosscut saw and splitting them with maul and wedge; maintaining 150 yards of gravel road, which led from Mission Road to the garage; dinner parties and afternoon teas—common year round; picnics in spring and summer; and skating parties in winter. He had always read extensively, and, in addition to scanning the medical periodicals daily, he continued to read books on weekends. Mother regularly attended church on Sunday, and Dad accompanied her when there wasn't anything else to do.

In mid-June, the light plant defected badly, and the Army Ordnance boys took it out to their shop to see what they could do with it. Once again, as happened quite often, the folks "camped out" in the log house for a few days, cooking over the fireplace or eating in the "shack," or in "Torgy's Cabin" at the north end of the property. The army brought in a substitute generator to serve until they could get ours running well, and that worked for quite a while before it, too, stopped. But by that time they had our plant working again and theirs was returned.

On August 1—his practice being covered by Dr. Earl, a navy physician—dad took advantage of an offer to make a trip for a week around the island with Bob von Scheele. Bob owned and operated the *Shuyak*, and periodically delivered mail, fuel, freight, and other goods to all the island villages and canneries. Dad was treated as an honored guest, often dining with cannery superintendents. He was welcomed by the villagers, as well, many of whom he knew as patients. He visited cannery dispensaries, and saw patients, usually in the village schools. The trip gave him a perspective on the mutual interdependence between the villagers and the canneries, and the communities' dependence on fishing. He found the island quite beautiful, and discovered that the forests of the north gave way to deciduous trees—cottonwood, alder, and birch—at the island's waist. Refreshed, he was happy to be home with "family," now only Mother and Smoky, our German shepherd I had brought home with me in 1943 from Willamette.

On August 10, 1944, the folks heard from the Beechers, in Seattle, that I had arrived and was shipping out. Within several days, they received a censored wire from me, saying only that I was sailing south. The ship I was on and its mission were censored. Its destination was the South Pacific, but only the skipper knew where.

* * *

IN KODIAK, life went on as before. Everyone was tired of dealing with the persistent problems of the light plant. One would expect that they would eventually be resolved, but this particular light plant was unique. Fortunately, the one solution to the problem would be forthcoming before long, in the form of an electrical cooperative. There must, however, before resolution, be a story of *one more outage*.

On the evening of August 21, Dad recorded in the diary simply "light plant off." They continued without power for a week, eating in the shack by the woodstove, until the plant was returned to power. The next day, "Ordnance fellows out to check plant—shut it off and couldn't start it again."

On Tuesday, August 28, they had a Rotary picnic at Sprucehaven that lasted most of the afternoon. Most had not yet seen the log home, and it evoked much favorable comment. The light plant was working. However, on September 2, it was not, and the big generator was installed, once more, in the afternoon. On September 3, about a dozen ordnance men, who had worked on the light plant, were invited out for a picnic. It lasted from 1:30 in the afternoon until ten o'clock at night. Nice fellows, they had a good time, although rain kept them indoors. Wouldn't you know—the big generator stopped working!

* * *

VARIOUS PROBLEMS DAD EXPERIENCED were not recorded in his diary, one which, early on, concerned his license to practice. Since his Oregon license was not transferable to Alaska, he was given a temporary permit pending his taking a license examination, which was a comprehensive test covering the basic and the clinical sciences and required considerable preparation. The law required that, when he was prepared, he take the examination in the presence of the judge. The judge was in the Kraft camp and obliged to support Dr. Jones. Sometime during the first year in Kodiak, Dad took the exam, and the judge told him he had not passed. Dad contested that judgment, and demanded that the exam be forwarded to Dr. Council, in Juneau, for review. Whether it was sent or not, or reviewed, is unknown, but he got his license without having to repeat the exam.

In addition, there were some in the Kraft faction that tried to discredit Dad from time to time. One of them publicly accused him of incompetence, and Dad finally brought suit against the man for libel, which quelled the matter. Some wanted to take over management of the hospital, particularly when he had his office there.

The Baptists wanted to bring in another doctor and, recognizing that Dad was competent and well liked as a surgeon, they were looking for an internist, who would have complemented the practice, but no one was available. They also wanted to manage the hospital, which was poorly managed in the first years.

In a May 16 letter, Dad wrote, "I am still keeping busy in practice, in spite of the fact that the dear New Deal government is subsidizing a man to run me competition." This casual aside didn't mention that he had been held responsible for the hospital management problem, which was largely because competent qualified staff were scarce, due to competition from the military, and the state had provided no payroll assistance so those recruited could not be retained. Since Dad's office was in the hospital, it would not have been unreasonable for folks to blame him for this. At any rate, the Hospital Board must have asked for help, which accounted for the fact that a Public Health doctor had moved into the hospital to practice and, presumably, to help manage the hospital. Some of this is conjecture, but the presence of the doctor in the hospital is not.

In a June 2 letter, he wrote, "Miss Oslin, the head nurse and acting manager, said she was getting tired of this new Public Health doctor. He had taken over an hour, the morning before, to take out a pair of tonsils, and that all of his surgery had been done by the army surgeon, who was going to be ordered not to come to town to compete with civilian practice."

On June 13, in a long letter, he spoke of many things: his practice;

the Normandy invasion, which had recently occurred; Rotary business; the status of Sprucehaven; and the Public Health doctor: "He has had about all he can take. The hospital is in worse shape than it ever was: the place is more in debt; Kraft's has cut off all credit until a balance of $1,500 is paid; it is greatly understaffed, with only three nurses working; the hospital is dirty. Now, the doctor has nervous indigestion, which is worrying him so much he is leaving Kodiak and probably will not return. What this new Hospital Board of Trustees will try next, I don't know, but everything they have done, so far, has been absolutely wrong, and they still do not ask advice from anyone who might be able to help them. The town is learning, however, and, if the [Public Health] doctor had not been leaving, I believe it would have been only about a week before he would have been asked to leave or else get another office. These things usually work themselves out in time. I have just gone ahead, said nothing, and am keeping busy."

Dad became involved with three patients left behind by the Public Health doctor, all of whom had failed to respond to their previous treatment. One, a young boy, who had an appendectomy and had subsequently developed peritonitis, was seriously ill. Another, treated for staphylococcal bacteremia [blood poisoning] without improvement, was found to have a deep abscess of the hip, which was drained. A third, originally, had a rib resection—two weeks before—for drainage of an empyema [lung abscess] by Major Smaha before the military was prohibited from coming to town to do surgery. This fellow was getting steadily worse. Dad found the empyema had expanded and, Major Smaha concurring, operated and drained it. All three patients recovered nicely.

* * *

OVER A YEAR OR TWO, Dad and General Corlett, now departed Kodiak, had become good friends. Dad had talked about enlisting in the Medical Corps and serving under him. The general liked the idea, but Dad, nearly fifty years old, was not likely to be accepted. The general, however, wrote the following letter to the Adjutant General to help him: "Enclosed herewith is a letter from Dr. A. Holmes Johnson, Griffin Memorial Hospital, Kodiak, Alaska, indicating his interest in the Medical Corps. I was intimately acquainted with Dr. Johnson during my twenty-month tour of duty in Alaska, and am familiar with his background and reputation. The details of his experience are indicated in the letter. It will be noted that he served as a Tank Corps Lieutenant during the last war. Others familiar with Dr. Johnson's record include: Lt. General S. B. Buckner of the Alaska Department; Brigadier General John Robinson, Commanding General A.P.O. 937, Seattle, Washington; and Colonel Hiram Yellen of the Medical Corps. Doctor Johnson is a man of the highest professional integrity and, in addition, has a background of experience which should make him especially valuable as a military surgeon.

"It is recommended that Dr. Johnson be commissioned in the Medical Corps in a grade commensurate with his age and experience. I should be delighted to have him in my command at any time."

After several months of negotiations, Dad was informed that there would be no waiver of the age requirement and that, furthermore, his presence was "essential" in Kodiak. Subsequently, on reflection, he wondered if his attempt to enlist was partly to seek respite from mounting pressures.

As mentioned, there was an eventual solution to the hospital problem, but to understand this, a history of how religion came to Kodiak is in order. Before the purchase of Alaska by the United States, the Russian Orthodox Church was the only church in the Territory. After the purchase, a dynamic Presbyterian minister by the name of Sheldon Jackson took it upon himself to see that schools were established to educate the Native people. He established mission schools in Southeast Alaska, but needed help to fund expansion to the remainder of the Territory. So in 1885, he called upon other protestant religions interested in missions to share the Territory. American Baptists chose Kodiak. The Catholics were not included in this agreement. The Protestants respected each other's territories for many years, so when the Johnsons arrived in Kodiak, the Baptist Mission was there as well as the Russian Orthodox Church. A Community Baptist Church was soon formed, and Mother and I became charter members. The Catholics followed in the 1940s.

The Catholic presence in Kodiak was sporadic at first, but a very special priest, known to me only as Father Gallant, came and stayed long enough to become well known. Dad took to him right away, sponsored him as a Rotarian, later finding that priests were not allowed to join civic organizations but the good Father had not asked. This tells you something of his "can do" nature. Tall, gentle, suave, and imposing all at the same time, he cut a noble figure. Dad, learning he was to travel throughout the country on church business, asked if he would keep his eye open for a Sisterhood that might be willing to assume management of the hospital. The story of what happened, as a result of that request, was verified by those involved:

One day, during his travels Father Gallant found himself in Grand Central Station in New York City. While strolling across the concourse, he spied two nuns in grey habits, and, remembering his charge, he approached and introduced himself. They were of the Order of Grey Nuns of the Sacred Heart. He was delighted to learn that one of the missions of the order was small hospital management. He wasted no time in telling them of Kodiak, describing the beauty of the surrounding sea, and mountains, and of the struggle to manage the new, sixteen-bed hospital, and asked if they thought the Sisterhood might be interested. They were on their way to the Mother House in Philadelphia, having just attended an inspirational meeting in upstate New York, in which they were encouraged to meet whatever needs arose. They saw this as an opportunity and promised to broach the matter to the Sisterhood and, later, inform him of the decision. They parted, the Sisters with his address and telephone number in hand.

They accepted the challenge with enthusiasm and the good Father was able to inform Dad, on September 19, that the Grey Nuns would soon arrive to give him the best service possible. Although, as noted, others were interested, four Grey Nuns of the Sacred Heart arrived on November 4, 1944. On the eleventh, their Superior, Sister Mary Monica Brennen, signed a contract with the City of Kodiak for the management of the Griffin Memorial Hospital. She, and Sisters Hilary Sheldon, Michael Cammarata, and John Berchmans Brazil would put the hospital on its feet, and the Order of Grey Nuns would remain for the next twenty-four years.

Their arrival in late fall was a notable one with little fanfare, and to tell you something about it, I quote from a talk given by Mother, many years later, at a farewell banquet in honor of the Sisters, on their retirement: "They found the village blacked-out, except for a decoy village beyond the military base. It was a strange experience for the

Sisters, that first stormy night. Sister Hilary told me that, as they sat in the blacked-out hospital, they wondered what might happen and if they would be able to cope with it. It was eerie to peek out and see nothing but darkness. Later that night, Dr. Johnson stopped by and offered help should any problem arise—we had an army field phone connected to the hospital by a mile and a half of field wire. Soon settled, they were happily welcomed by everyone, and we all grew to love them, for their devotion to the sick and their willingness to cheerfully undertake any task that came their way. They scrubbed floors, did laundry, and the cooking, when the lay help did not arrive."

The Grey Nuns of the Sacred Heart, with Dad, on the front steps of the Griffin Memorial Hospital (left to right): Sister Mary Monica Brennen, Superior; Sister Hilary Sheldon; Dad; Sister Michael Cammarata; and Sister John Berchmans Brazil, 1945. Kodiak Historical Society.

She said they also had many problems. They often had to borrow supplies from the military. Sister Mary Monica, the Superior, would call the Base and often receive the reply, "Sister we are unable to do that," and she would reply, sweetly, "Thank you very much, I hope you will be able to supply it in the morning." She usually got what was needed. Power was supplied by a generator, maintained, much as ours was, by Army Ordnance men. When the water supply ran low, as it did when

Dad had to close the hospital for ten days, the men brought and filled a water tank, and hooked it up to the system, thereby keeping the hospital open until it rained and replenished the supply.

Three of the Nuns were with Dad for most of the remainder of his practice and, incidentally, on into mine. Sister Mary Monica had an abundance of compassion, and was known to sit up all night with seriously ill patients so they would not feel fearful should they awaken to find themselves alone. Dad told Mother that she was as close to a saint as anyone he had ever met. Sister Hilary was a woman whose generosity was as large as her ample self, and she sat behind her desk in the hospital office, as administrator and business manager, for most of her remaining lifetime. Dad, a liberal, and she, a devout Catholic, could have studiously avoided religion in their frequent contacts, but each was too competitive to overlook an opportunity for a good conversational joust, which they enjoyed quite frequently whenever the opportunity arose. Also a trained librarian, she was a founder of Kodiak's library and trained others in its management as well, including Mother. Sister Mary Leo, small, energetic, and a first-rate surgical nurse, was one who could be feisty, and had a quick response to any gentle jibe.

* * *

THE NEW YEAR 1945 arrived with enthusiasm. In a letter on January 2, Dad wrote: "New Year's Eve, we were invited out to the Station, where we had cocktails with Captain Corning of the admiral's staff, then dinner with Captain Lowry at the Officer's Club, followed by a New Year's Party at the R.F.O. We had a very good time at the party as everyone had enough of the spirits of the night to be thoroughly happy and no one, there, had too much. Our party consisted of all the brass on the station, and occupied the admiral's section, although he was not there, being in Washington, D.C., on business. His chief of staff, Captain Fitzgerald, was in charge. All of these men are delightful company.

"Yesterday, after getting to bed at about 2:30 a.m., we arose and got ready to entertain most of these same men at a New Year's dinner. They came at 5 o'clock and, after a new 'Sea Breeze' cocktail or two, which they seemed to like, we had one of your mother's delicious dinners, ham being the *pièce de résistance.*

The end of the year terminated community unrest about the operation of the hospital and the competence of the surgeon, and eased Dad's practice in that regard. However, it had begun to look like he would be left with a solo practice of indefinite duration.

Chapter 18

The Workload Grows

1945

A S THE POPULATION OF KODIAK GREW, so did Dad's other activities and duties beyond his medical practice. As designated sanitarian of the city, he, Captain Lowry, and the Navy designee made routine monthly inspections of all eating establishments on Base and in town and graded them, frequently following up those that needed improvement. As president of Rotary, he presided at each weekly meeting and quarterly assembly, seeing that his committees functioned well. He continued on the bank board and attended Chamber of Commerce meetings. He had been appointed as Field Hospital and Civil Defense Director in 1941, and he continued in those capacities. Through his position of governor for the Alaska branch of the American College of Chest Physicians, he had recently became associate editor of their magazine. One blessing was the resolution of the light plant problem. Power was supplied to the village this year by the Kodiak Electric Association, a newly formed nonprofit public utility.

On January 3, Dad wrote thanking me for a Christmas card, which had infused their holiday dinner with good cheer. That dinner was celebrated with the Torgersons and their friend, Colonel Wall, who had brought a gift of champagne. Before they sat down, just as champagne was being served, there was a brisk rap on the front door. It was Father Gallant, who joined them for a drink. Dad wrote, "He is certainly an extrovert with a most engaging personality. I asked him how he knew just when cocktails were being served, and he said he had a special sense that kept him informed of the important facts of life. You would like him, since he is also quite sincere in his work and, like most of the padres I have met, not too narrow."

The Russian New Year, on the Julian calendar, was celebrated on January 14. A brief note in Dad's diary referred to this year's celebration: "Big Russian New Year's masked dance. I was M.C. Danced from 7:30 to 12:30, including five schottisches and three polkas, without tiring. Plenty of go in the old hulk, yet."

At the "masked ball," much of the fun was in trying to guess the identity of the masked person you were dancing with, male or female. Ah, you might say, "I could tell if I were dancing with a man or a woman." You would, however, not be taking into consideration that women often danced with women, at dances where men were scarce, and before the dance, men worked on eliminating some of the clues that might expose the gender of the masked partner.

A story about the John Malutin family was told by Annie Koppang, one of three remaining Malutin offspring at the time. Annie, by the way, was one of the first people in Kodiak to meet Dad. Right after his ship docked, he walked into Erskine's store, which was at one end of the dock. On impulse, he picked up an apple and threw it to the prettiest girl in sight. This was Annie. She was startled, of course, but she caught it and laughed. This was the beginning of a long acquaintance.

At the masked dance on Russian New Year's Eve, everyone attended a potluck feast at the beginning of the evening and then went home again to "mask." Annie said the family dressed independently, and went to the ball separately, so they wouldn't know each other. Each would try to trick his or her partner into divulging their identity. They might answer questions in a well-disguised voice or not answer at all. Sometimes they could be made to laugh and that could be a dead giveaway. Well, John Malutin was asked to dance, repeatedly, by an attractive blonde, who danced very well, and she said nary a word, so he couldn't figure out who she was and he was, of course, quite curious. At home after the dance, it was the custom for the family to sit down to tea, and discuss the evening, and John asked, "Did anyone see that blonde I was dancing with all night? She was a really good dancer but I don't have any idea who she was." Yes, they had all seen her, but no one could tell him who it might have been. A little later, when they were beginning to tire and think about going to bed, the door opened and in walked that very same blonde. Lo and behold—when the wig was removed, it was Moses, his own son. This, of course, prompted gales of laughter.

Toward the end of January, a letter from me stirred in him a need to philosophize, perhaps to teach. He asked if I had heard about the Brook Farm that was started by a Unitarian Minister in New England about 1841. A Transcendentalist, his idea was to combine the worker and the thinker in the pursuit of a society of liberal, intelligent, and cultivated, people, whose relationships with each other would permit a more wholesome and simple life than could be led amidst the pressures of competitive institutions. Truth, justice, and order were the governing principles. Each individual was free, insofar as he did not violate the rights of others. Charles A. Dane and Nathaniel Hawthorne were among the original trustees. Louisa May Alcott, Margaret Fuller, Theodore Parker, William Henry Channing, and Ralph Waldo Emerson were interested. It sounded good to Dad, but, as he said, "the participants were human, and there were differences of opinion, and the whole thing folded in about three years.

"Those were interesting times from a literary standpoint, as most of our great poets, essayists, and historians lived and wrote during the nineteenth century. Religion was looked upon with great seriousness, and the narrowness of Calvinism held back the Romantic movement in New England. The Calvinists believed that, since Adam, man is sinful and he has to keep fighting his sins, but the Unitarian movement, which brought forth the Transcendentalists, taught that we were children of God, instead of children of Adam, and that we could emulate God and grow into his likeness. It became a more individualistic religion, and more self-sufficing, which called for living in harmony with the divine. It rejected the sensationalism of Locke, and adopted the intuitionalism of the German idealistic school, with the humanitarianism of French thought. I wish I had more time to pursue this romantic age of American Literature, as well as review the French and German philosophies. There is so much to know, and so little time to ponder it."

In early February, he had two unusual operations: "The first was on a seventy-year-old lady from Simeonof Island, who came into town, about five months ago, with a large ovarian cyst, but also an intestinal hemorrhage and a thrombophlebitis of the left leg. After getting her over the hemorrhage and phlebitis, I found her blood [count] too low to tolerate an operation safely, so I sent her out with medications [perhaps iron] to build it up. A week ago, I felt it safe to go ahead, so opened her up and found the cyst to be much larger than a nine-month uterus and filled with about three gallons of fluid and adherent to all surrounding structures—intestines, peritoneum, and bladder—from which it had to be separated, carefully, raw areas covered with peritoneum, and abdomen closed, which was all done under one spinal anesthesia. She is now sitting up in bed and feeling fine and will be discharged the first of next week.

"The other operation was even more serious. A woman was brought into the hospital with severe pain in her abdomen, which would not lessen on medical treatment and showed signs of being a complete intestinal obstruction. By 3:30 in the morning, I felt it was not safe to wait any longer, so I had Sister John put the instruments on to boil, and called Commander Whiteford in for consultation. He came right in, and agreed that although all the signs of complete intestinal obstruction were not present, it was not safe to wait. Meanwhile, I had sent the Marshal after her husband and told him the news, and he said to go ahead. Under spinal anesthesia, this time with a good assistant in the form of Dr. Whiteford, we opened the abdomen and found a complete obstruction, with a loop of intestine about a foot long entirely strangulated by a band of adhesions. We severed the band, but the dark purple color of the strangulated bowel did not start to turn pink, so I resected that portion of the bowel, made an end-to-end anastamosis, put in 5 grams of sulfathiazole, sewed her up tight, and put her back to bed. This was five days ago, and today she is eating and having normal bowel movements, and, with her husband, is very happy about the situation."

This was when he finally learned that Dr. Douglas—who was to relieve him so he would be free to come visit at the Academy—had reneged, because he found his assistant was not yet able to cover his practice adequately. Dad wrote, "Maybe something else will break before the end of the year. We can hope, anyway." He encountered some variation of this story whenever he tried to find someone to relieve him, even when the workload increased to the extent that he needed a full-time physician. It didn't seem to occur to him, but his fees remained such that he could not afford to pay an adequate salary.

Dad's April 4 letter puts to bed the controversy that made 1944 such a difficult year. The controversy began with a letter written by Harry

Christofferson, at that time chairman of the Hospital Board, in January to the Surgeon General, accusing Dad of incompetence. It was because of suspected hospital mismanagement, which was not really Dad's responsibility, but it was made public and fanned controversy in an already fractionated community. Dad finally sued Harry for libel, and Harry wrote a letter retracting all of his accusations. His letter also said: "Rather than being exorbitant, his charges for personal services are, in fact, less than most of the minimum fees charged elsewhere for similar services. For example, his charge for an office call is $2, for a house call $4 dollars. Doctor Johnson charges $35 for a tonsillectomy, $50 for a maternity case, and his other fees are in conformity, being based generally on the fee schedule allowed by the Bureau of Indian Affairs."

Dad wrote, "I dropped the suit against Harry, since he signed a letter entirely retracting all he had said against me, which I believe makes everything right. At any rate, it preserves peace in town and—one can feel it—there is a good feeling, for which, I believe, Rotary has been responsible. I would not be surprised if this had much to do with the results of the recent election. We will try to have a good city here for you to come back to."

The "recent election" was of four City Council members, who replaced those belonging to the "other faction," some who had tried to make trouble for Dad. The new council consisted of Larry Wodlinger, Lee Bettinger, Stan Nelson, and Bob King, all good citizens. Dad wrote, "I am again beginning to believe in democracy. The first three men, especially Larry, have repeatedly been against measures wanted by the old regime. It looks like a new day is dawning for Kodiak, wherein folks care more about the welfare of their city than individual gain and animosities."

The letter also referred to a case that exemplified Dad's indomitable persistence in the face of great odds, especially with regard to the management of difficult patient problems. He had no qualms about doing whatever surgery was necessary, and often persisted in the face of what others might have considered hopeless situations. Jackie, a seventeen-year-old girl, had been ill for two and a half days with abdominal pain. Surgery, on March 23, revealed a ruptured appendix, which was removed, but peritonitis persisted. Following the initial surgery, there was continuing peritonitis, complicating pneumonia, and the formation of several abdominal abscesses, each requiring additional surgery and implantation of drainage tubes.

A week after the initial surgery, Dad had a difficult extraction of his crowned tooth by Dr. Sullivan. The process took three hours, since the roots of the tooth had to be chiseled off the mandible, and he had written, "I believe the extraction itself was harder on him than on me—but the aching jaw, since, is definitely my responsibility and, with an ear, throat, and jaw all cooperating in making life miserable, I have known brighter days."

In this letter, on April 4, still recuperating, he wrote: "Then, too, my little Jackie, who had the ruptured appendix and general peritonitis, takes a great deal of attention, more or less day and night. I gave up my hoarded stock of penicillin for her, which has been definitely beneficial. I have also given her two further operations for drainage of localized abscesses as they develop. This morning, I opened an intra-abdominal abscess on the left side under spinal anesthesia, and put in a couple of draining tubes. She is having a reaction from that this afternoon, but I am hoping that within a couple of days I can say that for the first time since the original operation she is out of danger. I have had to give her an indwelling duodenal drainage tube and feed her by vein for a number of days, but that has kept her resistance good so that, with sulfadiazine and penicillin, I believe we can pull her through. However, it is a worry."

On April 16, "My little girl with the peritonitis is now out of danger." And, on May 6, "Jackie is now up and about and will be leaving the hospital in another day or two." Thus ended a six-week ordeal for a spunky young lady and her surgeon.

✳ ✳ ✳

PRESIDENT FRANKLIN DELANO ROOSEVELT died April 12, 1945, and victory in Europe was declared on May 8. Now the United States was down to one war—the one in the Pacific—which concerned us more directly in Kodiak. The military would not be leaving soon. The social and community organizational responsibilities would continue for Dad. The intensity of medical practice would continue to increase slowly, commensurate with a steady growth in population. Along the way, the community had growing pains.

In June, Dad was re-elected president of Rotary. He had organized the club well his first year and emphasized participation by his perfect attendance. The club achieved and maintained near perfect attendance during his tenure and became the number one club in the district. He attended a formative meeting of the Masons called by Major Jackson, C.O. of the Marines, where he was offered, but declined, the presidency. He eventually did join the Masons, having been active in St. Helens, Oregon, and became Grand Master and an active Shriner, and Mother became Worthy Matron of Eastern Star.

That same month, the folks met three people who would become close friends and be seen frequently at Sprucehaven during 1945: Commander Lowry, the new Medical CO at the Naval Operating Base, an unpretentious physician with a good sense of humor, and Commander Kelly Byler and his lady friend, Verna Stimson. Kelly was the new Operations Officer at the Naval Air Station (NAS) in charge of all flights, and he offered to give Dad flight training on their Link Trainer. This happenstance resulted in enduring friendships, Mother included, as well as three early morning sessions a week for Dad on the Link Trainer.

Also in June, he wrote: "Elsie Carlson, of the Mission, had a baby boy. I was happy to see that the Baptist missionaries did not kick her out. On the contrary, Miss Marlin stood right by her throughout the pregnancy, brought her to the hospital when the time came, and stayed with her until the baby was born. This is much more Christian than the way it is done by some churches when someone errs—just kick them out so they won't contaminate others. I believe the whole thing has been a good lesson for the rest of the girls there. Miss Marlin, though technically classified as an 'old maid,' was compassionate and understanding and—one might say—as close to a saint as Sister Mary Monica

In mid-July, Kraft's store received and delivered the two-by-six, maple tongue-and-groove flooring, ordered a month or so before, and Dad was able to complete the floor of the apartment above the garage. He then moved everything they had stored in the apartment into the shack.

Grandma Sarah arrived on the *Denali* that month for another visit. She stayed three months this time, and during her stay rather than having to play Chinese Checkers every night, Dad taught her how to play bridge. While Sarah, a fundamentalist, did not believe in dancing, drinking, smoking, or playing cards, she did enjoy games, and was quite good at them. So this was a "liberal" breakthrough for her, and Dad was impressed that she, at eighty years of age, grasped the concepts of a fairly difficult game.

On August 13, Dad received a letter from me at a time when I must have been searching for answers to life's big questions. He responded that, at times, "There are more downs than ups—very logical and to be expected. Don't worry too much about the fact of God. Think about it, yes, and read along such lines when you can find time—listen to a good sermon once-in-a-while, or twice-in-a-while—but worrying about it does no good. You will reach a firm foundation sometime if you just persist, and when you finally become sure of what you believe, it will mean much more to you than if you take your grandmother's word for it, or my word for it, or even some minister's word for it. I think God means different things to different people, except Roman Catholics and such ilk who are told what to believe and not allowed to use their own judgment in seeking the Master Intelligence. I must confess that I am not fully settled on just what God is—I am still studying—but I am not worrying. I am sure that if we do the right thing by our fellow man while going through this life, we will have nothing to worry about in the future.

Sarah Johnson, Dad's mother, quietly reading her bible during one of her several visits to Kodiak, 1945.

It is logical to believe in God—that appeals to my intellect—but to believe that he is a personal God who knows the number of hairs on our head and sees each sparrow fall, I am not sure. It seems like an immense job but of course to God all things are possible. Don't worry. I am looking forward to having some talks with you at some future date and, perhaps, between us, we can arrive at some conclusion. I do know that I shall never believe in something that will not stand up to the light of truth.

"When the theory of evolution first came to light, most church people said, 'It does not agree with the Bible, so it is false.' More and more evidence for the theory came into view, but these people would not even read about it—their minds were closed. Now, of course, it is a theory no longer, because there has been so much [supporting] evidence that it has become a law. Still, many people refuse to believe it—including my mother. As I told her, if one's belief cannot stand the light of truth, it is false, and should be discarded, or, adapted to the new truths."

✳ ✳ ✳

AUGUST 14, VJ DAY, heralded the official surrender of the Japanese. Dad wrote: "Although I just got through writing you yesterday, I am at it again today. I felt that this would be one of the best ways to celebrate the Japanese surrender day. This is a great day.

"It has been a rather full day, aside from the big news. We got word this morning that a Congressional party from Washington was flying over from Anchorage to look over our city. We took the mayor, president of the Chamber of Commerce, some city councilmen, and the president of the Rotary Club and met the party at the airport. The army and navy briefly whisked them through the Base and then about town, getting them to the Victory Café in time for Rotary lunch.

"I had Governor Gruening of Alaska on my right, and our delegate to Congress, Bob Bartlett, on my left. Also at the head table were the senior congressmen of the delegation, Homer D. Angell of Oregon, Captain McDade, C.O. of N.A.S., and Colonel Wilson, C.O. of Fort Greely. As our guests, we had congressmen Marion T. Bennett of Missouri and Charles Robertson of North Dakota; Dr. Meredith Burrill, director of the division of geography, Department of the Interior; and I.M.C. Anderson, of the Department of Agriculture. We had some excellent speeches and, in all, a fine time. We sent them off again at 1:30 to continue their travels throughout the Territory.

"Two head men of the Shell Oil Company were in town yesterday. Larry Wodlinger and Lee Bettinger brought them out to see our house.

They felt Kodiak would probably be on the main airliner route to the Orient after the war, and they were planning to establish themselves here to compete with Standard Oil. With the party was young Boeing, who lives in Seattle and who knew a friend of the family." This was likely William Boeing, the founder of the Boeing Aircraft Company in Seattle.

This was a pretty special time, a time for rejoicing and introspection, and Dad was not one to overlook an opportunity for reflection. On August 19, he wrote a third letter in a week to me: "The Millennium must be at hand. That, and the discovery of the atomic secrets of the universe, will certainly start us on a new era—a potentially terrible era unless our mental and moral sense is adult enough to cope with our scientific knowledge, in which case we will see a beginning of the highest well being of mankind.

"My fear is that, due to the great augmentation of science on account of the war, we have reached a stage that ordinarily might have taken a century or more, and our moral sense may not have progressed to a level that will allow us to wisely control the power that has come into our hands."

In September, Dr. Lowry brought a new Navy nurse to dinner at Sprucehaven and, after the meal, while he and she and Mother and Grandma Sarah played Chinese Checkers, Dad read the charter of the United Nations. This was the product of an international meeting in San Francisco in June, in which Rotary had a significant part. It consisted of 110 Articles. It must have been a fairly lengthy Chinese Checkers game to have kept the ladies occupied, or Dad was a very fast reader. He felt the United Nations could be made to work, "as long as there is a will to keep peace in the world and build respect for each nation and all people."

It was becoming clear that Dad had gradually evolved intellectually and had discarded his early fundamental religious beliefs, one by one. This propitious occasion—the end of the war in the Pacific, the technological leap forward with the "splitting" of the atom, and the adoption of the United Nations Charter—prompted more comment: "I believe that I have found the church that more nearly expresses my thoughts than any other. This is the Unitarian Church. I asked Chaplain Miller, who belongs to this sect after having left the Presbyterian Church because he didn't honestly believe some of their tenets, to give me some literature on his church. He did so, and I find that it leaves all of these questionable things to a person's individual conscience."

* * *

ON AUGUST 24, Dad completed twenty-one hours on the Link Trainer. His instructor told him he had all he could give him, and he felt that he would be able to fly instruments under any conditions. His last lesson was to fly in on a beam with radio communication to the tower on altitudes and landing times, come in for a landing, according to instructions, and let-down technique to reach the field at an altitude of 600 feet, assuming visibility for actual landing. "I had to do this, with the roughest wind conditions possible and, believe me, when you are trying to fly a beam by radio that is filled with static and at the same time watch eight instruments, all of which are jumping all over the place, with a plane that is trying to jerk your head off, keeping all the instruments where they should be, continually compensating all of them so that you are flying on an even keel and at a given altitude as much as possible, you have your mind and your hands full. I made a good landing, however, and now I have graduated. The instructor says I should come out every once in a while to keep my hand in."

In September, the Reverend Mother Superior and the Mother Councilor of the Grey Nuns came to visit Kodiak. Dad enjoyed meeting them, and found them lively and bright. I had met them on a visit to the Mother House in Philadelphia. They had a pleasant afternoon visit at Sprucehaven before returning home.

"The Territorial Commissioner of Health arrived by plane Sunday, so I had to spend considerable time with him until taking him to his plane on Monday. He is Dr. Albrecht, a former Moravian medical missionary, who was located at the Matanuska Valley project until he went into the army three years ago. He is a good man, and I introduced him to army and navy people the next morning, and at lunch at the Officer's Club (RFO)." Dr. Albrecht became Commissioner of Health for the Territory of Alaska after his discharge, and remained in that position for a number of years.

In Dad's October 24 letter, he said: "Last night we had a dinner for Wilson Erskine and his wife, Babe (her initials are B.A.B.)." It began to appear that Wilson and Babe might be able to take the place of the senior Erskines in Kodiak society, for they appeared more and more frequently at various social occasions.

"Friday night both your Mother and I helped pack clothes for the Red Cross to ship to New York. Thursday I went to the Base to take another Link Trainer lesson. I am thinking of taking an advanced course while the opportunity offers. Wednesday, I delivered Mary Frost in the early morning hours. In fact, no sleep from three in the morning. That evening we were part of a big party at the Erskines'. I believe you will like Wilson's new wife. She is vivacious, a good hostess, and seemingly full of a lot of common sense. She loves it up here and is taking over as Mrs. W. J. Erskine would have been happy to see.

"The day before that, Tuesday the sixteenth, I did a caesarian section on June Wilson, getting a lovely baby girl for her and sending her back to bed in better shape than when she entered the operating room." This woman had heart trouble, and had become pregnant against advice, and having left Kodiak, returned, trusting Dad to deliver her baby. In addition to this, the Territorial Nurse, Miss Curtis, and I have tuberculin tested all school children and X-rayed all positive reactors. I am now going to have to tabulate our findings. We picked up two active cases, one being Zoe Sholl, whom I am now treating with pneumothorax.

"Oh, yes, my Mother's visit took up considerable time and energy. It was lovely to have her visit us, but after three months it is restful to have the house to ourselves again. During her stay, all liquor was put in the wine cellar, and the trapdoor was not opened once during that time. Mother would have felt badly if she knew we even smelled liquor—even though we are very moderate users of alcoholic beverages—so we didn't see any reason to hurt her feelings during her declining years. Consequently, when the gang was out last night, we had an 'unveiling,' and considerable fun was had over the martinis, which were especially good with a touch of lemon added to the gin, vermouth, and orange bitters."

On December 22, Dad, wrote a one-page, tongue-in-cheek letter. He noted that Mother had, as usual, mentioned that she wanted a Christmas tree, and he said, "Yes, of course, you would want a tree. It is very easy for you to want a tree. I get the tree—I put it up—good. I put on the lights. I come home the next day—nothing further done, so I put on the ornaments, then I put on the tinsel. After Christmas, I take off the tinsel, I take off the ornaments, I take off the lights, I take down the tree, and take it outside for burning—I even get out the vacuum, and clean up all the fallen needles. Yes, it is easy for you to want a tree. I added, 'This Christmas there will be no tree!' However, I expect that, this afternoon, I will get a tree and put it up, and put on the lights, and do all of the other things I have done every Christmas except when you were here to help.'"

The folks took Captain Lowry to a Rotary Christmas program at the Orpheum Theater on Christmas Eve, and then went to midnight mass at the Catholic Church, after which they stopped at the hospital long enough for Dad to deliver a baby, then went home for margaritas and a bacon and egg sandwich before bed at 3:30 in the morning. An ocean swim ushered in Christmas Day, followed by a late brunch, and a later dinner at Torgerson's. The old year was ushered out with a big celebration in the admiral's section at the R.F.O., where everyone had a good time, no one had too much to drink, and Dad danced with fifty girls.

On January 20, 1946, he wrote of the new Community Center: "The Red Cross gave the Legion Hall back to the city, and told them that if they wanted it for a community center, they would leave the furniture. The Legion agreed, and the city took it over. It is run by a board of city appointees: one each from Rotary, the Chamber, the churches, local Red Cross, Federated Unions, and the N.O.B. I am the city delegate and chairman of the board. When all are appointed, we will have a meeting, set up rules, establish by-laws, start a funding drive to raise $5,000, then find a good full-time director and his wife to put on a community athletic, recreational, and education program. I think it will be a fine thing for Kodiak."

Chapter 19

Solo Practice Continues

1946–1947

TOWARD THE END OF 1945, Dad wrote that Dr. Douglas was not able to relieve him, let alone join him in practice. He still hoped that one of several physician acquaintances would help find someone to relieve him long enough to attend my graduation from Kings Point the following April. He also mentioned that Woodley Airways, an Anchorage airline formed in 1932 that served southwest Alaska, had changed its name to Pacific Northern Airlines (PNA), and had increased its service to Seattle in l945. He wrote that, "Woodley had just received three new DC-3s, fully equipped, which will give us excellent service from Kodiak [starting in 1947]." Bob Hall, a seasonal pilot, would move to Kodiak in 1949, becoming the first resident pilot. He formed Kodiak Airways, which was the major local carrier for many years.

His next letter, of January 15, resolved the issue of a visit to the academy: "The sad news is that I have reached my last idea on getting relief in time to get out for your graduation. Everyone I have wired is unable to get away. Sorry, son. I tried my best, and I am disappointed, as you will be, but we must do our duty first, and my duty lies in Kodiak. I simply cannot leave these people with no one to look after them." This dedication would keep him on the job, alone, for the next nine years until I could join him in practice.

In early March, Dad gave a paper on the surgical treatment of the gall bladder at a medical meeting on Base, one he had prepared for presentation at the Alaska Territorial Medical Association in Juneau. I found a reference to that conference in a letter from Mother on March 5: "Dad has been swamped lately and his temper has been edgy. He really is remarkable, having been on the grind so long. He has been busy preparing a paper for the medical meeting in Juneau the eleventh and twelfth of June. I urged him to go, as it is the reorganization meeting of the Territorial Medical Association. Dr. Joel Baker, Chief of Surgery at the Virginia Mason Hospital in Seattle, is to be the guest speaker, and he wrote Dad, saying he hoped to see him there. He is the surgeon Dad sends difficult cases to. The Sisters wanted him to go, too. They sure back him up! I thought it would be a good idea for those Juneau guys to see what a good guy your dad is. Sister Mary Monica told me the other day that she just loves to see Dad come into the hospital, that he is just about the perfect doctor in every way. Sister Hilary feels much the same way."

The Grey Nuns wanted him to go for the prestige of the hospital, and were willing to pay half his fare, so he went. He enjoyed flying in one of PNA's luxurious new DC-3s. He said all the stewardesses either knew him or had heard of him. He enjoyed seeing folks he had met on visits to Anchorage for court testimony and employees of the airlines in Anchorage and Juneau, as well.

He visited the Sisters of Providence in Anchorage, and, in Juneau, the Sisters of St. Anne, each of whom managed their respective hospitals. He also had a good visit with Father Fitzgerald, the Alaska Catholic Bishop. His conference paper was well received, especially by the guest speaker, Dr. Baker, who referred to it several times in his own address at the final banquet. This undoubtedly made an impression, for one of the nurses approached him after the banquet and said, "From what Dr. Baker said, you must be an excellent surgeon." (Dr. Baker was a staunch supporter of Dad.) Governor Gruening, a nonpracticing physician himself, was also a speaker at the banquet. He and Dr. Baker were both made honorary members of the new association, which led to an invitation for all to dine at the Governor's Mansion the day following the conference.

This was a formative meeting and, besides the papers and presentation of cases, they passed a constitution and by-laws, and put together a Basic Science Act, which Dad was asked to present to the State Legislature. Before the meeting adjourned, Dad was elected vice-president of the Territorial Medical Association. The following year, he was elected president.

* * *

STATEHOOD WAS BECOMING AN ISSUE of controversy for some Alaskans. As a Territory, we could not vote for the U.S. president. We had a single delegate to Congress, who had a voice but no vote. Alaskans paid income tax, however, and the thought of taxation without representation became a groundswell of discontent among some folks, who began a campaign for statehood. Others, many of whom came to Alaska because it was a frontier, took pride in their independence and their territorial status.

Dad had met Evangeline Atwood, wife of the publisher of the *Anchorage Times*, at the governor's dinner. She was a statehood activist, and he invited her to Kodiak to speak to Rotarians on the issue. She remembered the invitation and came in April to speak on the advantages of statehood. Dad introduced her about, saw that she met everyone, and had her to dinner at Sprucehaven, with Torgy, the retiring mayor, and Lee Bettinger, the new mayor. The next evening, at the invitation of Torgersons, they all enjoyed dinner and dancing at the Montmartre, Kodiak's new club-restaurant.

In April, I graduated from Kings Point and Dad sent a wire: *Congratulations on your achievement proud of you much love Mom and Dad.* I had passed my exam for Third Mate's license. I was shipping to England on the *Paul Bunyan*, and so Dad sent me the addresses of our English relatives he had met as a young man en route to South Africa early in WWI, as well as in transit to and from France the following year. He was anxious that I should meet them all.

In May, Dad wrote, "My practice is getting busier all of the time. The town seems no busier, but I used to have time between patients, in the office, to get to the deskwork. Now, I have to do nothing but see one patient after another, as they keep filling the reception room. It looks like I may have to go down to the office on a Sunday, to catch up on the most necessary of my professional communications. I have been winding up my last year as Rotary president and have been busy getting the Community Center in shape for its new director, who is expected to come in on the Fish and Wildlife ship, *Crane*, this weekend.

"I removed a breast tumor from a man, did a plastic operation on a hand, had a run of operations on ingrown toenails, did an appendectomy on Mrs. Shupp and had her up the next day, removed a dermoid cyst of the ovary on another woman as well as her appendix, and did a biopsy of a cervix this morning. Several other interesting hospital cases, too, such as Father Edge with an enlarged prostate upon whom we tried a new treatment consisting of shots of ovarian hormone that worked well. Also tried the same treatment with the same good results on old Tom Nelson. Three pneumonia cases responded immediately to penicillin therapy, two kidney cases, one diabetic, some lymphangitis cases from canneries, a couple of alcoholic neuroses, an asthmatic.

"The governor of Rotary International District 101 made a visit to the Kodiak club in June and seemed very pleased at his reception. At both the assembly and the noon luncheon, he praised the club in the highest terms and said he had absolutely no adverse criticisms to offer. It happened, too, that the Kodiak club topped the entire district in attendance this month, a position it has been approaching for the last two years. I was elected to the Board of the Chamber of Commerce, and remain as president of the Community Center Board, and am trying to do my share in civic affairs.

"The Kodiak Realty Company purchased the Sunbeam Hotel and Totem Igloo Curio & Gift Shop and that entire property from Charles Madsen. This gives us that whole quarter block. After we are able to obtain materials and can build a new, modern hotel between the Sunbeam and the apartment house, we will call the Sunbeam the Baranof Annex, the hotel the Baranof Hotel, and the apartment building the Baranof Apartments. At least that is our present plan. What do you think of it? If we get all this completed and paid for, it will give me an independent source of income in about fifteen years so that I will be able to retire, if necessary, and leave the business to you."

This realty company consisted of Dad and Marshall Crutcher. Marshall lived in Ketchikan and was one of two certified public accountants in Alaska and had been coming to Kodiak to do tax returns for canneries. How he and Dad decided to join forces in a realty company, I don't know, but Marshall eventually replaced Torgy as president of the bank. In time, because of disagreements regarding ethics, Dad initiated an end to the arrangement and split the property, the hotel to Marshall, the apartment (known as the Felder Building, after its builder) to Dad.

In a letter from Mother, June 6, she said that a family had been hired to manage the Community Center, and Dad was attending the board's first meeting. The money had been raised, and Ken and Aileen Wade, and their daughter, Joy, had recently come to Kodiak. They were just the ticket—energetic, fun, and able to put together a variety of programs. It was, indeed, a fine thing for Kodiak, and became a focus of a lot of activity for youth and adults alike. Operating funds for the center were supplied, at least partly by an annual gala spring carnival, alternately sponsored by the Rotary Club and other local organizations.

Upon returning from England, I took a train across the United States and boarded the *Cordova*, arriving home August 1. I participated in the morning ritual dip with Dad, and helped him with Sprucehaven upkeep tasks. Many of the folks' friends had attractive daughters who lived on Base, and so I took a number of trips to and from the base to pick up and return these girls. To enter the base, you have to check in at the gate, and I became acquainted with an energetic young marine who was on guard duty. His name was Dan Hoag and, over a few weeks, we became pretty well acquainted. He came to dinner several times, and, in time, became an unofficial member of the family. I was happy that the folks took so well to Dan, for he was a big help around Sprucehaven, and would sort of pinch-hit in my absence.

❋ ❋ ❋

DANCES WERE HELD once a week in the Community Center, and we all went and danced with enthusiasm. Dan was included when he was not on duty. We learned a number of folk dances and Dad had learned to call square dancing, and took pleasure in introducing a new square dance every week or two to keep us on our toes. A high-energy activity, this was lots of fun and very good exercise. The center filled a number of functions for the town. There was a big kitchen, and potlucks and other parties were frequently put on by various organizations. Attached to the rear of the center, two Quonset huts were added to house a fledgling library that Dad and Mother helped initiate. Sister Hilary, a certified librarian, was instrumental in its development. She trained local volunteers to become library aides. Thus the seeds were sown of what would eventually become the A. Holmes Johnson Memorial Library.

It was a short, but good family summer. I departed in late September for Willamette to complete my premed education.

Dad's first letter was written on September 9: "Another Sunday rolled around, and I started out to get much work done out of doors. The weather was misty, but not the real rain that prevented work yesterday afternoon. I sawed enough wood for the fireplace for today, put the cold frame in order for the winter for Mother's pansies, which she thinks will do well if kept closed, put her garden tools in the tool shed from which she always takes them, for me to return again."

Frostie in her garden, where she spent happy hours each summer, August 1958.

"Frostie's garden" was one of Mother's major projects. It was a large, level, fenced-in area between the house and the lake, with a number of raised beds accessed on all sides from a network of pathways. She used a cold frame as a mini greenhouse, which allowed her to start a number of plants early, thereby prolonging the growing season. In addition, the long summer daylight hours in Kodiak's northern latitude made the garden very productive. Root vegetables and leafy greens grew rapidly and thrived. Cabbages were sometimes enormous. Rhubarb grew wild and when domesticated, became huge. A small breed of wild strawberry grew in one corner of the garden, an invader from outside the fence, and they had more flavor than those much later imported from Outside. Her flowers were beautiful and lush, often providing bouquets for gifts and social events.

Continuing with his letter, Dad said, "I also sawed out the plywood for the canoe repair only to find no crosscut saw—only the rip saw being in evidence. Charley, Norm Sutliff's father, who had moved into the garage apartment as caretaker, suggested you may have left it at Torgy's cabin, and as I was starting out to get it, Mother called me to the phone and I had to go into the hospital to sew up a waitress's hand. It is frustrating to be interrupted on weekends, while trying to work about the place.

"I delivered a baby every day last week. At least I averaged that, even though I failed one day and then had two babies the next, which is too many babies, too often. The first one called me out at six-thirty last Sunday morning with a marginal placenta praevia, which can be very serious, so took close watching until her delivery at 4:40 p.m., followed by a hemorrhage, which called for rapid packing to save the mother's life. This was Mrs. Lee Bettinger Jr., a lovely girl from New York. I'm happy to say that she is doing well.

"Three calls Monday night, culminated in a baby boy for Mrs. Martin Jensen at 7:30 a.m. Then, after Rotary, which served as a farewell to Torgy, who is soon to leave, I delivered Mrs. Chandler, who had an easy labor. Both of these patients have had complications, which called for really considered judgment as to their management, and I was happy to get them off my chest. This left only one more, really worrisome case, pending immediately—that of Jessie O'Brien, so I have been keeping her in the hospital. Wednesday, at dinnertime, I got a call saying that she was doing what I had feared—hemorrhaging. The nurses already had their orders so, when I arrived shortly, we took her into surgery and did an immediate caesarian operation in time to save her life. We put the living seven-month baby in the incubator, and both mother and baby are doing well. The Thursday baby came very early on Friday morning from an eighteen-year-old sailor's wife—a cute little thing with red hair. Friday's baby at 11 that night was another primipara.

"Tuesday, the Public Health boat *Hygiene* was in port, so I met with their doctors on health problems in the Native villages around the island." Ruth and Torgy and their daughter Theron were leaving for California, where Torgy would operate a bank in Cathedral City. They had been close friends of the folks during their time in Kodiak. Torgy's Bank of Kodiak had served well in providing financing for the growth of the fledgling community. Marshall Crutcher, the new bank president and his wife, Agnes, became family friends.

Dr. Lowry's tour of duty was soon to end, so the folks scheduled a farewell cocktail party in his honor in late October. They invited all the medical personnel at the N.A.S.—the medics, doctors, nurses, and dentists, including our local dentist, Gene Sullivan. Mother made delicious and varied hors d'oeuvres and Dad had mixed a batch of artillery punch which, "although tasting most innocuous, packs a deadly wallop." They built a roaring fire in the fireplace and committed one of their last sacks of coal to keep the fire going through the evening. Dr. Lowry would be replaced by Dr. List, whom Dad had met and was looking forward getting to know.

Christmas, my twenty-first birthday, inspired dad to provide a special gift for Mother, accompanied by a hand-written note: "To my wife of nearly twenty-two years—on our son's twenty-first birthday. My choice would still be the same. None other could be more true, nor more faithful than you have been, and none a better helpmate. I am a most fortunate man. It is with all the affection of your original lover, that I present these two rings, to replace those worn out in the loving service of making a true home for me. Wear them as a renewed and augmented pledge of my love and loyalty. From your husband."

And to me, he wrote a long philosophical message, which included: "You are now twenty-one—you have reached the age of political manhood and independence—you are now officially in charge of your own life, with all the responsibilities this connotes—your actions will now be your own in the eyes of the law, and your parents will assume only an advisory capacity. . . ." He finished by mentioning that he had placed five shares of Bank of Kodiak stock in my name, as a nest egg.

* * *

AS JANUARY 1947 PROGRESSED, it began to look like a cold winter. Mother wrote that Mission Lake was frozen to the bottom and consequently limited the water in the well, which was simply a shallow well at the edge of the lake surrounded by the little log pump house. By keeping this warm, enough ice was melted to provide some water, but not enough to allow the system to function continuously. The community water supply was diminished to some degree as well, and the city had to pump water from Big Lake into its own system and the Erskine system. Mother noted that it was difficult to keep the log home warm, as they were still heating with just the kitchen oil stove and the fireplace, which took a lot of wood splitting and fire-feeding.

"Our winter still holds on, and it is getting to the point where it is really inconvenient. The night it hit zero, in spite of two lanterns and the kerosene heater, our water pump froze, cracking the gizmos on top in several places. Morris Burnham, master welder, has taken it to the shop to weld it. It broke the nuts in half so he has to make new ones since they are very special. In the meantime, we (meaning me) are carrying all our water in buckets and pails (from the pump house) and taking sponge baths. We even have to carry water to flush the toilet. I hope we get it fixed before we run out of clothes. We are down to two sacks of coal, and the wood is getting low, too, about a third of what you split is left, so I am beginning to ration the living room fires. It is too cold to saw more wood—too hard on the saw. Anyway, Daddy hasn't time and he has bursitis in his shoulder, again, so doesn't even feel like splitting it, when he gets a few minutes. He was gone all night last night, and again from 10:30 until this morning. Of course, he gets some sleep, but it is easier to sleep at the hospital when someone is in labor, or he would be called in from home every hour or so. He has two more baby cases in today. When they deliver it will make six since Sunday, and it is only Tuesday."

Later: "The water pipes are still frozen. The pump is repaired and is working fine, but we will not have water until the pipes thaw. I took my washing in to Ruth, today, and washed everything. They had good water pressure today, but yesterday they didn't have any. The hospital lines are frozen, and the navy has a big tank and is pumping it into their lines. The hospital is full—twenty-three patients, with fifteen adults and eight babies. They have two babies in bureau drawers, since they only have six bassinets."

The cold snap ended in mid-February with an abrupt rise in temperature to the mid-thirties. The crystal clear, brilliant sunny days and fairyland moonlit nights were suddenly interrupted by a heavy, wet snowfall, followed by rain. Dad wrote that it was melting more rapidly than he had ever seen and, "everything was awash." The pond behind the Lyric Theater on Main Street became a sizeable lake and the Torgramsens (owners of the theater) had several feet of water in their house, as did buildings along Main Street around Tony's Bar. The water was two or three feet deep in the street, and could not be crossed without hip boots or a boat, so the town was divided in two. Peggy lived on the other side of the "moat" and didn't come to work that morning. By mid-morning, the Street Department had drilled through the frozen plowed snow berm on the ocean side of Main Street, in several places, and liberated the entrapped waters. But side roads remained flooded in a number of places, where water was trapped between the berms on either side. Even on base, the officer's quarters had a foot of water in the basements. Dad wrote, "Nothing has ever been seen like this winter in this century in Kodiak."

On Sunday, the fifth day of the thaw, Dad wrote, "Our lake [Mission Lake] had a foot or more of water over the solid ice so that it came up over the pool in the pump house and put all the floor boards afloat, coming nearly up to the log sill of the door. The little outlet stream was not enough to manage the outflow from the lake, so that a veritable river flowed over the road and the bridge to the ocean. I never knew, for a couple of days, when I came home at night, if the bridge was going to be there when I needed to leave the next morning or, finding it there, then, and getting to town, I had no idea whether I would be able to return to my garage at night. Luckily, the heavy rains that came down in a deluge on Thursday and Friday let up yesterday morning, and the outflow of our lake was able to resume its normal channel and flow under the bridge, which, being frozen fast to the ground on either side, had not washed out."

The roads remained icy and the pipes remained frozen until February 11. That day, they were thawed, and Dad removed his chains. Thus ended the severe cold spell, and the remainder of the winter was punctuated with short cold snaps.

As fate would have it, there was a slew of babies born during the cold spell, so Dad couldn't keep up with his sleep, let alone the chores. Mother wrote, "I had three mission boys shovel the snow from the road today in the high spots, so Dad won't have to do it. His bursitis has been bothering him again, and when he does get home, he's tired out. Larcy is going to split the wood until Dad's arm gets well. He came over this morning and split some logs, and Ronnie cut lots of kindling, so Dad won't have to do that. He was called at six o'clock this morning for another delivery. The poor baby had two clubfeet. It was the first deformed baby he's had, and he felt badly about it. He also has a child at the mission with suspected tuberculous meningitis, which is 100 percent fatal. He's pretty touchy today, and everything I say is the wrong thing. One can't blame him though, he's so tired. Just wonder how long he can carry on like this.

When he gets home tonight he can rest, since all the chores are finished. I'll have a fire going, and he can sleep on the davenport. Larcy is a good worker. When the weather moderates, I think I'll have him and Ronnie, both, saw wood so Dad won't have that to do."

* * *

DAD FINALLY BEGAN to realize that he wasn't paying enough to entice physicians to join him. His charges accomplished the purpose of not overburdening his patients, but they did not supply enough income to pay two physicians an acceptable salary.

In mid-March, however, he got a letter from a Dr. Clarence C. Bailey from Georgia, who was planning a seven-month vacation to Alaska and was in Seattle outfitting with a trailer, boat, outboard motor, and fishing and hunting equipment. He had contacted the Virginia Mason Clinic and met Dr. Baker, who told him Dad needed a man very badly to relieve him for a vacation. He suggested that he could fit his itinerary into five months, which would leave Dad two months in April and May. Dad called him on the phone and learned that he had surgical and obstetric experience, and decided that he could be trusted to manage his practice, so offered him $1,000, all office expenses paid, and his plane fare to and from Anchorage, which he gladly accepted. Still cautious, because of so many replacement doctors had not materialized, he said, "If there is no slip, which I have almost come to expect, we will start planning a two-month vacation." Two weeks later, on April 2, Dr. Clarence Bailey arrived in Kodiak.

On first meeting with "Dutch" Bailey, one immediately noticed that he looked at you with his left eye while his right gazed outward and upward toward the sky. When he spoke, his drawl immediately disclosed his southern origin. He had a warm and friendly smile, and was intuitively likeable. The day after his arrival, Dad took him on hospital rounds, introduced him to the Sisters and the patients, took him to the office to meet the staff and to familiarize him with the practice, and to dinner at the VFW Club with friends that evening.

The next day, Dad and Mother were scheduled to depart. That day, however, and one more passed before a plane could safely land at Kodiak and whisk him and Mother away for a much-anticipated vacation.

Chapter 20

A Vacation

1947

D AD AND MOTHER flew to Anchorage in early April 1947, where they spent a couple of days before their connecting flight to Minneapolis. They were invited by Evangeline Atwood for dinner the first night with her husband Bob and Dr. and Mrs. Walkowski. She was politically active and he, being owner and publisher of the *Anchorage Times*, was politically knowledgeable. Dr. and Mrs. Romig had them to dinner the next night. Dr. Romig was a fellow pioneer physician, sometimes known as the "dog team doctor."

They then flew to Minneapolis, where Dad visited the University of Minnesota Hospital, met surgeon Dr. Owen Wangensteen, watched him perform a gastric resection with a surgical team and an anesthetist, who had "enough equipment to fill a room," and visited clinics for a day or two. Mother traveled by plane for New York on April 9, while he went on to spend a week in Rochester. There, he visited the Mayo Clinic, and spent time visiting clinics and watching surgery in the affiliated St. Mary's Hospital. During his stay, he met many clinic physicians including several visiting from other countries.

In New York, he took the Long Island train to Freeport, where he rejoined Mother and Ruth Bishop, her brother Hewlett's wife. They drove to the Bishop residence in Freeport, which was to be their base of operations for the remainder of the month. They took a day to get settled, then drove to Patchogue, to joyfully be reunited with Mother's parents. Their little girl had left home twenty-two years previously and had only visited once, when she and I had come east in the summer of 1942. During their stay, they drove back and forth to Patchogue, and visited with other relatives on Long Island. They saw old friends at the

Methodist Hospital in Brooklyn, and at dinner, they recalled that Dad was inspired to climb an extension ladder to Mother's window in the nurse's quarters, one evening, to wish her a happy birthday.

He and Mother made a trip to Philadelphia to visit the Mother House of the Grey Nuns. There, they met the Mother Superior, a woman of warmth and dignity, and were delighted to see Sister Mary Leo, the sprightly nun who had spent two years as surgical nurse in Kodiak. They were taken to meet members of the staff at Temple University Hospital before returning to Freeport.

Dad flew to Boston, and spent three days at the Lahey Clinic, where he met with Dr. Frank Lahey and observed him and others performing surgery. Returning to New York, he and mother did some of the "city things" on their own. Hew, who was Atlantic Coast Director of the United States Merchant Marine at the time, took them to King's Point on a Saturday, to see my wartime alma mater. They were shown through the academy in the morning, took lunch in the mess hall with the cadets, and attended a regimental review in the afternoon.

The folks left New York on Tuesday, May 6, flying to Washington, D.C., where they were met by the Lowrys. The Lowrys took them on a mini tour of the capital, getting them to the airport in time for their 5 o'clock Chicago flight. Many hotels were full in Chicago—they did not make advance reservations at any of their stops—and they were fortunate to find a room at a newly opened hostelry at Chicago Beach. Dad was up at 5:30 the next morning and at the University of Chicago's Billings Hospital in time to observe Dr. Lester Dragstedt perform a vagotomy and gastroenterostomy. He then went to his alma mater, Northwestern, and put in a plug for me with the dean of admissions at the Medical School. Mother and he had dinner and went to see *Born Yesterday*, which Dad said was "an excellent comedy, with a moral." They left Chicago the next morning, routed through Denver, and Boise, to Seattle. There, they got a $10 room at the Olympic Hotel, had dinner in the Grill, and retired.

On Friday, May 9, Dad reported to the Mason Clinic and was warmly greeted by Dr. Baker, who turned him over to Dr. Capaccio, who was to do a medical workup on Dad. Dr. Capaccio performed the physical examination and arranged further screening X-ray and laboratory studies. That night, Dad and Mother went to Don's Oyster House for dinner.

Saturday morning, Dr. Baker picked Dad up and, with Dr. Durham, anesthetist and a scrub nurse, drove south to Aberdeen, where they performed a "pretty" gastric resection on a physician in their Catholic Hospital. The Sisters gave them a delightful lunch, after which they drove to Dr. Baker's brother-in-law's farm near Olympia, then to the annual meeting and banquet of the Tacoma Medical Society, where he heard a talk by Dr. Ruick on blood diseases and surgery.

Monday morning, Dad went to the Mason Clinic for his gall bladder series. While waiting for his final film, he watched Dr. Baker operate. After lunch he returned for a proctoscopy, then watched Dr. Baker perform a hysterectomy. He observed other surgeries and participated in clinical conferences the rest of the week, and on Friday, his summary medical workup was reported to have found only hyperacidity.

* * *

SATURDAY, MOTHER AND DAD caught a 7 o'clock flight to Portland. There, they took a taxi to his mother's home in Tigard, south of the city. Sarah was happy to see Dad, as well as Mother, whom she had always liked.

The next morning they went to church in Tigard, and in the afternoon Dad explored the house and the grounds. A beautiful Tudor home, it was set on an acre of land, with a well-manicured lawn in front, attractive shrubbery bordering the house, a separate double garage, and an orchard in back that had apple, cherry, and walnut trees, a vegetable garden, and a berry patch. This was to have been the quiet retirement retreat for the Bishop and his wife, but they had shared it only three years.

On Tuesday, they visited Portland's Good Samaritan Hospital, where Dad had been on staff. They visited the Medical Arts Building, where he had also practiced during the difficult years. In the afternoon, they visited the YMCA, where Dad had been the Northwest Regional Medical Director during their years in Portland. Then they rented a car to facilitate their visits to surrounding areas during the next week.

On Wednesday Dad visited the Portland Yacht Club, and then took Mother to lunch at the Oregon Oyster House before her appointments with the eye and allergy doctors.

Thursday, they drove to Salem in the afternoon, where they registered in the Senator Hotel, and then found me in biology class. They said, "It is hot!" They met some of my friends and professors, before retiring to the hotel for the evening. On Friday—it was still hot—they went with me to a student picnic at Pat's Acres, several miles north of Salem. That evening, we had a party at Normandy Manor, a nice club where my combo worked on Saturdays. (I had put together a quartet while at Willamette, consisting of piano, bass, trumpet, and saxophone. I played piano and arranged all the gigs. We played parties and dances, and a couple of nightclubs in Salem. It was called the KJ Quartet, for Kodiak Johnson.) We had supper, my parents met my friends, and we danced. Dad wrote that I played my own composition in their honor. On Saturday—still hot—they met President Smith and Dean Erickson, and heard my combo at the Manor in the evening before retiring. Sunday morning—still hot—they said good-bye after breakfast, stopped at Oswego to visit Kodiak friends, then drove back to Grandma Sarah's. Then they took the Streamliner train to Pendleton to visit Darlow and his family for two days, and returned to Portland. The weather continued hot.

On June 5, they flew to Seattle, and then visited friends in Bellingham and on Orcas Island, before returning to Seattle. They picked up $500 worth of silver from a Seattle bank for the Bank of Kodiak. They flew to Anchorage on June 12, and home to Kodiak on Friday the thirteenth, which may have presaged what was to come in the early days back home.

Chapter 21

Back to Work

1947–1948

T HE PLANE TO KODIAK was a drafty old army DC-3 freighter. They arrived home in time to have lunch with the Torgersons. This was followed by hospital rounds with Dutch Bailey to familiarize Dad with those folks who would now be under his care, then home to unpack. The folks went to bed early.

Within thirty minutes, Dad was awakened and called to the hospital for a patient with possible placenta previa. He stayed in the hospital to keep close watch, between snatches of sleep, until she delivered at 7 o'clock the next morning. This was followed by a circumcision, a chest tap, an excision and drainage of a carbuncle of the back, followed by office hours until noon.

It was a very busy first week home, during which Dr. Bailey was off on a Kodiak bear hunt, and Dad began to try to make sense of his records, which he said were in terrible shape. This, reading accumulated mail, catching up on past medical journals, writing insurance reports for patients seen during his absence, preparing a talk for Rotary, and attending Community Center and Chamber meetings kept him fully occupied for weeks.

Dr. Bailey returned with his bear and a broad smile, and Dad paid Sid Olds, local guide, for the hunt (as a gift, and perhaps an inducement for Dutch to sign a year's contract). Dutch had to wait a few days for a plane, so he was invited to dinner and he showed pictures of his hunt. In one slide, there was only one thin blade of grass between him and a very large bear. Embellished with his slow, Texas drawl, this and a few other tales were transformed into hair-raising adventures. He departed on June 23 on the same plane that brought me back for my summer vacation.

The Johnsons, recently arrived back home, were invited by the Sisters to the hospital for a welcome luncheon. Their home-cooked meals were special, and the occasion more special. The Sisters had been through a lot with Dad since their arrival. They were quite proud of their doctor, who had worked with them through the process, and they were fond of the family.

The remainder of the summer was warm and mostly sunny. On September 11, Charley and Hazel had the three of us to dinner in the garage-apartment at Sprucehaven. Charley had moved to Kodiak in the early 1940s. His son was Norm Sutliff, who came to Kodiak in 1939 with only a few dollars in his pocket, later started the lumber supply business, and eventually a True Value Hardware Store. Hazel, Charley's second wife, a singer he had met when he was a caretaker at Schroon Lake, a voice camp in upstate New York, joined him in Kodiak in 1946. Charley had finished a cozy apartment above the garage in my parents' absence. The rustic efficiency apartment had hand-made varnished bunks, cupboards, a wardrobe, and plank table, all nestled tidily within the log walls, and Dad was really pleased with it. Charley functioned as caretaker of Sprucehaven, and the place served as their rent-free home indefinitely. They became good friends of the family and we shared meals at both homes frequently. This occasion was my farewell party.

On September 17, my parents saw me off on PNA to Seattle, on the way back to Salem and Willamette, for my next year as a premed student. Dad wrote that day, saying that on the way home from the airport, he stopped to watch Charley help some Mission folks make a "set" with their beach seine. There was a warm, gentle breeze. Scattered clouds hung in a blue sky and hovered over the little islands in the bay. It was a day meant for stopping and watching. What was about to unfold was a local ritual, observed when the salmon were congregating near the mouths of the streams in the fall.

The seine had been carefully piled on the stern of a skiff. One man rowed the skiff out from the beach and another paid out the net as they went, swinging in a large circle as they came back to the beach. Then both ends of the seine were pulled ashore by hand, the belly being the last of the net to come ashore. This took about thirty minutes. The first haul produced sand, gravel and quite a lot of seaweed. Without hesitation, the net was shaken out, carefully piled on the skiff again, and the whole performance was repeated, producing two silver salmon this time. Undaunted, the process was repeated. Before the belly of the net was ashore, flashing silver bodies could be seen underwater, and as it began to emerge, there was much thrashing and splashing about as fifty-six beautiful silver salmon were pulled in and shaken out of the net. One was given to Dad, which Charley insisted on cleaning, and this served as the special entree for several meals for both couples. Subsequently, Dad and Charley put together a small beach seine for themselves, which provided fresh fish for them when used for subsistence fishing in season.

This brought to mind that, before coming to Alaska, the family rarely, if ever, had fish or shellfish. Such foods were not popular as a good source of protein in those days. When we moved to Kodiak, a community whose primary industry was fishing, we continued our meat-eating habits—even though fresh meat wasn't available—until, slowly, as we were exposed to fish in restaurants, and when invited to dinner, food prepared from canned salmon began to appear at the dinner table. As Kodiak grew, and the variety of processed seafood increased, so did our seafood fare. We evolved into a family in which fish and shellfish products became one of the most appreciated ingredients of our diet.

✳ ✳ ✳

MR. ERSKINE never fully recovered from Nellie's death, although after he returned to Kodiak following six months Outside, Dad reported that he was looking better. Later Dad began speaking in his letters of Mr. Erskine as needing a professional nurse, and I learned that he had developed multiple myeloma, a bone cancer, it had spread to the brain, and was terminal. Leisha Flood, a nurse-manager of the hospital for a time, became his nurse, they soon married, and Mr. Erskine continued to fail.

"Babies, babies, and more babies!" It seemed that few days would pass without a delivery. One could go back through the diaries and count the actual number of babies delivered but I don't think this was ever done. Dad was becoming busier, and busier, and it was no wonder, since Kodiak was probably adding at least 200 brand new souls every year, in addition to those who came from elsewhere.

On Sunday, December 7, Dad wrote: "It seems that this is going to be another winter in which the usual medical slump is not going to take place. Wednesday began by going over questionable chest X-rays culled from 1,200 taken under the tutelage of Dr. Marshall, who was conducting a mass tuberculosis survey for the Territory. There were very few that I did not have under observation already, which showed that the community had good medical supervision.

"The week ended yesterday with four operations in the morning. The first was a really difficult one on a young chap who had been brought in from Ouzinkie, first in 1944, in very grave condition with a ruptured appendix. I operated on him and found his appendix to be part of the separating wall of adhesions which, if broken down, would have given him a generalized peritonitis (much more serious) so I just put in a tube to drain the abscess and put him back to bed with intravenous plasma and glucose. He gradually began to improve, but got a fecal fistula that finally healed after about six weeks, and he was sent home, to return in three months to have his appendix removed. As he was well by that time he did not return, nor did he have any more trouble until this attack of acute appendicitis again.

"This time, I went through his old scar, removing it in passing, carefully going through adhesions and separating intestines from abdominal wall, continuing on through adherent loops of bowel, until I finally felt a mass, which I could separate from surrounding tissues with my fingers until I could get it up sufficiently to make sure that it was truly the offending organ. More adhesions were separated by finger until I could get above the inflamed area close to the origin of the appendix, at which point I removed the appendix, cauterizing the stump, and let it fall back into the abdomen. All debris and exudates were mopped out, and five grams of sulfathiazole powder was dusted into the area of inflammation and about all of the inflamed loops of intestinal tract, and the incision was closed without drainage. I am expecting him to do well and his report this morning is that his temperature is down and he had a good night and is feeling hungry, which is all good.

"After lunch, I was called back to town to see W. J. [Erskine], who had had another gastric hemorrhage from his old ulcer. He had been doing everything I had told him he shouldn't do, with regard to cigarettes, liquor, and diet. He was in good condition, though, and did not need transfusions, so we again put him on a stringent diet. While in town, I had to admit two more patients to the hospital, examine them, and prescribe treatment. They are all doing well this morning. We only have one empty bed in the hospital, so that will tell you something about how busy we have been—expecting fifteen or more babies before Christmas."

Christmas Day 1947, Dad wrote: "What a beautiful Christmas Day this is. The sun is shining, absolutely unopposed by cloud or haze—a clear day, that brings the distant mountains almost within touch. Speaking of sunlight and shadows, how many pictures have I seen with titles similar to that? Not one of these could begin to compare with the sight, and experience, one gains on tramping through our Sprucehaven woods. It is a veritable fairyland, and allows one to cast off all worldly care and thrill, again, to the *joi de vivre*!

"Dan and Joe were out last night. They were to get Christmas leave, but managed an overnight for Christmas Eve. I brought them out with me from the office yesterday afternoon. We had a roast beef dinner. Hazel and Charley came over after dinner, and we listened to the Christmas Carol, before we went to midnight mass at the Community Center, then to bed at 2 this morning. The boys had to be back at camp before 8 o'clock this morning, so they got up, got their own breakfast, and caught the 7:15 bus from the Beachcombers [a nightclub on the other side of Shahafka Cove from Sprucehaven], after doing their dishes, making their beds, and leaving us notes of thanks."

From one of Dad's Sunday letters, when my friend Dan Hoag was visiting that fall: "I got up a little before 7 this morning. Dan is out for the weekend, and, as he did not get much sleep during the week with his extra duties, I thought he would want to sleep in, and I knew Mother did not want to leave the "sack" until at least 9 a.m. So, quietly, I put on my bathing suit, ran down to the ocean, took my quick dip, and then—to my surprise—a flying apparition came swirling down the beach, into and under the water all in the blink of an eye. It was Danny, who had been lying in bed so as not to disturb Mother, and hearing me go out the kitchen door, was up and into his bathing suit, and was off, after me." That was Dan—full of energy and ready for action.

On the next to the last day of the year, a serious shipwreck occurred. Many who lived in Alaska coastal communities were fishermen. Travel between the villages, particularly before air travel was available, was by small boat. In wintertime, boat travel could be hazardous, since the weather could quickly turn nasty. This it did, on Christmas Eve this year, when a sudden snowstorm drove the *Spencer*, a cannery tender, ashore, on the peninsula across Shelikof Strait. The survivors, eight Chignik fishermen and two women, made it to shore, where they huddled together for five days. The blizzard finally subsided, and they were rescued and brought to Kodiak by the navy, on December 30.

The accident made the national news. Dad reported, "The two women were able to leave the hospital on the second day, in good shape. One of the men, who had loose rubber boots, had taken them off and rubbed his feet and, as soon as he recovered from exposure, he was able to leave. The other seven, however, are still in the hospital and, although they are recovering from exposure and their fevers are subsiding, six of them have feet that were frozen so badly that they will have to have amputations of varying extent—two, perhaps halfway to the knee. We are awaiting a line of demarcation between living and dead tissue. This is rather depressing for me, for these are all young men in their late teens or early twenties, and I dislike mutilating operations." Eventually he amputated eleven limbs, most of them halfway to the knee, and sent the seven men to Seattle to be fitted for artificial limbs.

These were all members of the large Skonberg family from Chignik, most of whom are still alive, and they love to tell the story of their "adventure." They were particularly proud of their amputations, for, when they arrived in Seattle to get their artificial limbs, they were told that their "stumps" were the best they had ever seen. Most of them live in Kodiak, now, and they still brag about Dad.

* * *

THE YEAR 1948 was much like previous years. Dad was forever on the move, rarely sitting still, noticing all the beauty that was around him, but taking very little time to indulge in it. He was not content unless he was accomplishing something, and furthermore, accomplishing it quickly and efficiently. He had a great tendency toward perfectionism, and, in my case at least, and perhaps in Mother's, he could be indulgent of those who were not quite of that tendency.

On January 4, Mother was at church, and Dad was sitting in his comfortable armchair by the fire, musing how, in such a rustic and beautiful setting, "one tends to feel at peace with the world." Then the radio reported fighting and death, in Palestine and in China, and political warfare in several European countries. He thought, "One tends to lose some of that peaceful feeling, and sits, wishing for a truly peaceful world." In spite of many technological advances, which made our material existence more pleasant, he felt that the world was still not very civilized. "There must be a balance between intellect and knowledge, religion and morals, beauty and poetry, and relationships." In *Problem Island*, a book he had read, the author pointed out that a society may be very rich in material things and still not be civilized. These things were, in a sense, the apparatus of civilization, because, under proper direction, they made for material well being, and a civilization could get on better if it had this for a basis, but they did not make significant progress toward true civilization. He said, "As a matter of fact, it is true that civilization and Christianity seem to have progressed together, and it is Christianity that teaches grown-up ideas of selflessness and brotherly love, and the search for the good, the true, and the beautiful, which is really the aim of true civilization."

In Dad's day, psychiatry was something most doctors thought was "whistling in the wind." Dad commented, "I have been re-reading a bit of psychiatry lately, and find that it is taking a much more sensible attitude than it did in the past, and that Freud is getting it ironed out into some reasonable semblance of logic. When you consider a neurosis simply the result of stress that upsets a person's intrinsic mental and emotional equilibrium, the stress being internal as a result of conflicting feelings, or external because of external events, you can begin to make sense of it. The person's mental state is designed to cope with events in such a way that they do not create stress and lead to mental illness, just like one's immune system is designed to cope with events to prevent physical disease. Mental equilibrium depends upon heredity, and the sum of all cultural and intellectual influences stemming from the environment. If this is overwhelmed, the equilibrium fails, and compensatory mechanisms—basically neurotic—are mobilized." He continued, "The psychiatrists outline some of the neurotic mechanisms for coping with stress, as well as some of the physical symptoms that can result. Then comes the study of the subconscious mind, which is always fascinating, and the means of psychotherapy that are becoming helpful, and which all doctors use either consciously or subconsciously in their practice."

* * *

DAD'S LONG SEARCH FOR AN ASSOCIATE now appeared to be on the verge of fruition. In late February, he wrote to me: "I received a letter from Dr. Bailey about a week ago in response to a letter of mine to him, asking if he were ready to settle down to a practice yet. I told him I would be glad to have him with me in Kodiak until you were through school, and then the three of us could carry on until I retired—that when you came up, I would semi-retire for a few years and let you two carry on. He asked a number of questions regarding living expenses, expected income, and, especially, if there would be time off each year for hunting and fishing. I answered all his questions, and should hear from him before another month is past. One thing he wanted to know was how you felt about it, so I told him you had liked him when you met last summer and I was sure that this plan would meet with your approval. If it won't, let me know. I believe we can get along with Bailey as well as anyone that would be likely to come here, and I expect to keep full control of the office until you come."

Meanwhile, Dad had to wrestle with his ambivalence about my scholastic performance. I was senior class president, more involved with class and music activities and not enamored with quantitative analysis, a difficult chemistry course, which involved a lot of work. His perfectionism demanded more of me, and yet his affection for his only son allowed a degree of indulgence. He had difficulty juggling the two while trying to encourage my performance without jeopardizing my affection.

In a letter, written near the end of March, he mused once again on the world situation. "The world situation does not seem to be very stable these days, does it? If it were not for the payments on wars, past and possibly future—if we could cut all world armies and armaments down to local police forces, and let past war veterans earn their way like other civilians—think of the billions of dollars that could be spent on the underprivileged. There might need be no one in the world lacking a proper home, and clothes, and food, and how much happier everyone would be. How childlike and selfish and ignorant we are. There is far to go before civilization has progressed to any real degree in international relations. Even the United States is not ready as yet: we, perhaps as much as any other nation, refuse to give up any of our own prerogatives to a world body, and until we can see problems from a global standpoint instead of our own personal view, we will never have world peace. I know of no nation, not even Britain, that has reached that state."

Chapter 22

Shared Practice

1948–1949

ON JUNE 2, 1948, Dr. Clarence "Dutch" Bailey arrived to join Dad in practice. His decision to come seems to have rested as much upon the opportunity to hunt and fish as it did to practice medicine. He had stopped to see me at Willamette, and didn't hesitate to tell Dad how much he had enjoyed the visit, and that he looked forward to practicing with the two of us when I finished my training.

Dad met the plane and took him to Sprucehaven, where he would be a guest until some of his baggage arrived, and then he would move into an apartment in the Felder Building. Dad liked him and was sure that we would have a pleasant association throughout the years. The extra doctor would take some of the load, and their arrangement would allow Dad an afternoon and alternate weekends off first call. He would still need to be on call for surgical emergencies.

Saturday afternoon, Dad and Mother had a gathering at Sprucehaven for Dr. Bailey, so that the navy doctors, dentists, and nurses, as well as the commanding officers, could meet him. Dad wrote that, "We had about forty people out and all had a very good time. Admiral Jack Perry was in for the weekend, so we asked Admiral Montgomery to bring him along. We took the two admirals, Mrs. Montgomery, and daughter, with Captain List and Dutch to dinner at the Montmartre afterward."

Mother was too overwhelmed to go to dinner. Dad understood, but attributed it to menopause, not realizing that his demands played a considerable role in her problem. Dad wrote to me, "We are going to have to watch Mother, and be thoughtful of her for the next couple of years, after which she will be alright. However, if you have not already made any commitments, it would be much better not to have anyone here this summer, who would not do his full share of everything about the place and fit harmoniously into the scheme of things. She doesn't mind Danny, because when he comes out, he helps set the table, helps with the dishes, and is more of a help than a burden. Use your own careful judgment—but I think she would appreciate it if you can get home as soon as possible after your commencement."

Dad's comment was the result of my mention of the possibility of bringing a friend home for a visit that summer. Al Isenberg, a fraternity brother who owned a motorcycle, had taught me to ride on a borrowed bike that spring. I had bought a gutsy Indian motorcycle, and we had decided to be the first bikers to negotiate the recently completed Alcan Highway across Canada and into Alaska, which had been built to ferry military equipment to bases in Alaska. The idea, hatched between us, had grown irresistible.

June was a busy month. Since summer vacation was imminent, there were no more letters, but Dad picked up his story in the diary. Sunday, the folks had a seagull egg for breakfast—no comment on its taste. Monday morning, Dutch and Dad made hospital rounds together, beginning the indoctrination of the young doctor. That afternoon, Dad helped him get settled in his new apartment, and, on Wednesday, Dad had his first afternoon off. He would perform most of the non-routine surgeries and assist Dr. Bailey with his operations.

The hospital was full, with one bed in the hall, on June 15, when Dad received the wire from me on June 19 from Edmonton, Alberta, indicating that I was bringing home a guest. He wrote that Mother had "cleaned the cabin for the boys." On June 30, when he realized that we were taking a long time to make the trip, he sent a wire to the Mounties at Edmonton, putting them on our trail. Presto, the very next day, we arrived in Kodiak by plane. The motorcycles followed a week later by ship.

Because Dad had spent some time as a cyclist delivering messages while at Camp Colt waiting to be shipped overseas, he was familiar with motorcycles, and he wanted to try my bike shortly after it had arrived. It was a sunny Sunday afternoon, and Dad and Mother were enjoying the sun with the Wagners on the front terrace when I, having been out for a spin, zoomed up and dismounted. Mrs. Wagner, a lively lady, wanted a ride, so I took her for a short spin after which Dad wanted to give it a try. The road led down a short hill and then meandered left to eventually cross the bridge at the lake outlet. Dad hopped on, kick-started the bike, and roared down the hill at the bottom of which I expected he would slow down. Instead, he went faster and was across the road and into a clump of small spruce trees. Before I could reach him, he was up and had extricated himself and the bike from the spruce, and was ready to go again. He could not lose face in front of the admiral and his wife. It turned out that his experience was with bikes whose throttles operated exactly the reverse of those of my day, which is why he went faster when he meant to slow down. His second try was more cautious, and went off without a hitch.

With Dutch there, Dad had more time to spend with us and on his other activities. There was the usual maintenance of Sprucehaven, now made easier by Dan, Al, and me. The extended family all went to every square dance at the Community Center, where Dad had become quite the professional dance caller. The folks helped with picnics for the young folks, and included us and our lady friends at their social affairs. They seemed to enjoy Al, who stayed through July, although he was somewhat of a daydreamer, and Mother was heard to say that she had never seen anyone spend so much time drying one dish. After Al left, Dan spent the first two weeks of August on furlough at Sprucehaven. In late September, I returned to Willamette, to begin my final year.

* * *

DAD MENTIONED THAT W.J. WAS NOT DOING WELL that year, didn't say much about it. There was no longer mention of his going out of the house. He began to spend most of his time in bed. His multiple myeloma would have been painful, and his nurse-wife, Leisha, provided appropriate medication as needed.

Dad, since living in a community known among big-game hunters all over the world as the home of the Kodiak bear, thanks to Charley Madsen, and as a village where many earned their living from the sea, felt he should give these activities a try. Sport fishing was touted as a most desirable, relaxing pastime, and he tried surf casting several times off the beach at Sprucehaven. But it didn't take long for him to decide that fishing might be good for some, but was not productive enough for him. His experience as a hunter was no more successful. He and Charley went duck hunting four or five times, and, though they did see many ducks, they were often not accessible. When they were, and they were able to shoot one or two, the birds would invariably fall into the sea out of reach. They succeeded in bringing home at least one duck, which they proudly exhibited between them in a *photo*graph taken on the front terrace.

In October, a Mr. Donnelley and Mr. Acheson were guests for dinner at Sprucehaven. They owned and operated a general merchandise store in Flat, a village in the Iditarod Valley of the Territory, and had purchased the W. J. Erskine Company store. Bob Acheson, Dad wrote, was the younger of the two and had moved to Kodiak to manage the store. His brother had remained in Flat to manage that store. Mr. Donnelley had no children and had helped the two brothers set up the business. He would be coordinating the two stores for a while, and then would probably retire to Seattle. They were pleasant folks, and Bob and his wife, Betty, whom they later met, became fast friends of my parents.

Charley Sutliff and Dad, with a duck, back from the one successful hunt of three, which they decided would be their last, late 1940s.

"I should have written you two days ago, but events wouldn't permit. The major event was an urgent call to see W.J. at two o'clock Thursday morning. He was feeling well the previous few days, but he got one of his sudden pneumonias, and when I reached him his lungs were full of pulmonary edema. He opened his eyes when I came in and said,

'Hello, Doctor,' then lapsed into unconsciousness for nearly two days. On Friday afternoon, December 24, 1948, the grand old man died." Dad had to "take Leisha in hand, make arrangements for the funeral, wire Caroline and Wilson on Christmas Day, and, on Sunday, meet Wilson's plane to keep him in tow and keep him from drinking too much." On Tuesday, there was an Elk's memorial service, and W.J. was buried on a hill next to Nellie's grave, which had a panoramic view of the harbor. The will, read after the funeral, "left his estate to Caroline, Wilson, and Leisha, one-third to each so that, although no one was satisfied, no one was too put out."

Wilson and Dutch were guests at Sprucehaven over the Christmas weekend, and after the ceremony, Wilson flew home. In a sense, 1948 saw an end not just to the Erskine Company, but of what was formerly the Alaska Commercial Company, originally the Russian-American Company.

* * *

BECAUSE I WAS NOT AN EXCEPTIONAL STUDENT, Dad was concerned that I might not be accepted in medical school. In January 1949, I was about to enter the second semester of my senior year, although I already had enough credits to graduate, when he wrote: "My main concern about this situation, is that, if you do not have a full schedule, or a little bit more—you are going to play around, and get into habits, which have been your downfall in the past. It would be much better for your character and study habits not to go to school at all. You see what I mean, don't you?" That is the closest he came to telling me to quit fooling around and tend to business, something his dad had done, finally, when he found himself ill prepared when entering medical school.

In Dad's letters he observed, on one occasion, that Dutch was somewhat like an overgrown boy and, being single, seemed to need some extra attention. Dutch left the last day of February to attend the annual Alaska State Medical Association meeting in Juneau, it being his turn. This would occupy the first few days of a six-week vacation, during which he would be taking a month's postgraduate training in problems of the eye, and a couple additional weeks of vacation. He would return in time to cover the practice, so the folks could take a planned vacation, so Dad was temporarily back in solo practice again, with plenty to do.

One week into it, on March 6, he wrote: "Had a fairly busy week, like old times. Did a caesarian operation last Tuesday night on one of Dr. Bailey's patients, a sixteen-year-old girl, who already had had one caesarian nearly two years ago. She was also becoming toxic and, the next day, started to have convulsions, for which we had to give her intravenous medications, but she is all well now. About 3:30 the next morning I had one of my own OBs.

"Thursday was a rather typical winter day in my practice. I arose at 7:30 a.m. and did exercises, took a cold shower, then had breakfast, and studied for nearly an hour, arriving at the hospital at 9 o'clock for rounds. Wrote up three histories and physical examinations—short form, of necessity—interpreted six X-rays taken the day before, started an IV medication on a pneumonia patient, removed sutures from a post-op patient, and did a circumcision on a newborn. Office at 10 o'clock, where I saw about twelve patients with all sorts of maladies until about 12:20, when I went home to lunch, after getting the mail and doing a little shopping for Mother. Back at the office, for another busy session from 2 to 4:30, where I squeezed in some insurance reports between patients. Bank directors meeting, another trip to the post office and stop at the hospital, then home for dinner and the evening, if no meetings or calls. One simply has to keep going with a systematized schedule and everything comes out even with not too much trouble. Of course, I have grown up with it here and take it in stride, although I do expect that it would be a bit difficult for a newcomer and I can see Bailey's difficulties when he relieved me in 1947. He will be more used to it when he returns."

Mother must have observed the caesarian Dad performed on the girl, because she wrote, "He can certainly turn out a lot of work and seems to like working alone better than with someone. He's so quick, most folks get in his way. I watched him do a caesarian the other night with just Sister Mary Leo helping. He did a beautiful job. I was proud of him. Sister said it was such a pleasure to work with him, he was so sure of himself, and everything moved so smoothly they never worried about anything. I hope you inherit his skill in surgery, since by the time he's ready to slow down, he'll need you. He thinks you are 'a natural.'"

One of several interesting cases Dad had during this period was a baby whom he was called to see at 4 o'clock one morning. The baby had intermittent vomiting and diarrhea for a couple of days, followed by no bowel movements and continuous vomiting, the day before admission. Dad wrote that, "This sounded like an intestinal obstruction which, if mechanical, meant an operation fairly quickly to save life. It was an important decision to make—to operate or not to operate. If it were a paralytic type of obstruction, an operation would make matters worse and might prove fatal. I must confess, the case had me scratching my head. I did not feel, somehow, that it was a mechanical obstruction, although all signs seemed to point to it. I spent some time studying the case. We could not get an enema in or out. No gas could be gained from a rectal tube. The baby's belly was blown up like a tire and it was vomiting bile. I finally put in a return flow and ordered hot stupes to the abdomen, and I went to bed for a couple of hours. At nine o'clock the next morning, the baby was worse and its abdomen seemed about to burst and its vomiting was fecal in character. I still felt that there was no mechanical obstruction but told the Sister to set up the surgery and that if there was no improvement in another hour we would operate. At 10 o'clock there was no improvement. We scrubbed, and Sister Mary Leo was ready for the operation. I donned my gown and gloves, and was about to paint the abdomen for a local anesthetic when I heard the escape of a little gas from the baby's anus. I said, 'Hold everything,' and we waited fifteen minutes. The baby's stomach was definitely less tense so I told Sister Mary to cover the sterile instrument table and Sister Superior to take the baby back to bed. In fifteen minutes it had a good bowel movement and was out of danger. I breathed easier." It seemed that Dad was governed by some sixth sense.

* * *

IT WAS APPROACHING NINE MONTHS of Dad's new practice with Dutch. Dutch had gained considerable experience, and Dad felt he ought to be up to managing the practice. His contract had three months to go and, since his sister Dorothea would be in the country visiting Grandmother Sarah, Dad felt they should schedule a sojourn Outside. Dutch would return in April, and that would be a good time.

A letter on April 10 heralded this approaching vacation. They had arranged the purchase of a 1949 Pontiac, which would be available on their arrival in Seattle. He wrote, "We will be happy to be with you again! I expect you will be able to run up to your grandmother's for a few days when we will be there, the last week in April. Dorothea, and Frank Spears, her second husband, will reach the West Coast in time to be at Darlow's for Easter, where Mother will meet them. [Frank was multitalented: he was a painter, he designed sailboats and sailed them, he was a radio announcer, an actor, and a singer.] Then they will all go up to Mother's place in Portland for the next week or two. We can all be together during the last week in April. If you can only stay a day or two of that week, they will understand. We don't want you to take so much time out of your schoolwork that you will not be able to get off early to go up the Alcan Highway with us. I must be back in Kodiak before the middle of June. At any rate, in a couple more weeks, we shall be together again for a short time, and then, in another three or four weeks, we will have a summer before us."

That spring, we learned that my applications to medical school were rejected. I was assured, however, that if I could demonstrate my scholastic ability in graduate school, I could qualify for entrance to the University of Washington in 1950. And so I applied to the University of Michigan, where there were two leaders in the field of genetics, an interest of mine. If accepted there, I intended to obtain a master's degree in zoology.

Mother and Dad flew to Seattle in mid April, and spent the night at the Olympic Hotel. Their car would be available for them in a few days. While there, Dad visited several hospitals, made a side trip to Everett to confer with Arild Johnson, architect for the new Kodiak school, visited with several Kodiak friends, shopped, and stopped for oyster stew at Skippers and Von's several times.

On Saturday afternoon, April 23, they drove from Seattle to Salem in their new Pontiac, to pick me up and take me back to visit the family. We drove the fifty miles to Grandmother Johnson's home in Tigard, where Dad's sister Dorothea, her husband Frank, and Emily, a younger cousin, had recently arrived from Cape Town. His older brother, Darlow, and wife, Alta, had come from Pendleton, their current parish, for a few days. This was the first family get-together since the death of the Bishop, whose spirit, nonetheless, was present. The afternoon was spent catching up on each other's lives. They previewed Frank's paintings—he'd had several showings in London—and listened to some of his recorded songs before dinner. Dinner was enlivened by Darlow's fine sense of humor.

After breakfast in the morning, the folks dropped me at the bus station, so I could return to Salem. Mom, Dad, Dorothea, and Frank, and Emily left for a drive down the winding Pacific Coast Highway, with its beautiful countryside and the magnificent ocean vistas, to Los Angeles, where Dad would attend a medical meeting. They also drove all over Southern California visiting folks they knew, mostly military families who had been in Kodiak. Dad attended his meeting, and then they headed north.

They spent several days in San Francisco, and arrived in Salem in the evening of May 26.

There were a few more busy days in Seattle, before I arrived by bus early the morning of June 9, to accompany them in their new Pontiac on an adventurous trip up the still-unpaved Alcan Highway. We drove east through the beautiful Wenatchee Valley, stopping for lunch in Cle Elum, had tea at the Grand Coulee Dam, and spent the night at Bonner's Ferry, Idaho. The next morning, we went through Customs at Kingsgate, and entered British Columbia.

The highway was accessed through Canada, its origin being in Dawson Creek, B.C. North of Edmonton, the roads were largely unpaved, and settlements and facilities were increasingly far apart as we went farther north. There was wilderness as far as the eye could see, and many unique, frontier communities. But we hurried on, because Dad was intent on arriving home by June 15.

We got to Anchorage late one afternoon, five days from Kingsgate. We visited Avery and Maxine Roberts, before retiring at the Westward Hotel. The next day we attended Rotary as guests of Elmer Rasmuson, then president, where Dad gave a short talk. We shipped the car home, and boarded PNA to fly south to Kodiak. A taxi took us to Sprucehaven, where Hazel and Charley had the log cabin clean, cozy, and warm, with a fire in the fireplace, and we could sit down, take a deep breath, and relax, after our whirlwind Johnson vacation.

Chapter 23

Solo Practice, Once Again

1949–1950

THREE MONTHS ON HIS OWN apparently caused Dutch Bailey to decide that he wasn't a pioneer physician, or at least didn't want to continue as an associate in such a busy practice. His initial one-year contract was up, and within a week or so, Dad was back in solo practice. Dutch was going to take up practice in Palmer, a community north of Anchorage, where it would be easy to arrange various big-game hunts, and he would be getting married in the fall to a girl named Julie.

The summer passed in the usual fashion, each day starting with a swim in the ocean. An occasional houseguest would be invited to join in, and a few did. For Dad, the cold swim replaced a cold shower from about the first of May to the first of October. It gave him a vigorous start to the day, even when he was short on sleep. Besides, it was a family tradition. Dad's mother, Sarah, took a cold bath every morning until the age of ninety-six, when she could no longer climb in and out of the tub. She attributed her rapid aging thereafter to having given up her cold tub. The Johnsons stand by this custom, and think everyone should try it. From a state of morning lethargy, a cold shower—no diluting with warm water—instantly sets one dancing about the room, toweling with vigor, and creates a momentum that persists through a good part of the day.

Solo practice was like old times, only more so. Activities included chairman of the Community Center Board, which involved organizing the annual fund-raising. He had become chair of the building committee for the School District. And he continued as a director of the bank, city Health Officer, and chairman of Civil Defense and Hospital Units. So once again, there were only cursory notes in his diary.

On September 15, Dad wrote: "Saw Bob off for his year at the University of Michigan, Ann Arbor, for his master's degree in genetics. Lonesome house." The next day, "Ocean swim alone—raining." And that evening, "to conference on housing with Admiral Wagner and Captain Dow at N.O.B."

* * *

SPRUCEHAVEN WAS STILL EVOLVING. Dad added an oil furnace, which was ready for use before Christmas. It was installed by Vinnie Root, who managed Kodiak's plumbing and heating needs, and whose work was perfection. Vinnie was a tall, fun-loving Norwegian whose wife, Mary, was, in Dad's opinion, most beautiful. Vinnie had a fine tenor voice, and, at a party, would invariably join in with singing old-time favorites in harmony. With a little coaxing, he would entertain everyone with, "Rita, My Clam-Digger Sveethaart," in perfect "Svedish" accent, and the "Street Urchin's Melody."

On December 14, Mother invited all the schoolteachers and several other women to what was becoming an annual church Christmas tea at Sprucehaven. There was no big Christmas dinner party this year, but the folks had an open house on December 26. On New Year's Eve, the folks were invited to a cocktail party at the Base, after which they were guests of Admiral Wagner at a formal dinner dance. These rare formal affairs gave Dad an opportunity to wear his decades-old but still elegant tuxedo. He and Mother, in one of her beautiful formal gowns, made a handsome couple.

As chairman of the Building Committee, Dad was charged with finding property and a means of financing for the new Main School. He had been in touch with the Territorial governor, who found that some of the property belonging to the Army Communication Corps might be available. The land had been deeded to the army after the purchase of Alaska to provide communications during the period of military rule, and it continued to serve as a telegraph and long-distance telephone facility for the community until we developed our own system. There was more land than needed, and it appeared that some would be available. It was in an undeveloped, heavily forested area, within a mile to the north of town, and the committee selected a couple of desirable sites.

The School Board met on February 10, with the Council and the C.O. of the Signal Corps, to define the property desired. They then awaited a visit from Governor Gruening, who was arriving the afternoon of February 12, at which time they would discuss the issue and inform him of their preferred site. An evening reception was held for the Gruenings at the Officer's Club on Base, by Admiral and Mrs. Wagner. The next morning, at a meeting with the School Board, they were happy to learn that the favored site would be available to the city for construction of the school. That evening, there was a final banquet at the Elk's Club where the governor spoke. Governor Gruening was effective in convincing the federal government and the army to release the property for the school. I heard him speak several times, and was impressed by his ability to speak without notes, and, when ticking off points at issue on any given subject, to remember all of them.

Mother's letter described the dinner: "They served cracked king crab, with lettuce, tomato, and cucumber salad, rolls, apple pie, and coffee. The crab was prepared by Tiny Cichoski, local fisherman, and was delicious. We had all we could eat. Thirty-two crab served 120 people, and there were more available should they have been needed."

Dad learned that, not long after Dan returned to New Jersey, his mother had become ill. In time, it proved that this was a terminal illness, and Dad was concerned that, since Dan didn't seem to have much in the way of family, her death would be a heavy blow for him. Since returning to his home in New Jersey, Dan had become acquainted with Dad's nephew, Darlow Botha, one of Dorothea's sons by her first marriage, and they had become good friends. Both wanted to come to Kodiak that summer.

* * *

DAD WAS RARELY SICK. When he was, he rarely let it get him down. When it did get him down, he rarely stayed there. On February 28, in the afternoon after a Rotary luncheon, he wrote that he was "not feeling well." The next morning, he wrote: "Fearful vomiting during night—wanted to die—temp. 101 degrees in a.m. so to hospital for penicillin only available by injection. Lay in stupor most of day except to admit patients, verbally, and give necessary orders. Those shots! Not too sick to dread them!" And the next day: "Temp broke at 2 a.m. after which awful aching, of all muscles, ceased, and I was able to sleep. Felt good today, but stayed in bed on penicillin and diet another twenty-four hours. Read *The Seven-Storey Mountain* by Thomas Merton to please the Sisters." And the next day: "Up at six 6 o'clock, to examine a possible appendix case—removed cast—incised abscessed finger—made hospital rounds—did circumcision—admitted more patients—busy until noon. Then home, and rested the rest of the day."

When I arrived home from Michigan on Saturday, June 24, Dad met me at the airport. I now had my master's degree. I went to Rotary with Dad on the last day of his third year as president. Dan, Darlow, and Beverly, Darlow's bride, arrived on the first of July. This trip was to be a honeymoon for the newlyweds, and Torgy's cabin served as their home for the summer. Dan stayed in Dad's den.

The Kodiak community had a great party on the Fourth of July. The celebration had been well organized for years by Ray Martin, the energetic manager of PNA. There was always a parade, often led by Johnny Gibbons, a tall, handsome engineer who sported a neatly trimmed mustache and a broad-brimmed hat, and rode his beautiful white gelding. There were races for kids of all ages, pillow fights, boxing matches, carnival booths, games, and an evening banquet, followed by a dance with a local accordion and guitar band, where schottisches, polkas, and round dances were enjoyed to exhaustion.

Darlow and Beverly stayed a month before returning home to Baltimore. On their day of departure we had a farewell dinner with Charley, Hazel, and Dan, and then took our cousins to the airport.

For the rest of the summer, Dan and I helped with chores on the property and also worked the ships as longshoremen to earn a little money. I had been accepted at the University of Washington Medical School, and on September 18, I left for my first year.

* * *

DAD HAD MET MILO FRITZ, an ear, eye, nose, and throat (EENT) specialist, on one of his infrequent visits to Anchorage. Milo had traveled all over Interior Alaska, removing tonsils and adenoids to prevent ear infections and subsequent hearing loss in children. Dad thought it would be wonderful if Milo would come to Kodiak and hold a clinic, to provide eyeglasses and consult with Dad on patients who needed speciality care. Dr. Fritz agreed, and he and his nurse came on Sunday, October 29, set up in Dad's second exam room, and held clinic all that week. This was the first of many itinerant clinics in Kodiak, and saved folks who needed these services an expensive trip to Anchorage.

Chapter 24

Staying With It

1951–1952

THROUGH THE CHANGING STAFF at the Naval Operating Base, over time my parents met and made many lifelong friends. Among these were Generals Corlett and Buckner, in the early war years when Kodiak was the home of the Integrated Alaska Command. Captain Lowry, the first medical director of the Base Hospital, spent a lot of time at Sprucehaven, and was host to the folks at functions on Base. These folks and, later, Admiral and Mrs. Wagner, Colonel "Pep" Shaeffer of Field Artillery, Dr. and Mrs. Liszt, Dr. and Mrs. Gillespie, Kelly Byler and Verna Stinson, were some of their closest friends from the NOB. Captain and Mrs. Kaitner arrived in 1950 and became friends, as did Admiral and Mrs. Caldwell. The admiral was instrumental in getting Dad to join the Navy League, which was a citizens support group for that branch of the service. Captain Roberts, whom the folks knew on his tour in the early 1940s, returned in 1951 to oversee construction of the army dock.

The Erskines, and Merrill and Louise Coon, who were in Kodiak when we arrived, were among several who really called Kodiak their home. The folks lost two of their first and closest Kodiak friends when Nellie and then W.J. died. After Torgy and Ruth Torgerson, Avery and Maxine Roberts, Frank and Elsie Lahtonen, and the Cliftons arrived in the early 1940s, they were great friends of the folks'. The Torgersons kept in touch, even after Torgy sold the bank and moved to start the Desert Bank in Cathedral City, California. The Roberts, the Lahtonens, and the Cliftons left in the late forties. Bob Acheson, who had taken over the Erskine Store, and his wife, Betty, became close friends. Many of these folks eventually retired to homes Outside, but Kodiak was home to the Johnsons.

The start of 1951 might have been considered bleak, if it were important to Dad to find a partner—or an assistant—to help him with his practice. But the fact that I would complete my medical training and could join him in five years seemed to result in his lack of further attempts to look for more than short-term assistance. Early in January, his diary notes a balancing of the previous year's accounts, which indicated that he had spent over $28,000 and collected "about the same in office and surgical fees." Dad was extremely busy during those five years, and journal entries are skimpy.

* * *

MOTHER'S LETTERS often provided interesting comments: "You should see our little weasel eat cottage cheese. Does he love it. He knows I feed him, too. Yesterday morning, while we were at breakfast, he came out and indicated he wanted something to eat. I ignored him. Dad said he kept looking up at me, and cocking his head, and running back and forth and in circles, where his dish usually is. He's so cute. We haven't had a rat all winter." That little fellow had been around for quite a while. I was told that he became tame enough to run up Dad's leg to take food from his hand. One Saturday morning, when it was time to change the sheets, mom pulled out the built-in linen drawer under her bunk bed and was startled to find the little fellow nesting there. Equally startled, he stood up on his hind legs and began to chatter angrily as if to say, "Just what do you think you are doing in here?"

Dad surprised me with a visit to Seattle on February 20. He showed up at my 11 o'clock Public Health class, only to find that I didn't. He finally found me at 1:30 p.m. When he explained why he had come, I understood. From his affiliation with the Portland Yacht Club, he was an enthusiastic sailor. He, like a surprising number of folks, nurtured a dream that, one day, he might own a deep-sea sailing craft, which could provide the freedom to escape the ordinary life and ply the seven seas. I knew of this, and had discovered a ketch for sale, at the University Boat Mart, and had written to him about it. He wrote back, providing me with a long list of items to check, which I had dutifully done. The ketch was a ten-ton 38-foot, double-ended, deep-sea cruising ketch, with bowsprit, standing room in the main cabin, and a six-foot keel. We went over the boat with a fine-toothed comb, had it inspected, and made arrangements to have the sternpost and some surrounding rot replaced by the owner. Then Dad returned home, after a one-week stay. Dad was the sailor, not I, but I would monitor the repair and negotiate possible purchase.

Prior to Dad's visit, Mother had noted that he had been extremely busy and had begun to get irritable, which only happened when he had been unable to get a good sleep for several days. After he returned, she wrote: "The trip did Dad a lot of good. He needs a change, once in a while. He hasn't seemed to mind his calls so much, and is quite cheerful."

She also wrote, "I sure had a round with the rats when Dad was gone. I had to beat one to death. He was stunned by the trap and I wasn't going to let him get away." She hadn't seen the weasel for a week, but she had seen rats so she began to set traps. She caught several. "I even caught Teenie Weenie [the weasel] in a trap, but found him right away and lifted the spring. He shook his head and ran away so I guess he was all right." This insult was too much for Teenie Weenie, though, because he was never seen again.

One of the wonderful things about Kodiak is its unspoiled environment. In Dad's day, there were numerous wild creatures in and around town, and there are many still. At Sprucehaven, there were many varieties of ducks and gulls at sea and on the lake. Occasionally on the sea side, we would see sea lions, harbor seals, pilot whales, and orcas (usually in pods), and occasionally a sea otter, floating on its back with an open clam shell supper on its tummy. There are endless varieties of songbirds in the woods in springtime, some of which nest there. Kingfishers keep watch for salmon fry in the lake, and many ducks have little ones in tow in the spring. Frequent summer visitors are Canada geese and trumpeter swans. Ptarmigan are plentiful in the hills and rabbits are everywhere. There are brown bats, tundra voles, ground squirrels, marmots, and a few varieties of fox. Roosevelt elk and Sitka black-tail deer live on the island, and the famous Kodiak brown bear (*Ursus middendorfus*) is our prize resident mammal.

March in Kodiak may have come in like a lion, but it did not go out like a lamb. In mid-month there was a blizzard that deposited three feet of snow in drifts overnight and, as fate would have it, Dad was called in the wee small hours for an OB case. He spent half an hour digging out the road and got his truck halfway to the gate, when Charley arrived with his 4-wheel drive Jeep and managed to push through to Mission Road and take dad to town. He found the OB case only in very early labor and returned home by taxi and was dropped at the gate. Walking in, he was "chased by another taxi to tell him another OB had been taken in." It took him another 20 minutes of digging to get that taxi turned around and headed out. This got him back to the hospital at 4:30 a.m. The second patient delivered at 6:20 and the first patient, at 11:00 a.m. There was another blizzard during the night of the 27th. Winter continued on into mid-April, and it was May before the ground thawed and Dad could do his morning swims.

On March 20, mother wrote, "Dad had a rugged weekend last week—or was it a week ago already? He lost two patients, one a heart case, the other Tom Stiles, whom you will remember. Tom had been ill for some time. He had been through the Virginia Mason Clinic and spent about six months under treatment. [He had been in Kodiak long enough to think of it as home, and had returned to spend his days there.] Then caught the flu and couldn't overcome it." Tom Stiles was Director of Civil Service, whose employees provided support services for the Base from its inception, and the Base-to-town highway was originally named Tom Stiles Road.

On April 2, Dad took the time to note the following in his diary: "OB case with baby at 12:15 a.m. Another baby during the morning. Another at 6:45, and another at 11:06. Four babies in one day—a record." That was also the day he accepted the presidency of the School Board, in which capacity he continued to pursue the transfer of the ACS property, the design and construction of the new Main School, and the solution of the problem of access to the site. Two weeks later the Board hired a surveyor to make contour lines for the school grounds and Dad sent a wire to Juneau, and the architect, regarding the latest school plans, commenting that it looked like we would get a grade school and a gym.

Mother wrote that her father, "H.J." Bishop, was planning on celebrating his eighty-seventh birthday with them at Sprucehaven, and Mr. Tuthill, Hazel's father, would likely be coming with him. They subsequently arrived together on May 6, and spent three weeks at Sprucehaven. Dad brought the men to meetings he thought might interest them, and took them on excursions throughout the sixty miles of the road system. The old gentlemen—H.J., Tuthill, and Charley—

engaged in a few domino games during their stay, and Charley emerged the champion.

I spent some time looking for a doctor who might be interested in working in Kodiak. I had put Beech Barrett, a UW resident in internal medicine, in touch with Dad, and they had apparently kept in touch for, in his diary, on May 23, was a note that Beech had wired and was coming as an extern. An extern was part of the training program for residents, and the physician-mentor was only required to provide travel and living expenses. This was a boon, and would take some of the pressure off Dad for several months.

∗ ∗ ∗

ON THE NINETEENTH OF APRIL, Dad heard General Douglas MacArthur's speech before Congress. He had been following the war in the Pacific, and was impressed with the general. He put the following note in his diary: "MacArthur's address was a true masterpiece at playing on the heart strings as well as appealing to the intellect." As anyone who heard the general speak would agree, he had charisma and was a compelling leader.

∗ ∗ ∗

ALL THIS TIME, we were awaiting the return of the woman who owned the ketch in order to discuss purchase. On April 1, Dad wrote: "Mother suggests *Windbird* as a name for a boat." Finally, on May 14, an entry in the diary noted a call from me announcing, "The ketch is ours for $7,000." Dad got a bank loan for $5,000, which provided enough to meet the price but it took two weeks for a final review of repairs and alterations. On May 28, Dad noted, "Purchasing 38-foot ketch, *Windbird*."

On June 1, Dad turned his office over to Dr. Gardener, Lieut. MC, USN, for a month. A few days later, he and Mother flew to Seattle. I met them on arrival at Boeing Field, and drove to Portage Bay, and got them settled in at my houseboat across from the university. From there, we could access the *Windbird* easily, for she was moored at the boat mart on Portage Bay just across University Bridge.

For the next two weeks, we scampered about Seattle, finding things to complete outfitting the boat. On June 13, the boat was declared shipshape, and after lunch the mooring lines were let go, and we departed under power. We three were to take the direct route across the Gulf of Alaska to Kodiak.

The Windbird, dockside, June 1, 1952.

In the afternoon of the second day, after leaving Cape Flattery on the northwest edge of the Washington coast, we encountered a late spring, fair-weather gale, which soon created heavy seas. The storm tore a few sails, upset our 12-volt batteries, and disabled our motor. When the wind slacked and the seas moderated, we were able to come about and limp back, under sail, to Neah Bay, just inside the cape. There we spent two days mending sails and repairing the damage, before returning to our point of departure and putting our girl away for the season.

* * *

IN MID-OCTOBER, Dad was re-elected president of the School Board and remained active in the pursuit of the new school, became more active in the Chamber of Commerce, and continued his involvement with the Community Center. In his diary, there were several entries concerning equipment purchased and work done on the *Windbird* in Seattle, and some noting the receipt of *Coast Pilot* and navigational charts covering the whole anticipated route to be followed, hopefully, the next spring.

Also in October, "To musical, for cultural examples—Donald

Gramm with Schapiro himself, as accompanist." Yes, his intent was to set an example and encourage support. And on the thirteenth of November, "Second of concert series—excellent." He was surprised to find a performance of such high caliber. This signaled the beginning of the Alaska Music Trail, which brought aspiring young artists on tour to Alaska communities at affordable costs. The founder of this series was Mr. Schapiro, the local sponsors being the Business and Professional Women's Club in which Mother was active.

Mother and Hazel Sutliff had become really good friends. They hiked and ice skated together, and truly enjoyed each other's company. Mother, Hazel, and Alice Given worked together collecting local wild flowers and ferns and taking *photo*graphs of them, and Hazel's collection would eventually reside in the Baranov Museum and is the most complete in Kodiak. Mother often used the slides to give lectures for the military wives.

Baranov Museum, Kodiak, Alaska, the old Erskine house, c. 1960s.

Dad was too busy to write but Mother kept me informed of his activities to some extent. A letter written on January 2, 1952, talked about Dad: "Dad and I went to the Wyatts' New Year's Eve, then on to the club for dinner. It was the usual New Year's party—noisy but not too bad! Dad had a wonderful time dancing with a lot of new young ladies. It did him good. He has been gay as a lark ever since." He loved being the life of the party—especially among the young women. In the same letter there was also a comment about my newest girlfriend: "Marian sounds like a well-balanced girl of whom you can be proud. What are her parents like?"

She noted that Dr. Louise Ormand, an internist, was coming to cover his practice in July, so he could come down and bring up the *Windbird*. He wanted to come in June, but this was up in the air, until he determined if his practice could be covered by one of the navy doctors until Dr. Ormand arrived.

On May 22, I wrote that Tutti Frank, a friend, shipwright, and a mechanic, was finishing up a number of odds and ends, and had re-ringed and re-installed the motor on the *Windbird,* and it had just been put back in the water. "It looks like a dream. Brand new coat of paint, topsides." I added that I would have her hauled out again, after finals on June 13, at which time I could finish painting the sides and the copper bottom.

Mother wrote: "Dad still doesn't know when he can come down. The young medics are leaving and replacements aren't here, as yet. The New C.O. is a very nice chap, and, I believe, will be cooperative, but he's new. We will just hope and pray something turns up. Dad is anxious to make the heart clinic at the University on June 16. I hope he can. I think he is tired, and he needs six weeks away. I wish he could have two months. I think he is a remarkable man, to carry on as he does."

Mother flew down early, on June 5. She brought charts and other equipment, and busied herself, purchasing and storing what was needed, such as linens, dishes, and groceries. I had finals that week. Dad managed to get his practice covered and flew down in time to help with final arrangements. Marian had been invited and, with her parent's permission, would accompany us on our Alaskan cruise. This time we would take the Inside Passage as far as Cape Spencer, then brave the open ocean, following the coast to Seward, and then down to Kodiak.

Chapter 25

Voyage of the *Windbird*

1952

ON JUNE 18, the ship's log documented our departure from University Boat Mart, under power, at about 5 in the morning. Soon under the University Bridge, across Lake Union, through the Lake Washington Ship Canal, under the Aurora Bridge and through the Fremont Bridge, we cleared the Ballard Locks and entered Puget Sound. All hands were feeling pretty chipper, but it would be unusual if Marian didn't feel a bit anxious, looking forward to a deep-water voyage in close quarters with her prospective in-laws. I certainly admired her courage for going along.

After breakfast, at 9 o'clock, the ship *Princess Marguerite*, passed us bound for Victoria, B.C., with a full load of tourists. Eventually, we hoisted sail to a nice westerly breeze, which took us to Friday Harbor for a brief stop, then to Parks Bay, where we rendezvoused with Jerry and Pat Stevens, sailing friends from Portland who were cruising Puget Sound in their 40-foot cutter. We moored alongside their boat for a few hours and took pictures of the boats from the crosstrees of the *Windbird* before retiring.

The next morning, we stopped at Friday Harbor again and topped off the water and gas tanks. By noon we cast off, and hoisted the sails to take advantage of a nice easterly breeze. This took us into the Strait of Juan de Fuca, past Victoria, up Georgia Strait, and then to Nanaimo on the inshore side of Vancouver Island, where we tied up at the dock in our first Canadian port and went through Customs.

The following day we headed across Georgia Strait for Jarvis Inlet, off the direct course, to visit Princess Louisa Inlet, which we had learned was a must-see. The boat cut though the ocean quietly, with only the hum of the breeze in the rigging, the waves swishing against the hull, and the occasional cry of sea birds to break the silence. There came a subtle inner ease, a soothing of the soul, something all sailors experience, that explains, I suppose, why they sail whenever there is even a light breeze. This carried us into and along Malaspina Strait, behind Texada Island, to Pender Harbor, and beyond, where we dropped anchor in an unnamed bay in time for dinner.

June 21 was an adventure. We left early enough to navigate fifty miles up Jarvis Inlet to reach the narrows at the entrance to Princess Louisa Inlet in time to catch the tide. The *Windbird* could not make headway against the ebb tide, which barrels through the narrows at 6 to 10 knots, faster than her top speed. Nor would it be wise to go though on the flood tide, for she would be racing through so fast, she wouldn't be under control and could strike one shore or the other. We arrived near the end of the ebb tide and elected to go through against the subsiding current. This made for a slow but safe passage, and as we emerged into the wider inlet, we faced an awe-inspiring sight. The inlet extended before us between perpendicular, solid rock walls, 1,000 feet high. The water was deep blue, concealing a depth beyond the reach of our anchor. We could have put out fenders, sidled up, and tied directly to the wall, but we moored alongside the Malibu dock, instead, which was a float made fast to the left wall just a little beyond the narrows. It was nearly 6 o'clock, and marked a thirty-five-mile day.

Mother and Marian lighted the gas stove for dinner, which heated rapidly and was easy to control. We all loved the hiss of the burners, which heralded not only a delicious meal but also the associated warmth. Marian loved the baked potatoes that came out of that oven— crisp, almost scorched skins and perfectly cooked interiors. The galley looked aft on the cockpit through a porthole, and when under way on chilly days, a cup of hot soup or coffee could be passed through to warm the helmsman.

We spent the next day in the inlet, motoring slowly up the canyon to its head, in a little over half an hour. Here, the perpendicular walls had relented, and blended into a steep, heavily forested slope. We tied to another floating dock not far from the rushing Chatterbox Falls. Dad and I donned our bathing suits and took a little shower under the edge of the falls in water not one bit warmer than the ocean in Kodiak.

Marian thought we were a bit loony. We then took a picnic lunch, went ashore, found a trail, and walked through the lush green undergrowth of the forest along the waterway. As the rush of the waterfall faded, we sat down on a bench and ate lunch. Then we returned to the float, cast off, and reached the Malibu dock in late afternoon, in time to retire early so we could arise to catch the tide at 4 o'clock.

In the morning, we docked at Powell River long enough to fill the tanks, and resumed our northward course, now back in Georgia Strait. We arrived at Refuge Cove on Redonda Island, and berthed at the oil dock, having logged seventy-nine miles for the day.

The next day we arose to an overcast sky and departed Refuge Cove early. The aroma of coffee, and frying bacon, wafted through the companionway, lightening the mood if not the sky. At 9 o'clock we docked at Yaculta and filled the tanks before negotiating the tide rips in Johnstone Strait. At noon, we tied up to a log boom behind Lotte Island for a quiet lunch, and reached Port Neville at 6 o'clock, where we berthed at the Standard Oil Dock. The oil companies were quite hospitable, and allowed us free moorage.

We left Port Neville, shortly after four in the morning, and stopped for an hour and a half in Alert Bay. This village was started in 1870 when two English explorers built a saltery, the embryo of an eventual thriving fishery. The population by early 1900 was predominantly Native. We had time to visit the burial ground, with its totem poles—one the tallest in existence—and an old Native ceremonial house. The village had just been incorporated six years before. Groceries stored, we went on to moor at Port Hardy for the night.

June 25 dawned overcast and gray. By mid-morning we were into Queen Charlotte Sound, which was open to the sea and a brisk onshore breeze, and, we hoisted sail and stopped the motor. The breeze brought with it a three- to four-foot swell, and placed the *Windbird* on a heel, occasionally dipping her starboard rail. She swished though the seas at a good pace, joyously tossing waves off her bow while the wind, equally joyously, blew it into the faces of those in the cockpit. Marian retired below for a nap, and we Johnsons exhilarated in the wind and salt spray. Marian, we later learned, was "scared to death," and went to sleep so she wouldn't have to face the prospect of drowning at sea, seriously doubting the sanity of her prospective in-laws.

We moored, overnight, midway across the sound, in Safety Cove, and continued early the following day under overcast skies. At 5 o'clock, we started looking for a place to anchor. None showed nearby on the chart, so we ventured cautiously into what appeared to be a small bay. This was not too wise, but with Dad at the helm, me on the bow, and the boat moving very slowly, we thought we were okay. I could see the bottom rising beneath us. It began rising more quickly, and I turned and shouted, "Put her astern." It was too late. We gently slid up onto an underwater reef. The tide was falling rapidly and attempts to back off were unsuccessful. We were "hard on" in minutes, the *Windbird* listed to port, resisted all ingenious attempts to float her free, and eventually rested on her port belly, lower than the keel, which left her on a sixty-degree heel. We slept on the cabin sides, until the wee hours, when the incoming tide righted her, and we were able to move to Muncie Bay, only forty minutes away, where we dropped anchor in eight fathoms of water. We slept better when we were afloat, and upright, and we slept late. We were none the worse for wear from the night's experience except, as we discovered that morning, all the clothes stored in the port lockers were steeped in bilge water. This required that we spend a couple of hours in the first available laundromat to restore everything to its original condition.

Windbird at anchor in Safety Cove, off Queen Charlotte Sound, British Columbia, June 25, 1952.

We departed Muncie Bay at 11:30 that morning. We were now in the narrow channels of the Inside Passage most of the time, so we traveled under power for the next several days. On July 1, we encountered a light rain, which became a deluge by the time we arrived in Ketchikan, in the afternoon. The log registered 831.5 total miles. We topped the fuel tanks at the oil company dock—thirty-six gallons—$8.75. Everything was soaking wet, so we lit the oven, and hung the clothing up to dry. It was still pouring.

Elmer Johnson, Dad's accountant, who did an itinerant business in Kodiak, showed up at dockside to welcome us, and invited us to dinner the following day. He was in ordinary raincoat and hat, and seemed to ignore the rain, which, to us, was a deluge. After he left, Marian and I donned dry clothes and rain gear and went uptown to the Elk's Club to share a few beers and some dancing.

Fortunately, the next morning dawned clear, and we could hang things outside to dry. We spent two days in Ketchikan. We had the ship-to-shore radio adjusted, had a mechanic check the motor, had dinner with Dad's accountant and his wife at one of the local restaurants, and were invited to brunch by Dr. Wilson, whom Dad had met at the state medical meeting in Juneau.

The morning of July 4, we picked up a favorable breeze and set sail. An hour later, we encountered a school of dolphins, which cavorted about the bow for fifteen or twenty minutes. That afternoon, we sighted four or five more, and two sperm whales. When we were under sail, we found the animals of the sea more friendly. In mid-afternoon we tacked into Exchange Cove, dropped the sails, and anchored in two fathoms of water, logging a 76-mile run for the day. It was overcast and there was light rain. My sleep that night was interrupted by a vague sense of concern. I could see the open companionway against the lighter sky. All was quiet. I dozed off for a few minutes and awakened again with a mild sense of alarm. Was the companionway tilting a little? No—my imagination was working overtime from the grounding the previous week. Dozing, perhaps fifteen minutes, I awakened again. There was a definite, slight list to port. We all arose and confirmed the fact that we were aground. Veterans, now, we removed the clothes from the port-side lockers to keep them dry and settled down to wait. The tide went out, left us high and dry at a forty-five-degree angle, and came in again to float us by 9 o'clock, and we were under way fifteen minutes later. We found the port side lockers dry so the ladies re-stowed the clothes, while Dad and I pulled the anchor aboard and got under way.

We reached, and entered, Wrangell Narrows at noon and, negotiating it against the tide, were given a toot by a cruise ship on its way south. We were under full sail at the time, the motor needing a rest. We stopped for the night at Petersburg, at the north end of the narrows, continuing north through Frederick Sound to Stephens Passage the next day, still nursing the motor, which was not behaving nicely. The second day out of Petersburg, the motor developed a serious-sounding knock and we went under sail again. In eight hours the wind ceased, and—with some foreboding—we started the motor again, nursing it along at half speed, and reached Juneau at 1:26 the morning of July 9. The log registered 980 miles, the last 150 miles or so on a failing motor.

It took a good part of two days for a mechanic to re-create a functional motor. We spent the time visiting and sight-seeing. We visited the famous Mendenhall Glacier, introducing Marian to one of Alaska's special creations. Dad introduced us to Dr. Whitehead, of the Territorial Licensing Board, and let him know that I would be joining him in practice in a few years. We left Juneau at eight in the morning, feeling pretty good—the motor no longer smoked or knocked— and before long, we rounded the southern tip of Douglas Island into Stephens Passage and headed northward, under full sail.

Dad was a "seat-of-the-pants" sailor, often making judgments on intuition, which simply meant not wasting too much time poring over charts for details. This usually served him well. This day was special—a sunny afternoon, all sails full, a spanking breeze, the *Windbird* performing grandly, tossing aboard a little spray from time to time, an exhilarating ambience, perfect for intuitive sailing. We needed to round Point Retreat upon which was a Coast Guard light, to head south along Lynn Canal to Icy Strait, which would, soon, take us into the Gulf of Alaska.

Allowing fairly good clearance, Dad began to swing around the point at a distance that felt right to him. It didn't feel right to me, and I said so, but he was a man of conviction, and didn't feel we needed to check for details. With a loud, grinding crunch, we came to an abrupt stop. At once, a bevy of white-suited sailors emerged from the lighthouse, rushed to a dock high above the water, and began to tediously lower a lifeboat by hand. Meanwhile, back at the reef, we looked over-side to assess the situation. We couldn't tell much, but Marian saw a halibut swimming along the reef, almost close enough to touch. We checked the tide, and found that it would soon be slack high water, and we would have to get off quickly, in order to avoid another night aground, this time in a more vulnerable location.

The Coast Guard launch arrived, and they thought we were almost over the reef, but time was running out. There was still a spanking westerly breeze, and we had an inspiration. We hoisted all sail, used power to swing around broadside to the wind, which then heeled us over and lifted our keel, and allowed us to sail off the way we had come. The boys invited us to dinner, so we sailed under the lee of the point, dropped the anchor, unshipped the dinghy, rowed to shore, climbed the 100-odd stairs to the top of the cliff, and entered the cozy warmth of the station. A square building that served as home for a small cadre of sailors, it also supported an automated signal light on its roof. With a quart of bourbon and two women in hand, we were welcome, indeed, and enjoyed a good meal and a fine visit.

We left early in the morning, to reach Indian Cove, where we made fast to a fish trap for the next night, prepared to enter the Gulf of Alaska the next day. We would be setting sea watches in the morning: Dad on the four-to-eight; Mother and Marian on the eight-to-twelve, and I on the twelve-to-four.

We were under way shortly after four o'clock, and passed Cape Spencer two hours later, at which time we had traveled a total of 1,085 miles from Seattle. Heretofore, we had measured our progress by distance measured on the chart. At this point, we shipped the yacht log, which would record our distance traveled through the water. It was good that we had a working motor, since there were only light and variable winds all day. By midnight, we had logged 110 miles and we continued on to moor alongside another vessel at the cannery dock in Yakutat shortly before 7:00 the next morning. While waiting out an expected storm that did not materialize, we walked to town and found a fishing village that, historically, was once an unsuccessful Russian farm project. The next day we sailed sixty miles, paralleling the Malaspina Glacier to Icy Bay, which we reached at dusk. We could see icebergs floating inside the bay and were reluctant to risk collision—visibility was fading quickly—so we anchored in the swells at the entrance to the bay, which required posting watches until morning to be sure we didn't drag anchor. We were rocked—rather vigorously—all night.

Under way again, at a few minutes to ten, we set a course paralleling the Bering Glacier most of the day. We eventually passed Cape Hinchinbrook, the eastern entrance to Prince William Sound, and dropped anchor in Zaikov Bay on Montague Island.

Arising early, we were greeted by a drizzle and a gray overcast sky, which could not cloud the beauty of the island-studded sound to the west of Montague Island. We departed at 6 o'clock for an eight-hour run to Port Ashton in Sawmill Bay, where we tied up to the Standard Oil Dock and topped off the water and fuel tanks. The next day dawned clear and beautiful, the mountains—still snow-laden—gleaming in the sun. We left the sound, under sail, for the first half of the eight hours to Resurrection Cape, in view of the giant Ellsworth Glacier all the way.

Rounding the cape a little after noon, we passed by Fox Island and entered the bay named for the first shipyard in Russian America, where, in 1794, "the Phoenix, named after the beautiful bird of the legend, was literally lifted out of the forest in the bay called Resurrection." For the next three hours, we were flanked by forested hills on both sides, blending into mountains bearing a mantle of snow they never shed completely, as we approached Seward at the head of the bay. We moored in the small boat harbor, and spent the next day ashore.

Dad had become acquainted with Dr. Bannister and his wife in Seward, on his way to Anchorage to testify a few years before, and with blue sky and sunshine, Mrs. Bannister drove us to Moose Pass for lunch. It was warm and, to the four of us, seemed almost tropical. At each community, Dad usually knew several folks. As president of the Medical Association he knew most doctors. Mother, active in the library, knew many of those belonging to the State Association. Neither were wont to sit around when there was someone to visit, so when in port they kept busy calling on folks they knew. If Dad didn't happen to know the medical folks in town, he introduced himself. We were frequently invited to dinner, and were often loaned a car to use during our visits, which made sightseeing much easier. The log has little record of these onshore activities so the few, included, were resurrected from memory.

We left the boat harbor at five o'clock in the morning, and by six were beginning to encounter a shifting, dense, marine fog. As the fog became denser we slipped into Sunny Cove, and anchored, to await clearing. It was flat calm, and the sun was penetrating the fog but not dispersing it. We waited two hours with no change except, perhaps, a little brightening, suggesting that the fog layer might have thinned. Dad suggested I should climb the mast and see if I could get above the fog. I did, and when I reached the crosstrees I was looking over the top of a snowy-white layer of cloud. I could see for miles. I could see islands poking their tops above the fog. We weighed anchor, and with Dad on the helm with the chart, and me on the crosstrees, as his eyes, we soon reached open water and clear skies.

We traveled down the coast of the Kenai Peninsula until nearly ten o'clock in the evening when we anchored in a little bight on the northern shore of Nuka Island. The next morning, we left our little bight, and powered through Nuka Passage. Hoisting sail, when we merged into the Gulf, we sailed south, passing Gore Point at noon. The wind was increasing fairly rapidly so that by one-thirty, we lowered the main, tied it to the first reef points, and headed for shelter. We reached calmer water in a couple of hours, dropped the main, and proceeded under power to anchor in two fathoms of water in the first cove in the West Arm of Port Dick. In the morning, we encountered a strong head wind and heavy sea, so returned, to anchor, in the same cove.

Windbird *coming down the channel before arriving in Kodiak, July 25, 1952.*
photo taken by a hiker on Pillar Mountain.

Up early the next morning, Dad and I took a quick swim—part of the routine, just as at home. After breakfast, we powered to Gore Point, then headed south under a single-reefed main, with a stiff breeze and five-foot seas. At noon, we could see Kodiak, and, as we passed the Barren Islands, the wind eased, somewhat, and we shook out the main, hoisted the stays'l and our speed picked up. Approaching Kodiak, Marian shouted excitedly, "Look—look there," at the same time pointing off the port bow. We looked, and immediately saw that what excited her was a school of killer whales, or orcas, quite far off, swimming directly toward us in single-file, surfacing rhythmically as they came. While we watched they were closing the gap between us fairly rapidly, and Marian asked Dad, "What do you suppose they will do when they get closer?" And Dad said, "They will probably just swim around us." Approaching, however, they didn't change course, and as they neared, the girls were quite apprehensive, until, at the last moment, the leader dove under the keel and surfaced on the other side, on the same course, followed by all the others, one by one, approximately fifty in all.

Next, as we approached Seal Rocks, north of Marmot Island in the Kodiak group, we could hear a faint bellowing. As we came closer, we could make out hundreds of sea lions hauled out on their sizable rocky island. The bellowing got louder, and a few of them began leaping into the water and swimming in our direction, soon followed by the rest. Soon they were all around us, honking and bellowing a welcome. They followed for a mile or two, and when we entered Marmot Strait they turned back. In two hours we were anchored in King Cove on Afognak Island, across from Marmot Island, less than a day's run from home.

King Cove was a cozy little bay, protected from the ocean swell by Marmot Island, across a narrow strait to the east. The surrounding hills kept it sheltered from all winds so that it was always tranquil. At its southern end, beyond a sandy dune covered with beach grass and a few alders, lay a land-locked lake. It was a beautiful place to spend the last night of an eventful voyage. After supper, Dad and Mother did some packing, while Marian and I rowed to the beach and walked the short distance to the lake. It was nestled in the surrounding hills, which were mirrored in its calm surface. Marian found some artifacts, suggesting that the site had once been a Native village.

We spent a quiet night, arose early, to clear skies, anxious to get home. It was July 25. We donned our *Windbird* sweatshirts, gifts from the Crawfords, for our arrival. There wasn't much wind, but we hoisted the sails to dry them under way, and proceeded on a southerly course toward Kodiak through Marmot Bay. We arrived in five hours, tied up at the Standard Oil dock, and took on thirty-seven gallons of gasoline. A few folks had seen us on our way in, and came to welcome us home. We posed for pictures, side-by-side on the ship's railing. We left in thirty minutes, retracing our last two miles, to drop the anchor in Shahafka Cove, off the point at Sprucehaven, having logged 1,942 nautical miles from Seattle.

Windbird *and crew, at the dock in Kodiak after arriving from Seattle, July 25, 1952 (left to right): Mother, Dad, Marian, and the author.*

Chapter 26

World Without End

1952–1955

ONCE HOME, going through the accumulated correspondence, we found a letter with some disturbing news that upset my Dad and made Mother quite angry.

The hand-written letter was addressed to Dad, from Dr. Turner, Dean of the UW Medical School, and a more detailed, typewritten letter to me. Each said, essentially, the same. The second-year faculty had recommended that I withdraw from medical school because of my performance that year. They added, however, that, should I choose not to heed that advice, I could re-take the course on laboratory medicine that summer, and, if I passed, they would reconsider. Even if I were allowed to continue, however, I would be on probation. Dad was, of course, disappointed, but, in his usual fashion, would make the best of it, but Mother was angry. They had supported me completely. I had let them down. I had allowed my pleasures, Marian, my music, the houseboat, and the *Windbird* take precedence over my studies. There was no question—we did not accept the advice. Marian and I returned to Seattle, where I set up a program of study to salvage my career and regain the faith of my parents.

Hazel and Charley had kept Sprucehaven in good shape, and Dr. Ormond—with occasional help from the navy surgeon—had taken good care of the people.

The *Windbird* was anchored off the point at Sprucehaven, and could be seen from the sun porch. She would need a permanent mooring before fall. Hazel and Charley got the first day-sail. Charley really enjoyed it and was a natural sailor. When the wind, the weather, and the practice allowed, Dad took other friends sailing, and Charley was often on board as crew. In no time, Charley became a first-rate sailor, and accompanied frequent day-sails, during August and September, and, because of unusually mild weather, into October.

On August 19, Dad and Mother were the only civilians invited to a dinner for General Omar Bradley and his staff. The next day, Dad and Mother flew to Anchorage, where he presided over a four-day meeting of the Alaska State Medical Association. They attended a dinner that evening at the Atwoods, with Governor Gruening, Mr. McKinney, Assistant Secretary of the Interior, and his wife, engineer Mr. Beaudieu and his wife, who was president of American Women Veterans. Dad still seemed to make friendships wherever he went, including influential folks in Alaska. Mother was elected president of the medical association auxiliary. Dad visited the Draft Board to check on my status—I had recently been called to the recruitment center in Seattle—and found that I was still deferred as a medical student.

My parents had thoroughly approved of Marian on our sailing voyage, and we looked forward to getting married although no date was set. I think the folks did not want to encourage us until they were sure that my position in medical school was secure. In a letter to me on August 27, Mother wrote, "Dad and I are thinking of you in these last days before your exams and hoping you have it cold! We will be anxious to hear, so let us know as soon as you can." One week later they received a wire saying that I had passed and was still a medical student. In mid-September, the folks encouraged Marian and me to set a date for the wedding if we wanted to. I think they felt that I probably would do better with Marian at my side. Of course we wanted to, and with the permission of Lloyd and Isabel James, Marian's parents, we set the date for Sunday, October 4.

One night, in late September, in one of our driving, southerly, equinoctial storms, the *Windbird* pulled anchor and was blown onto Mission Beach. Dad was able to pull her off and move her to temporary moorage at Alvine's Boat Works, downtown. This made the need for a permanent mooring urgent.

Dad and Mother came down two days before the wedding, and showed up at the houseboat at 5 in the afternoon—a total surprise. Lloyd, Isabel, and Marian came over, and Dad took everyone to dinner, after which Marian went to a wedding shower. I was still attending classes and studying, went home to study, and the folks went to bed. On Saturday evening, at the James's residence, Dad showed slides of the *Windbird* cruise for everyone.

The wedding party, October 4, 1952 (left to right): Marian, the author, Mother, and Dad.

Sunday afternoon, the folks came to the houseboat, where my best man, Harold Systad, and Marilyn, his wife, were waiting to drive everyone to the wedding. Harold was a high-school friend and his Dad worked in construction at the naval base. They drove us to the James's residence, for a quiet, private wedding, that, according to Dad, was "very impressive," followed by a reception.

Dad was up at 7 o'clock the next morning, got himself to the airport, and was home and back to work that evening. Mother would return in ten days. Dad batched it in Mother's absence, even throwing a couple of dinner parties on his own. He cleaned the whole house, polished the bottom of the copper pans, and caught up on chores that were overdue. He was invited to dinner at the hospital and enjoyed himself thoroughly with his respected friend Monsignor Gallant and Father Mahar.

Concerned about the *Windbird* moorage, Dad called a Coast Guard commander recommended by Bob Acheson, and was relieved to find that he would help. Within a couple of weeks, he came up with a four-ton concrete mooring block, which was delivered on a barge. It was dropped into place in Shahafka Cove. That same afternoon, Charley and Dad brought the boat home and made her fast to the new moorage. Then followed a period of winterizing when, since there was no way to dry the sails on board, the folks had to live around them as they hung, drying, from the crossbeams in the living room. Then they were bagged, and stowed, and she rode at her new moorage, in view from the sun porch.

* * *

IN THE MEANTIME, Mother returned home, and life for Dad became normal once more. The end of the year was approaching, and Dad was having his office remodeled and had to work around carpenters and plumbers for a week or so. During the holidays, he and Mother gave a dinner party for the members of the School Board: Bob Hall, who had built and operated an air taxi service on the Near Island Channel, and his wife, Helen, a nurse; Gil Jarvela, one of Bob's pilots, and his wife, Bonnie, who were members of the Community Baptist Church; Paul Dupler, the current town lawyer, and his wife, Sue; Marion Lynch, the Public Health nurse, and Patrick, her husband, a building contractor; and Ivor Schott, the new Superintendent of Schools, whom dad thought was a great improvement over the man he replaced, and his wife, Helen, who taught kindergarten.

On New Year's Eve, there were five couples to dinner, only one of whom had been in Kodiak as long as Dad and Mother: Louise and Merrill Coon. Also present were the Crutchers and Achesons. Bill Smith, current president of the Bank of Kodiak and his wife, relatively new friends, and the Haases rounded out the party. They had the usual cozy fire, which often served as an open grill for broiling steaks. After dinner they played Canasta and Tripoli. They then rang in the New Year, 1953.

In mid-January, Dad entered a note stating simply that he made a "plastic repair of a severed nose—good result after removing gangrenous end of flap." In addition to major surgery and a variety of orthopedic surgery, including complicated and compound fractures, he also did plastic, or reconstructive, surgery. If it needed fixing, he would fix it. Had it been otherwise, more than a few of his cases would not have survived.

* * *

THIS WAS A BUSY YEAR for the School Board. Dad remained as president and much of their business centered on the new school, its design, the eventual awarding of bids and its construction. A Parent Teachers Association was formed, and Dad attended some of their meetings. He was elected president of the Library Board as well, and remained active with the Chamber of Commerce. Dad continued to be active in Rotary and, at mid-year elections of the Board, he received the highest number of votes once again. He was pleased, but did not accept the presidency again.

Dad and Mother, at her induction as Grand Matron and Worthy Patron, Order of the Eastern Star, 1953.

On the tenth of July, there was a church reception for the new preacher, the Reverend John Molletti. He stayed in Kodiak many years, and his wife Dorothy became Dad's receptionist.

On July 11, I had arrived back in Kodiak, having successfully completed the probationary year of medical school and the first nine months of marriage. I would serve an externship with Dad during the summer, which would count as part of my medical education. Marian also soon arrived, and we became involved in the life of Kodiak for the next six weeks. Having found a Dr. MacFarlane on Base to cover for him, we went on a week's cruise as a family. In late August, Marian and I returned to Seattle.

Managing the *Windbird* afloat during the winter had become a problem, so Dad decided to put her to bed ashore and she was taken to the dry-dock put in a cradle that would support ten tons of sailboat. "*Windbird* to bed in a cradle—above high water—infamy—a grownup boat in a cradle. She looks proud and perky but a little subdued. She doesn't have the bounce she had at her moorage, especially when the wind blew—now she ignores wind and waves!"

There had been babies, babies, and more babies born during 1953, and this trend continued over the holidays. Hospitalized in the midst of these were a man with a fractured hip who had been put in a body cast, a man with a coronary, a patient with toxemia of pregnancy, all of whom required continued close attention.

On January 22, Mother wrote: "Dad is very busy these days. At present the navy isn't doing any civilian outpatient work. A new medical reservist arrived, who had to leave his newly established practice in Los Angeles, and said that he didn't come back in the navy to treat civilians, and it was against navy regulations anyway. This was true. The navy doctors had to agree not to treat civilians, so they were added to Dad's practice, but one of them told Hazel it wouldn't be for long. Hope they stick to that policy when you come up, Bob. In the meantime, we'll see." So Dad became even busier, and he did not write much in his diary for three years.

On January 30, Mother wrote: "Dad has been under the weather for a couple of days. He didn't feel well Wednesday morning, but carried on anyway. I was upset too, so we thought it was something we'd eaten. However, that evening Dad was feeling so 'all-in' that I took his temperature and it was 100.8. He was supposed to go up to a School Board meeting, but I put my foot down. I went out in the snowstorm and took his papers. It was blowing and snowing like mad. In the morning we called Jean MacFarlane and she came in and took office hours and hospital calls Thursday and Friday." Dr. MacFarlane had covered the practice when we took the family cruise the previous August. She was married to a navy doctor and was free to help Dad when needed. This was a boon for Dad, particularly with the increased load.

* * *

IN 1952, Dad had bought Pataud, another shepherd, with an impressive pedigree. Unfortunately, he was paranoid and suspicious of everyone, particularly strangers, probably the result of too much inbreeding. Dad did not want to reject him, however, so over the next two years, with the help of Smoky, he gradually taught him to trust the family. He and Smoky became great friends.

Mother wrote: "One day in early March, Charley was taking a load of lumber down to the cabin. Smoky and Pataud had followed, but when Charley was unloading the truck he noticed that Smoky wasn't there. He left the truck, and went back on foot, and there was Smoky at the side of the trail—dead. He had apparently been playing with Pataud and just dropped dead. Nice way to go, as I would not have liked having him shot if he became helpless. Pataud is like a lost soul without him. He used to get him up every morning and follow him around all day. He always backed him up when he barked at something and chased intruders for him. He looks for him in his doghouse every morning. Smoky was a faithful friend and we will all surely miss him."

Smoky, our German shepherd, awaiting a ride in the truck, 1954.

With the added load of civil servants, Dad's responsibilities began to look like a "world without end." If Dad could just last through that year, I would join him in his practice in mid-1955.

The federal government had decided to make the Base the permanent headquarters of the Seventeenth Naval District, and a town housing project for naval personnel was nearing completion. This meant that the population boom, created by the war, was a permanent part of the economy. This was good news, but not for navy and Civil Service families that were housed in makeshift houses and trailers that were being condemned. Although the Aleutian Homes housing project was to be completed in October, at which time these families could rent one of the units, those who owned trailers, without adequate sewer, would have to move or sell them.

* * *

THE FOLKS' FIRST GRANDCHILD was born on April 15, 1954, and we named him Craig Holmes. Shortly thereafter, I was accepted for a rotating internship at the Methodist Hospital of Brooklyn, which pleased them both. Mother's brother, Hew, and his wife, Ruth, would be most pleased to provide us with a home away from home during weekends when I was off duty. The internship began on July 1, and the folks would not see their first grandchild until he was over a year old.

About babies in Dad's practice, Mother wrote: "Dad still insists a mother needs ten days in the hospital to get the baby in routine and her strength back and her nervous system under control. Our public health nurses say the mothers and babies in Kodiak are far better organized than in Anchorage and in better health, so I guess A. Holmes is a very good obstetrician. You can't beat his statistics.

"Thursday night, Dad delivered a baby at three o'clock in the morning; Friday morning, at four o'clock; another tonight—has just gone in again. Has two more due now." Babies didn't always come this close together fortunately, or there would be no way for Dad to get any sleep.

Then came the Christmas Tea, which Mother and Betty Acheson co-hosted. "The tea was a great success. Florence came out and helped and we ordered all the food from Naughton's Bakery. Since it was Russian Easter week, we served kulich (Easter bread), tiny tarts with salmonberry jelly and mincemeat, and petits-four teacakes in pale green and yellow. We also had mints to match with tiny jonquil trim. One end of the table, I set with a samovar for tea and Russian hurricane lamps—the other end with a silver service for coffee. I told the group a little of the early history and about Russian Easter service."

Florence Welch, whose husband came to Kodiak with the first civil service contingent, had become mother's "girl Friday." Florence's husband had retired and become a painting contractor and she was extremely capable. Without Florence, mother would not have had the energy to entertain as often as she did.

* * *

THE FOLLOWING MAY, the folks had a dinner for Dr. Phil Moore, an orthopedic surgeon from the Sitka Mount Edgecumbe Sanatorium. All the navy doctors and wives were invited, fourteen in all. Dr. Moore volunteered the information that he thought a two-year internship, one of which was in general surgery, would fit a young man for general practice better than anything else, a suggestion for me to consider.

Later in May, "Things started out with a boom at 6:30. Some fellow shot himself in the head but didn't finish the job, so Dad grabbed a cup of coffee and beat it for surgery. At 8:30, Dr. Moore is going in and they are going to put a pin in a leg. Dad has six babies due before Saturday. Looks like they are waiting for the weekend. He still has his cold. He has a cough now that is bothering him, and I wish he could shake it."

Dad could anticipate having a permanent associate in one year. His workload had reached the point where it seemed that consideration of an additional year of internship was out of the question.

The *Windbird* had been beached all winter and well into spring. Dad had taken all the spars and hatch covers off during the winter and sanded, varnished, and replaced them. The sails had been replaced or mended. The deck and cabin sides had been repainted. In June, at the first sunny opportunity, Dad and Charley finished painting the hull above the waterline and copper-painted the bottom. On July 1, the Cat came out and launched her on the highest tide of the month, and she was afloat at her concrete-block moorage, ready to sail again.

It was the custom to hold a Fourth of July picnic at Sprucehaven. This year the fourth was on Monday and the picnic was on Sunday. Mother wrote, "Dad took all who wanted to go for a sail."

Charley Madsen had not been up to par for several months and had developed heart failure. Being a stubborn Dane, he did not admit to his illness until he was forced to by a heart attack. This brought him to the doctor whose advice he then could ignore. He was 70 years old. Dad wanted to put him in the hospital but he would have none of it and stayed at home. Advised to go to bed, he sat up in a chair in his living room and, after a few days, died quietly. Thus departed the stalwart wilderness trader and big-game hunter.

✳ ✳ ✳

THAT SUMMER DAD took to the air to practice his flying skills. Mother mentioned that he had encountered fog on a recent flight, which he did not enjoy, "but it gave him a feeling of satisfaction to be able to handle the situation." He had to fly low over the water, using the compass to get from point to point, to make it home safely. "He had a wonderful flight a week ago on a perfectly clear day. He circumnavigated Kodiak completely, stopping at Karluk to see the Kim Clarks because Shirley had been ill and had written him. After the visit, as he started to taxi for the takeoff, he noticed the two of them jumping up and down on the beach and gesticulating, so he opened the window and looked out. Their dog was sitting on one of his floats. He had almost gone flying!"

In August, Dad and Charley began working on the small cabin—-the one-room frame structure the Torgersons built at the north end of the property years before. They were putting in a small stone fireplace at one end of the small living room, an adjacent bath, and kitchenette with sleeping loft above, a workshop-entryway, and insulation. This cozy little cottage would be our house when we arrived the following year.

In September, Mother wrote, "Dad is under the weather today. He's been working very hard—diarrhea and nausea again, same as last time. Poor man! We will be so thankful when R. Holmes can take over when he's sick so he can at least take time to be ill!" There had been several such episodes and a couple of upper respiratory infections that year—more than usual. This may have been due to fatigue, from more work and less sleep.

In late October, she wrote: "I'll be so glad when we get the cabin fireplace finished. Then Dad can go down there when he wants to rest, and be out of touch with the phone for an hour or so. He tried resting yesterday afternoon, and the phone rang constantly—mostly for me. He lost sleep, and had several very ill patients, which took their toll.

"Dad is getting a big kick out of hearing about your cases, Bob. He loves it! It sounds as though you are truly interested in internal medicine, which is good. Dad has had some very difficult medical cases the past month. I am sure he would have been happy to have 'Dr. Bob' around to help carry the responsibility and discuss the cases. He will, no doubt, tell you all about them."

In mid-November there was an open house at the hospital, in celebration of the Grey Nuns' tenth anniversary. Mother said: "I poured at tea from four to five. They had Dad's picture framed and up in the hall, along with the Pope's! Anyway, Dad was pleased. The new admiral came, which pleased the Sisters."

Dad was "counting the days until July," according to Mother. "He was called last night at 3 o'clock for a primipara, and didn't get back until 8. Of course he rested some of that time, but didn't sleep. He said, the other day, 'I'm bone tired! I don't believe I'd make it another year alone.' Of course he hasn't gotten away at all since the week's trip to Afognak. Probably what he needs most is a change away from the practice."

Early one morning, Charley called saying he couldn't awaken Hazel. Dad went over immediately and found that she had died. She had been feeling fine but complained of a headache when she went to bed. It was a shock to everyone, as sudden death always is, although there is some consolation in knowing that it was a blessed way to go for there was little suffering, if any. It was a great loss. John Molletti conducted a beautiful memorial service at Community Baptist Church. His son Norm took Charley in with them, feeling that he would be too lonely in his apartment. The folks let him know he was welcome to stay, for they had become great friends, and secretly hoped that he would decide to do so, which he eventually did. Mother wrote, "You can imagine how swamped Dad is without Hazel in the office. As if he didn't have enough to do—she did so much for him. We can only hope that help will come from someplace."

"Torgy's Retreat," the cabin converted by Dad and Charley for Marian and the author, 1955.

In April, when I was on surgical rotation, bored with scut work and getting little hands-on experience, mother wrote, "Son, you will probably learn more surgery from your Dad than you would in most internships. Dutch Bailey said he wouldn't take anything for what he learned from Dad—it was invaluable. He said this after he had been in practice in Palmer." She also reported that, "work was progressing on the high school, and that there are 680 kids in school since the Aleutian Homes have been occupied." This was work Dad had begun.

In the few months before our arrival, Charley and Dad went to work nights and weekends on the cabin. The plumbing and the electrical work was finished, but there was apparently much left to do and the time remaining before our arrival was rapidly diminishing. Many hours were spent completing the fireplace chimney, which was made from rounded beach stone and had to go well above the peak of the roof. In addition, before he went to work, Dad was flying each weekday morning for an hour, to pile up enough time to get his solo pilot's license.

In May, in a one-page note, Mother wrote that friend and bank president Marshall Crutcher had an inoperable brain tumor, and his son had suggested that he be replaced. Torgy had been contacted, and Mother and Dad were delighted to learn that he and Ruth would be returning to stay. She had thought they were sold on California, but they seemed quite happy to be coming back in Alaska.

Chapter 27

A New Leaf

1955–1959

AFTER COMPLETING MY INTERNSHIP in June 1955, we packed all our belongings into a U-haul trailer, and the three of us drove across country, up the Alaska Highway, and flew to Kodiak in mid-July. Dad met the plane, and was just delighted to see his first grandson.

The Bank of Kodiak welcomed me home, when I returned to join Dad in practice, summer 1955.

At Sprucehaven, over dinner, we all reminisced a bit about our times at Brooklyn Methodist. Then we were shown to our newly completed nest in the woods, and we settled in for the night. On the second morning of our return, Dad and I made rounds at the hospital and then went to the clinic, where we each had an office and an examining room, and we began our joint practice. This, for Dad, would be like "turning over a new leaf," to start another page in his book of life. He would have some time to himself during the week, and perhaps eventually even some extended time off.

Having just completed a hectic year, particularly the last few months when remodeling the little cabin became paramount, Dad had geared himself up to meet the demand. With our arrival, some of the pressure was off, but he hadn't unwound entirely. While using the table saw the first week after our arrival, his left hand slipped into the blade, seriously injuring his fourth finger. Nerves and tendons were severed, and repair was beyond me. But the Base surgeon responded and did what he could to repair the damage. The wound subsequently healed well, but resulted in a stiff finger, fortunately not on his dominant hand. He was able to perform surgery again within a couple of weeks.

Marian Johnson and her young son, Craig, were passengers on this flight when the Piper Super Cub, piloted by her father-in-law, crashed in Mission Lake in 1955.

Dad had purchased a Piper Cub on floats after he got his license, and was anxious to show off his ability as a pilot. So one afternoon, on a calm day in September, he took Marian and Craig for a short flight. The sun was out, the sky was blue, and they had a beautiful flight over the area around town and the Base. Returning, as he approached to land on Mission Lake, the afternoon sun reflecting off the lake's unruffled surface made it difficult to establish how near he was to the water. He had used most of the lake before touching down and, attempting to quickly reduce speed, his stiff finger struck the throttle and he was briefly airborne again. There was no lake left and his flight was abruptly stopped as his right wing wrapped around a telephone pole on the shore. The plane, of course, was disabled, but the passengers were fortunately unhurt. Shortly after they disembarked, a twelve-year-old boy, who had been walking along Mission Road and witnessed the event, stopped to declare, "Pretty bum landing, Doc." The only casualty was mother, who, having heard the crash, had run to see if they were all right and tripped over a line stretched across the road from the boat cradle, and skinned her knee.

The rest of the year we adjusted to working together. I contributed some of what Dad was missing in internal medicine, and he managed whatever surgical problems arose, tutoring me as assistant or as primary surgeon with him as the coach. We complemented each other. I was never able to learn enough surgery to replace him, but the navy was willing to provide a surgeon for emergencies and when he took time off for a vacation. We took call on alternate days and weekends, allowing each other free time. If there was a surgical problem that was beyond me, Dad was still on call even on his days off. If he had a medical emergency and needed help, I was available. Neither of these two situations occurred frequently, so it was a great improvement for him.

* * *

ON JANUARY 1, 1957, Dad's diary was renewed: "Spent the entire day helping Frostie take down and put away Christmas decorations and clean up a mess of spruce needles." Spruce were the only evergreens available on Kodiak Island. They differ from other Christmas trees, in that they dry and drop their needles within a few days of being cut, even when the base is immersed in water, which is consumed at the rate of two quarts a day. Consequently, they are less than ideal for use as Christmas trees or decorative boughs. They drop their needles in the forest, as well, making the soil acid and attractive to mosses and ferns, which grow in profusion, creating a fairyland in the deep woods of Kodiak. They are, however, a housekeeper's bane. When it is wet outdoors, needles stick to the shoe soles, even after wiping, and are tracked into the house by unaware visitors. It is a custom in Kodiak to leave your shoes at the door, which is done widely in Alaska.

The next day, Dad performed a spinal tap on a five-year-old child from Unga, who proved to have tuberculous meningitis. This was one of the most depressing illnesses encountered, for there was no treatment and it was always fatal. This child died three days later. Tuberculosis was rampant in the Territory until Dr. Charles Fraser, a Public Health physician, was retained as Tuberculosis Control Officer. He took it upon himself to organize a program through physicians and public health nurses, all over Alaska, that brought it under control within a few years.

On Saturday, Dad took my weekend call, since it was his last before a two-month short vacation. He admitted a cardiac patient. He and Mother went to the Achesons' for dinner that night, during which he had eight phone calls and admitted two patients, whom he examined on the way home. Sunday morning he returned to the hospital for an Rh-negative OB, who finally delivered by mid-forceps at 4:30 in the morning. He slept until 9 o'clock, then cleaned the house "for Frostie."

Monday morning Dad noted, "Bob did an exchange transfusion on a jaundiced Rh-positive baby." This was a relatively new and effective treatment for Rh babies, which I had learned at Methodist Hospital. (When an Rh-positive baby is carried by an Rh-negative mother, the mother can build up antibodies against the infant's blood cells that are foreign to the mother. Her antibodies attack the infant's red blood cells to destroy them, and this situation, when unchecked, can be fatal to the fetus. The objective of the transfusion is to replace all the positive cells in the baby with Rh-negative cells that will not be attacked. The procedure is often life saving.)

On Saturday he wrote, "Completed packing for a two-month trip, and left Kodiak on the morning plane in full sunshine." Their trip was a combined vacation and business trip. He went by himself, to attend the Territorial School Board Convention in Petersburg, of which he was secretary. Mother would join him in Seattle. Petersburg was not on the primary air route and was reached via Ellis Airlines out of Ketchikan. (Ellis Air was founded by Bob Ellis, a famous Alaska bush pilot, who helped to develop early aviation in Alaska.) At the Mitkof Hotel, at a reception, he met folks from school boards all over Alaska, and attended daytime business sessions for two days. Then he flew back to Ketchikan.

In Ketchikan, he visited the hospital, and happened to catch Drs. Wilson, Moore, and Salazar. Dr. Wilson's two sons had joined him in practice, and one had been a fraternity brother of mine at Willamette. Dr. Phil Moore was the orthopedic surgeon from Sitka, and Dr. Salazar was the doctor whose wife Dad had delivered in Nome when he was company physician in Bristol Bay the summer of 1937. Dad then departed for Seattle, and checked in to the Benjamin Franklin Hotel. Mother was scheduled to arrive that evening but her flight was delayed because of fog.

Their trip took them to places such as New Orleans, Florida, The Bahamas, New York, New Jersey, and back to Portland, and they visited with family and friends everywhere. The final two weeks were spent in Seattle, during which both Dad and Mother had complete medical examinations. Dad was given a clean bill of health at the Mason Clinic, but Mother needed to have a hysterectomy, which extended their visit. The day following her surgery was their forty-second anniversary.

In April, Dad spent his spare time painting and furnishing a Quonset hut as a temporary museum for the Kodiak and Aleutian Islands Historical Society, of which he was president. The historical society was becoming quite active. There were monthly meetings, each followed by a program, having to do with regional history, archeology, anthropology, and natural history.

That summer, a boat harbor was built along the south shore of town, to accommodate the expanding Kodiak fishing fleet. The boat harbor provided shelter for downtown as well, which had one winter been pummeled by a southwesterly gale of hurricane force that showered the whole area with spume, coated the houses on shore with ice, and flooded the streets. Dad moved the *Windbird* from its hazardous mooring in Shahafka Cove to a protected slip in the boat harbor. A few months later, as fate would have it, another southwesterly gale struck. The dolphin at the outboard end of the slip gave way, putting the *Windbird* and about ten other boats in jeopardy. By the time we arrived, a local fisherman had moved his big vessel against the dolphin and was holding it against the wind, under power, until it could be stabilized, which saved the day.

On July 3, Sarah arrived for the summer, which meant that the alcohol would again be out of sight. Dad attended church with her, although reluctantly. He said, "Took Mother to church. Terrible sermon. Mother loved it!" She was an easy visitor, though, requiring little attention. She was content to sit quietly and crochet or knit. On an August afternoon, Dad took her for a drive out the roads south of town to view the fireweed, which was, "perfectly beautiful." In late summer, the sudden blooming of fireweed's fuschia-pink flowers on barren hillsides is a reminder that fall is coming.

The friends most mentioned by Dad that year included the Hinckels (Jack was the agent for Union Oil Company, which had moved to Kodiak in competition with Standard Oil); the Torgersons, who had returned to stay (Torgy was again the president of the bank); the Schotts (Ivor was the Superintendent of Schools and was instrumental in the successful transition from the old downtown school); the Hobbs (he was the admiral and commandant of the Naval Operating Base); and, of course, Charley. Jack and Mayor Bettinger had been involved in getting federal funds for Aleutian Homes, the 343-unit government housing project, whose fuel contract went to Union Oil.

In late September, Dad went to Fairbanks with Ivor Schott for a joint meeting of the Alaska Association of School Boards and the Superintendent's Advisory Commission. The president, dean, and a number of faculty from the University of Alaska were present as well. Dad was elected president of the association. He gave a short acceptance speech at the final banquet, in which he told of Kodiak's program. The conference was a continuation of his interest and involvement in education, and was the start of a long presidency.

On November 17, Bruce Keers arrived for a visit. Bruce had been a fellow intern at Brooklyn Methodist, and he and his wife, Jo, were close friends of ours. We had often spoken of practicing together in Kodiak. Serving at the Air Force Base in Spokane, he had boarded a military flight to Kodiak to look things over for a few days, and we were expecting him. I met the plane when he arrived on a dark and stormy night, thinking, "What a grand impression he's going to get of Kodiak." Dad and I exposed him to the practice at rounds, and showed him the office. We loaned him a car to sightsee. The days were short, because the winter solstice was approaching, but he managed to cover a good part of the road system. The sun only came out for a few hours one day, and, for no reason at all, he raved about Kodiak, saying, "Bob, you didn't tell me it was so magnificent—that the mountains were so big, and everything was so beautiful." So Bruce liked it, and Dad liked him, and he was a very good doctor, and this spoke well for a future joint practice.

In December, Dr. Bill Mills, orthopedist, and his nurse, came to Kodiak from Anchorage, to hold an itinerant clinic. Dad and I knew him, and had consulted him by phone for difficult fracture cases. This was the first of several itinerant clinics, which, along with the clinics of Milo Fritz, increased specialist access for local residents.

* * *

AND SO WE MOVED INTO 1958, and both of us were fairly accustomed to a dual practice. Dad was still not ready to retire, and did not feel free to leave me in solo practice for an extended period. He was still bound by his love of Kodiak and what he was doing, and his personal commitment to his practice and to me.

It was the year of the schools. Dad had early on realized the essential need for education in order to perpetuate society and, in particular, the democratic way of life. He had shepherded the new school—and the new road—into existence. Since he was elected president of the Territorial Association of School Boards, he had been researching education—the process and the objectives—and forming his idea of where we, as Alaskans, should be directing our efforts. He began to speak of educational goals at various local organizations, as well as to appear on Armed Forces Television, which had recently been inaugurated. He began an ongoing dialog by mail, with Alaska school boards, intending to stimulate their interest. In April, he attended the annual convention of the Association of National School Boards in Miami. On his return he gave a summary talk to the local school board and PTA, and sent copies to Alaska school boards.

"This year," Dad wrote, "Kodiak fishermen caught more king crab than any port in the nation." The *Deep Sea*, a floating crab processor, owned by Howard and Lowell Wakefield, had appeared in Kodiak in 1950. This became Wakefield Fisheries. The industry grew rapidly, as others joined in, and achieved this status in only 8 years. John Gibbons, president of the Chamber of Commerce, convinced the city that we should declare Kodiak the, "King Crab Capital of the World." We quickly put together a festival to celebrate it on the first of May. The Junior Chamber's scuba divers were the major attraction as they leapt off the dock into the boat harbor, and emerged with giant king crab,.from the depths. (By 1979, king crab would make Kodiak the top fishing port in the world, a title it held until the crab fishery dwindled in 1983.)

Newly caught king crab, just unloaded from the crabber alongside the dock, ca. 1958. Kodiak Historical Society

As president of the Historical Society, Dad had taken on the task of getting a museum established. The Quonset hut he was preparing for occupation was set on a piece of property that had been purchased by the Rotary Club. He completed the structure during the year, and it kept open part-time by volunteer curators. It functioned until a more appropriate structure could be found.

In his diary he spoke of a treatment for fracture of the clavicle (collar bone) that is no longer used. This involved an open reduction and wiring the fractured ends of the bones together. The discovery of two such cases and a follow-up removal of wire (and scar) of another, treated the year before, caught my attention. It was interesting to me, because the current way to treat these is to allow them to heal themselves, the rationale being that they cannot be immobilized anyway and that open reduction is fraught with a risk of infection. This new method occasionally leads to deformities that are particularly distasteful to young women. Dad's open technique did not lead to deformities, and seemed to work well for him.

On June 5 of that year, my friends the Keers—Bruce, Jo, and their children Susan, and Cindy—-arrived. The plan had the potential for Dad to soon be in a position to travel more—in short, semi-retire. This plan had a reasonable chance of success, for Bruce was really taken with Kodiak.

In planning for Bruce's arrival and his own semi-retirement, Dad had decided to surrender his office in the clinic and move to his den at Sprucehaven. He would continue to do surgery and make rounds on his surgical patients and to see those for whom we needed consultation. We would assist him in surgery, learning in the process, and graduate to surgical procedures under his supervision until we mastered them. We would never match his intrepid approach to serious problems nor his surgical expertise. In a few weeks, the Keers family fit right in, in every way. Bruce and I decided to take emergency call on alternate days and weekends, because we knew Dad would always be on call for most serious emergencies.

The *Windbird* was one of the things Dad wanted to spend more time with, and her care had grown to fill more and more of Dad's (and Charley's) leisure time. During the previous winter, when the boat was cradled, Dad dried and repaired the sails (in the living room). He and Charley stripped, sanded, and finished all the woodwork, including the masts, booms, tiller, and skylights. The masts were painted, the rest varnished. The bowsprit had been broken and Dad spent hours making a new one. He made new floorboards for the cabin and cut and cemented linoleum to fit. He varnished the woodwork in the cabin and repaired the head and bilge pumps. The motor and a new auxiliary charger, much like the generator in the pump house in previous years, had numerous vexing problems. This had led to the need for a tow from time to time, which is most embarrassing for a sailor.

Chapter 28

The Vacation
1958-1959

IN SEPTEMBER, Dad was busy preparing for an extensive vacation trip that he and mother were looking forward to. He planned to visit friends and was selecting slides for showing. They had booked passage for early November, and planned to attend a convention of the Alaska Territorial School Boards in Ketchikan and visit friends in Portland and California on the way.

On Saturday, September sixth, Tina and Jack Hinckel threw an enormous going away party for the folks and many of their military and town friends came. Following this, they attended a bank farewell dinner for the Torgersons, who were also leaving, and another farewell dinner for them given by the Sisters at the hospital three days later. That was a sad occasion for they did not anticipate returning.

They left for Ketchikan on the twelfth of September, where Dad officiated at his first meeting as president of the Alaska Association of School Boards. In Seattle they visited a few friends and in Portland they spent two weeks with Mother Sarah at Villa Ridge Drive. This freed Darlow and Alta, whose parish was then in Tigard, so they could travel to California to visit family, while the folks used their Rambler to visit old Portland friends. Then to Los Angeles, by train, where they purchased tickets for their trip to South Africa on the SS *Friesland*, a Holland-American Line vessel.

They boarded the ship in San Pedro on the 4th of November, and were surprised to find two dozen roses, in silver vases, in their stateroom. Marian had called the company, and the Captain had purchased them himself.

The accommodations were excellent—and spotless. The ship was well outfitted, with dining salon, dance floor, bar, swimming pool, game room and deck games. The officers were perfect hosts, and joined right in the passenger parties and games. There were Indonesian stewards, and Mother was amazed that they scrubbed the stateroom floors, walls and ceilings every day. Pieter, the second steward, took a shine to Dad and was a frequent opponent at ping pong as well as part of a bridge foursome from time to time.

The Friesland

The *Friesland* was a cargo-passenger ship, primarily outfitted for carrying cargo, but providing quite nice facilities-including air-conditioning- for a dozen passengers. The passengers were convivial and were accommodated at two tables in the dining salon, where they came to know each other quite well. All were welcome on the bridge, and free to roam the ship. Meals were exceptional, often featuring Indonesian cuisine, and celebrations were frequent and fun. "Aboard ship," Dad wrote, "we labor from grapefruit to dusk: reading, sunning, ping pong, table-shuffleboard (Sjulbok), walking, swimming, conversing." And so it went for four weeks.

Not long after breakfast, on December second, Lion's Head and Devil's Peak of Cape Town emerged through a low-lying haze. South of town rose a flat-topped mountain shrouded by a low-lying cloud. The day was calm, and the cloud had slowly spilled over the edge, creating a remarkable resemblance to a tablecloth-thus, it had been named, ''Table Mountain."

Dorothea, Dad's, "little sister," and her husband Frank Spears, met the ship and shepherded them through Customs and across town to

Veritas, their home, where they spent a very pleasant six weeks. The Spears household was a busy one. Hilary and Johnny, the two boys, were young adults. Hilary built Spears-designed racing sailboats, and Johnny worked in a law office. The parents had a busy social schedule and so did they, with a circle of personable young friends. Frank, and the boys, were avid sailors, and Dad, in addition to helping Hilary build Spearheads, accompanied them to the yacht club frequently, to watch the races. The Spearhead was a fast boat and the boys good sailors, so the races were exciting.

Dorothea was a remarkable woman-intelligent and creative. She was a poet and, like some, a philosopher, with an unusual capacity for understanding the human spirit. She was pensive, in a handsome sort of way. That is, her face reflected her character—it was interesting—while still being attractive. Her hair was white, worn short, with a slight natural wave and was combed simply no-nonsense. She had a slight postural tilt to one side, due to a mild scoliosis, which added a touch of mystery. Physically active, she walked to and from the local post, the grocery store, and tended her gardens. She loved flowers, and they showed it. Her poetry was often about flowers.

Frank was an actor, an artist, a sailor, and a radio announcer. An Englishman, he had unruly hair, bristling eyebrows, bushy chin whiskers and definite opinions. He loved his Queen and hated his Prime Minister. He thought Socialism the best form of government, and St. Petersburg the most beautiful city in the world. He had been exhibited, from time to time, in London. He was a realist early in his career, and his works were quite good. Later, feeling restrained by reality, he became a surrealist. A painting, in that style, of "St. Petersburg," captured well its extraordinary beauty!

Dad's pace was slowed slightly, the last two weeks, by what proved to be Infectious Hepatitis, but he, in his fashion, did not change plans. On the fifteenth of January, they bid farewell to the Spears, packed their brand new Austen rental car for the three-thousand-mile drive north to Mombasa, not counting side trips, and departed. They followed the east coast highway a good share of the time. Feasting on scenery between towns, and on generally fine food in restaurants and hotels, they arrived in Durban on the 6th day. Four hundred miles further, they took a break in Johannesburg, made several side trips and returned on the eleventh day, to turn in the Austin which had registered 1,748 miles.

They visited the Diamond Mines; Pretoria, the capitol of South Africa; Victoria Falls on the Zambezi River, which separated Northern Rhodesia (Zambia) from Southern Rhodesia (Zimbabwe) before each of these became separate states. Leaving the Falls, they went to Bulawayo, and by rental car over what had been an ox-cart trail in 1917, to the Old Umtali Mission. They were welcomed by the staff, and Mother was shown how Dad, as secretary to his father, filled many other shoes that helped make the mission a success. Mr. Gates, who originally imposed upon him to become printer, and publisher, came to dinner and they engaged in pleasant reminiscence late into the night!

Up at dawn, they were on the road by six o'clock and to Salisbury at ten o'clock where they had a bath, and took a much-needed three-hour nap. They flew on to Dar es Salaam, twelve-hundred miles distant, on the Indian Ocean, in what was then Tanzania. They went through customs preparatory to departure from Mombasa, and joined a safari to see hundreds of game animals in the Royal Nairobi Game park, before flying to Mombasa on the tenth of February.

There they rendezvoused, by intent, with the Bergs, who had been table-mates on the *Friesland* voyage, and reminisced on several occasions during their two days before departure on the "MV Afrika," This, a well-appointed tour ship, took them through the Gulf of Aden, Red Sea, Suez Canal and the Mediterranean to Venice, where they spent three days, explored the Grand Canal from end to end, and visited every edifice of note, before boarding the train for Zurich.

They passed through Padua, Verona and Milan to arrive in Zurich that evening. They were in the middle of the Alps in Switzerland: Mecca for winter sports; neutral through two world wars; home of the United Nations; privy to money handlers who could keep secrets; harbor for spies and counter-spies; land of intrigue and romance! They spent three days exploring and absorbing some of its ambience, while awaiting the delivery of a newly purchased Volkswagen. After a tour of Rotary International Headquarters, they began their exploration of western Europe on their own.

First to France where Dad spent his time in the war, then back to Switzerland to visit the regional headquarters of the United Nations in Geneva, along eastern France to Nice and the Mediterranean to Spain, then across the Alps to western France including, of course, a week in Paris. This was followed by Belgium and the Netherlands before crossing to Dover in England. In England they spent time at Oxford, visited all living relatives, explored London, and returned to America via San Pedro and Seattle.

When they arrived back in Kodiak, on a Sunday, July 5, 1959, Dad stepped into a new role—that of semi-retirement, surgical consultant, and relief physician for his two associates. In his absence, Alaska had become the forty-ninth state in the union.

Chapter 29

Semi-Retirement

1959–1962

D AD HAD NOT ANTICIPATED the effect the new role of semi-retirement would have upon him. When they got home he was abruptly confronted by his new life. Symbolically, he had been relieved of his *raison d'être,* which had sustained him through many decades. True, he continued to preside over the Alaska Association of School Boards and remained active in other organizations, and he and Mother continued in their role as hosts of the military, but he was no longer sole provider of medical care for his people—in his mind he was no longer needed—and he became depressed. He kept this to himself, but it was obvious to mother and to Marian, and they talked about it. It eventually seemed to pass, but it may have left its mark on him.

The staff at the grand opening of the new clinic in its new location
(from left to right):
the author, Marian, Jo Keers, Dr. Bruce Keers, 1959.

On his second day home, Dad went down to inspect the new clinic, which had been designed and built to occupy a third of the ground floor of the Johnson (Felder) Building. After Dad had divested himself of the Sunbeam Hotel, where our most recent office had been in the annex, we needed a new home. Bruce and I had designed it, consulting with Dad by letter during his foreign travels.

Dad and Mother, founders of the Holmes Johnson Clinic,
at the grand opening, 1959.

In semi-retirement Dad resumed his diary that summer. His entries were somewhat skimpy, no longer documenting a full-time practice. They included his surgeries, consultations, and community activities, which they expanded to include year-long involvement with the Masons and Eastern Star, and, in March, with the newly formed chapter of the Navy League, of which he was elected president. The family also hosted young performers, part of the Alaska Music Trail Winter Concert Series.

On August 3, Dad noted, "Bob is away for two weeks on *Windbird*, so I am paid a salary to take his place." Four days later, his mother, Sarah, arrived for a three-month visit. She was 96 years old, and Dad noted that she was "chipper."

In November, Dad and Mother attended the Alaska Association of School Boards annual meeting in Palmer. Dad was the evening speaker the first night, and his talk, "Observation of Education in Several Countries," was well received. They found time to look up

Dutch Bailey, there. Dutch and Julie were proud to show the folks their new home and forty-acre tract.

On November 23, the bank directors considered a proposed merger with the National Bank of Alaska. A merger with this major Alaskan bank could be of great benefit. Some thought it might dampen the personal aura of a small town bank, but after discussion, the merger was tentatively approved.

Dad's mother, Sarah, left on November 27, and life at Sprucehaven became more relaxed, particularly for Mother. There were daily entries in the diary, if only a sentence or two, from then until the end of the year. On December 11, Dad wrote, "Daily chores: filling wood box; filling lantern in pump house; sweeping walks; shoveling snow, at home and apartment house; *Windbird* maintenance; occasional hospital visit, after surgery; helping with Bob's house, when idle; work in study; shopping."

Marian's parents, Isabel and Lloyd James, arrived on December 22 for the holidays. They stayed at the log cabin, and had breakfast with my folks and the remaining meals with us in the little cabin. Dad took them on a tour of Kodiak, and Mother put together a smashing dinner for all of us and the Keers on Christmas Day. The Jameses left for Seattle on December 29, and 1960 soon dawned quietly for the Johnson family.

✻ ✻ ✻

IT WOULD SEEM that Dad should have had more leisure time. But he had changed little, still regarding idleness as wasted time, and maintained an active interest in just about everything. Early in February, he put his printing skills to work to run off several jobs for Sig Digree, editor of the *Kodiak Mirror*, helping him catch up with his workload. Next, he decided to learn how to upholster furniture. Wes Rhodes, the furniture dealer, showed him the technique, and he subsequently reupholstered one of our couches well enough to merit praise from Mother. He spent a lot of time on the *Windbird,* repairing sails, repainting, and varnishing woodwork, even replacing the motor that was rebuilt after her purchase. And he helped a lot on our new house, which was being built on the cliff halfway down the property.

Dad spent a week in mid-February building bookcases for and painting the manual training shop at the old downtown school, to provide a more suitable place for the town library, which then resided in two skid shacks attached to what had been the Community Center. Then he helped move the books, and mother and Sister Hilary cataloged them. That evidently inspired him to begin cataloging his personal library, which he estimated at over 1,000 books.

He spent quite a bit of time in his den, arranging, sorting, and filing his papers, cataloging his books, and labeling and segregating his many slides. He prepared commentary for anticipated public and private talks, with slides, showing segments of their trips.

He was re-elected president of the local School Board and remained active in the Alaska Association of School Boards. He had observed schools in Europe and Switzerland while on their trip, and he gave talks on "Education in Europe and America." He spent hours studying and formulating goals of education, and was influential in the state as well as in the local school educational system.

He turned to the task of building membership in the Masonic Lodge, which had never been very active in Kodiak. He and mother helped Eastern Star and Rainbow Girls grow into vigorous organizations. There were meetings of one or the other most weeks.

"Doc" and Harriet McKechnie, the admiral and his wife, had become close friends. They were interesting and fun-loving folks, and they spent good times together, either at Sprucehaven or on Base. This was their last year in Kodiak, and they were replaced by Rear Admiral and Mrs. Caldwell in April. As was the case with the military, friendships were often limited by transfer to another site although some, as in the case of the McKechnies, lasted a lifetime.

February 27, the bank merger was approved. The success of this could not have been imagined, and the stock increased in value and split repeatedly until, fifty years later, even a certified accountant could not unravel the complex history to compute capital gains on resale of stock.

Early one spring morning, the Russian parsonage across from the Orthodox church caught fire. The blaze was well along when the volunteer fire brigade arrived with the emergency pump cart. To their dismay, they found the tide was out and their supply hose would not reach the water. The fire had trapped the Orthodox priest in his bedroom. He quickly chose the only way out, which was through the window. Dad wrote, "On entering the hospital for treatment of his second degree burns, he wryly remarked that he created quite a stir in the neighborhood when he backed out the window clad only in his pajama top. In the hospital, it was discovered that he weighed well over 250 pounds, but he did not seem concerned about this, whimsically noting that some referred to him as a 'whale of a man.' "

We learned that the priest, Roman Sturmer, and his wife, Xenia, had escaped Russia during the Bolshevik Revolution. As a commander in the Russian Imperial Navy, he was "high society" and, as such, was not welcome in the new bourgeois society, nor was she. She had, in fact, been arrested and, put in a line-up for execution by a firing squad, had fainted just before the triggers were pulled and been left, among the bodies, for dead. Somehow she escaped and the two found each other, and managed to escape to a Russian community in California, where he became a priest. He was later assigned to Kodiak, where they were well received.

Dad and Mother were taken with the Sturmers, so they planned dinner get-together for them. After dinner, beginning with a retelling of the escapade of the parsonage fire by the good priest, the evening became hilarious, and a big step was taken toward developing lasting friendships. Xenia's infectious laughter was undoubtedly a big part of it.

On April 1, Dad and Mother attended a formal reception for Rear Admiral Caldwell and his wife at the Officer's Club on Base. That day there began a friendship between the Caldwells and the Johnsons.

April was proving to be a significant month in Dad's life. He introduced one more item into his life by getting a group together to form a Platting Commission and, of course, was elected chairman. Up until that time, Kodiak had grown, more or less, "like Topsy," and it was time for some type of planning. This proved to be a very complicated task, but Dad stayed with it, feeling it was important for Kodiak to expand "logically."

On the twentieth, the Republican Club asked Dad if he would be a candidate for State Senate. Seeing the need, he agreed. His attitude was that, if the public wanted him, he would serve, but he would not go out of his way to campaign, which meant that he wouldn't be likely to cancel a planned Hawaiian vacation.

The U.S.O. had terminated in Kodiak at the end of 1959, and Dad had been negotiating with Sears Roebuck for the lease of the ground floor of the Johnson Building. He was pleased to receive a phone call from Anchorage on April 21, indicating that they would lease the space on his terms. It wasn't long before a lease was signed and Sears moved in and set up business.

Monday, at 5:30 a.m., Dad, Lou Veerman, Jack Hinckel, Merrill Coon, and Emil Knudsen boarded a Navy DC-3 in the company of Admiral Caldwell, his aide, and a couple of sailors. They took off, had breakfast on board, and were on their way to a Navy League Conference in Los Angeles. They stopped at Anchorage to pick up the Anchorage bunch and continued to Seattle. They flew a short hop to Sand Point, where they picked up the Washington contingent; then, Portland, for the Oregonians, finally reaching Los Angeles at 5:15 p.m.

Wednesday, the admiral and captain re-joined the Kodiak group, to attend the sessions with them. There were "many Vice Admirals, Rear Admirals and Captains present," among a total of six or seven hundred Navy Leaguers. Meetings were held in giant tents that had been erected for the conference. Leaguers were transported, in multiple buses, to appropriate sites to witness demonstrations. They observed a review of naval vessels, a simulated attack and capture of a beachhead, an impressive series of maneuvers by the Blue Angels, a demonstration of infiltration and setting up of an established position by the marines, and they were given an address by the Secretary of the Navy. The Leaguers left the conference impressed with the might of the American Navy.

One highlight of the year, not too dramatic, was Dad's candidacy for State Senate. In mid-May, he attended a forum sponsored by the Kodiak Electric Association, where the candidates for Senate and House gave their views on education. Dad knew his stuff on this subject. He took the time to compose an essay on his political beliefs for a brochure that the Republican Party produced. I was appointed his chairman and, between us—two totally untutored in politics—a campaign was mounted. I was about as busy as he used to be, and he was out of town two weeks in midsummer, and spent the last six weeks, prior to election, in Hawaii. If elected, you could be sure he would stand by his principles and would be an effective senator. But his failure to really engage in his campaign did not bode well for his election.

Bruce's parents came to visit on a Monday in mid-July, and the Johnson women put on a "coffee" for forty women to meet the mother of the "new" doctor. Both families got to know each other quite a bit.

Marian and I had met them at their Brooklyn home when I was an intern. Dad took the whole Keers family for a cruise around the local islands, which was a thrill, for they saw whales, seals, puffins, and eagles.

Professionally, Dad consulted with us on various questions, and officiated at all major surgeries. He believed I was a "natural" surgeon, but I never achieved the confidence that comes from complete faith in one's own proficiency. Dad seemed to have inherited that natural confidence which, together with his training, made him willing and able to tackle—and often successfully resolve—the most extreme emergencies. In the early days, this confidence enabled him to deal with issues, such as tooth extraction, for which he had not even been trained. In August, he was called on by Dave Henley, a local rancher, whose prize bull had broken his leg. Dad responded to the call and helped Dave set and cast the leg. "Animals are not terribly different from human beings," he said.

✳ ✳ ✳

ON SEPTEMBER 5, 1960, Dad arose at 3 a.m. for a Navy League trip to Nome on the Admiral's plane to meet the atomic submarine *Seadragon*, which had just completed a trip under the ice from the East Coast. This was the first transit of the Northwest Passage in history. Ceremonies were held on the USCG cutter *Northwind*, followed by a visit to the submarine, a Chamber of Commerce luncheon where they met the scientists and Nome residents and heard a full account of the trip given by Commander Steele. Then, back at Anchorage, they were hosted by the general in command of Elmendorf Air Force Base for dinner. They returned to Kodiak that night.

On September 18, a Sunday, the following brief notes were found in the diary: "Filled ditch at cabin. Marian had a baby boy at 11 a.m. Did all outdoor chores preparatory for winter. Bob and boys for dinner." That baby boy would have been his third grandson, Jimmy.

✳ ✳ ✳

CHARLEY HAD STAYED WITH HIS SON, NORMAN, for a bit after Hazel died, but he had returned to the garage apartment he had so lovingly furnished and "rejoined the family." A mint julep with Charley had become a weekend afternoon ritual for Dad, on the front terrace on sunny days. And so they continued their friendship.

The pre-election vacation, which began on September 23, was scheduled to coincide with a Pan Pacific Surgical Conference in Honolulu, Hawaii, of which Dad was a board member. The opening meeting of the conference was impressive. Doctors had come from all over the world, and there were 1,350 in attendance. The conference lasted two weeks, with sessions every day and visits to local hospitals. Dad visited the State Tuberculosis Hospital, where the superintendent indicated that Hawaii, like Alaska, had a problem with tuberculosis control as it had—in the past—with leprosy, a related disorder. He particularly liked the session on gastrointestinal problems, including pancreatitis, gall bladder disease, liver tumors, and gastric carcinoma. In the final business session, Dad was reappointed to the Board.

They looked up Marian's uncle Kenneth Kearns and Maile, his wife, who were active in the Masons, and attended several Masonic functions there with them. A story was told during one evening that, during the Pearl Harbor attack, a U.S. bomb had fallen into their living room. Fortunately it hadn't exploded, so they only had to have it removed and to repair their roof.

On November 9, I sent Dad a wire, telling him that the state elections had been held and he had not been elected. He was not surprised.

They left Hawaii and flew to Portland early November 13. Darlow picked them up at 7 a.m. and drove them to the Rose Villa, a retirement home on the Willamette River in Tigard, where Grandmother Sarah, now ninety-seven, was living. They stayed a month, visiting family, seeing old PYC and medical friends in Portland, St. Helens, and on the coast, and finally returning home on December 30, 1960.

＊ ＊ ＊

THE YEAR 1961 was physically busy, for Dad assumed all his own maintenance tasks: the apartment house—repair of doors and windows, furniture and upholstery, flooring, cabinetry, alterations, and construction; the *Windbird*, which, being a wooden boat, required frequent care—scraping and repainting spars, decks, and hull, drying and sewing sails, tinkering with the motor and generator to keep them operational; Sprucehaven—simplified by the purchase of a chain saw, which reduced the time and energy required to cut wood; building shelves and doing maintenance on the Kodiak library; and helping me with our new home, which was almost a full-time process in the last few months of the year, when he and Charley built the entire outside of a large fireplace and chimney.

In January, Dad was nominated by his Rotary Club as a candidate for District Governor, District 504, in the 1962–63 Rotary year. During the following months, he was interviewed by a panel of past district governors, and was selected as governor, to begin his year with visitations to other Rotary Clubs, in July 1962.

In mid-January, he became chairman of the City Planning Commission, which had evolved from the Platting Commission he instituted in April 1960. This effort involved "much study" of the plans put together by Alaskan cities, Palmer and Ketchikan, and required considerable negotiation and tact in order to reach consensus on many different issues. Each decision had to be open-ended, often due to unforeseen changes in the community, so it was an unending task. By the end of January, Dad called an organizational meeting. Everyone attended and each was assigned a subcommittee. They held regular meetings after that to review committee work and, in late March, adopted a program, after which Dad wrote up Bulletin #1, and planning had begun. He stayed with the planning commission throughout his remaining years.

Later in January, he attended an informational town meeting on political organization. Since the Territory had become the forty-ninth state (in January 1959), the new legislature had been exploring ways to provide services to those areas outside of incorporated cities. Currently they were investigating a borough system, and Dad, of course, wanted to be sure he, as a citizen, knew what this was all about.

Now that Marian and I had vacated Torgy's little cabin and moved into our partly finished new home, Dad turned his attention to sprucing up the cabin. This involved putting in a furnace and a hot water heating system, painting walls and ceilings, and laying linoleum in the addition he had built for us. This was just another item that took a month or two, working part time, and resulted in a cozy little guest cabin, improved by the addition of central heating.

Sunday, March 12, was Dad and Mother's thirty-sixth wedding anniversary. They had come a long way from the starry-eyed romantics they were in Brooklyn. They spent the day together, went to church on Base, called on Admiral and Mrs. Caldwell, drove up to the Ski Chalet to watch the races and enjoy lunch, and spent part of the afternoon in front of the giant fireplace in the lodge. The Ski Chalet was built by the navy on a mountain pass between the Base and Antone Larsen Bay on the other side of the north end of Kodiak Island, about an hour's drive from town. It was for the public and ski equipment was available free of charge. Kodiak folks could easily enjoy a day on the slopes.

By mid-year, the Planning Commission had become quite busy sorting out property conflicts and establishing subdivisions as the community grew. With the construction of the Naval Operating Base in 1940, Kodiak had instantly become a boomtown. In ten years, the little village grew, from a total population of 550 to an area population in 1950, excluding navy families, of 3,264, of whom 1,700 resided within the city.

When Marian and I had moved to Kodiak in 1955, the area population was about 5,000, with about 3,000 in the city. All that growth resulted in a cluster of properties among the few roads, some of which needed resurveying to resolve perceived conflicts. This explains the evolution of the commission into a Planning and Zoning Commission as the work became more complex.

* * *

IN JANUARY 1962, Dad noted interesting consultations: an intestinal obstruction in the young son of an Episcopalian minister, requiring surgery to remove an inherited Meckel's diverticulum and to untwist a segment of small intestine that had wound around it; surgery for closure of a ruptured duodenal ulcer, and treatment of resulting peritonitis; and another case of peritonitis from a ruptured gall bladder, which required removal of the gall bladder. These were serious conditions, but all did well.

Most cases of peritonitis were the result of ruptured organs, including appendices, which occurred in patients from remote locations who, coming to town by boat, often arrived too late to prevent rupture. Most did well, however, partly because Dad did not hesitate to open and drain abscesses when they occurred and partly because bacteria remained sensitive to sulfa drugs and penicillin—the only two antibiotics available. None of these had died.

* * *

IN MARCH, Dad wrote to the State Local Affairs Agency to inquire about borough government, and laid plans for a public meeting to look into the prospects of a borough for Kodiak, which would function as an agency for governing the larger Kodiak area. The Kodiak Island Borough was formed the next year (1963), taking over area-wide powers of taxation, education, planning and zoning, health care, and waste disposal.

On a Sunday in March, Dad and Mother had dinner with the Achesons, who had become their best friends. Dressed for the beach, since there was a minus tide, they went clamming after dinner. The evening was chronicled by Dad: "Acheson's for turkey dinner. Clamming after. I fell, and nearly fractured my skull." The next day—cold packs to right face all night but severe pain, relieved by morning—to hospital for X-ray, rested most of the day." The second day: "More X-rays— three fractures in zygomatic arch—one through entire inferior orbital fossal bone—crack at temporo-mandibular fossa, read most of the day." The third day: "Winds of great force—temp. to 12 degrees, some desk work, much reading; stayed inside, healing rapidly, swelling going down already." The fourth day: "Windy and cold. Much damage done about town. Garden tool house blew over and two trees broke off. I stayed inside although feeling O.K." The fifth day: "Facial colors turning yellow and green, healing rapidly; spent most of the day at my desk, on conference speakers. Clear and warming. Garden tool house covered with plastic until fixed, to keep contents dry." The sixth day: "Desk work until tired, then out in warm sunshine to cut kindling, bring in wood, sweep terraces and walks, and explore the beach."

Sunday, a week following the injury, he returned to a full schedule of activities. Today, he would have been referred to an ophthalmologist for evaluation and, certainly, advised to undertake a more extensive period of physical inactivity. But this behavior, of complaining very little and being minimally distracted by the injury, was an example of his English "stiff-upper-lip-ism."

* * *

ON MAY 21, Dad and Mother, knowing Dad's year as district governor was coming up, decided to attend the annual Rotary Convention in St. Louis in June. They flew to Seattle, and the next day, they began their trip east by car. They visited several national parks, and many sites of historic interest, and made several stops. On June 6, they arrived at the convention, and registration was the next day. The speakers were outstanding, including RI President LeHarry.

They drove east as far as Evanston, Illinois, the regional center of Rotary in North America, and they were shown through headquarters and saw the extent of Rotary's work in America and the world. Next stop Cedar Rapids, Iowa, then it was straight west on U.S. Highway 30, transferring to U.S. 6 for lighter traffic, and continuing, to arrive in Denver on the third day, where they stopped for a swim in the afternoon. The temperature was ninety-six degrees in the shade. It was cooler the next evening, when Gordon and Mary Ibbotsen, who had sailed with them to Africa on the *Friesland*, had them to dinner and showed slides of their trip. They drove west over the Continental Divide, visited Utah's Bryce Canyon and Zion National Parks.

Then, it was up the coast to Oregon. They rented a cottage on the ocean just north of Cannon Beach. And Dad rented a second cottage for Dorothea and Grandma Johnson, whom Darlow and Alta drove down to stay a few days. Dorothea was visiting from Africa. Sarah, who was now ninety-nine, insisted on swimming in the ocean with them. On the morning of the June 29, they returned to Portland, where Darlow's family now occupied the Bishop's retirement home in Tigard. That evening, cousins Roberta and Carol, and Carol's Methodist husband Larry, joined them for an outdoor picnic dinner. Sarah, Dad's mother, reached her one-hundredth birthday during their visit. The family celebrated with her at the Villa, and she received greetings from folks all over the world.

Dad and Mother drove Dorothea to Seattle on August 7, and the three of them flew to Kodiak. At home, Dad found the lawn nearly knee-high. He was compelled to mow it that afternoon. The next day he arose at 6 o'clock and, after raking and re-mowing the lawn, commented that, "it was beginning to look like someone lives here."

Dorothea, Dad, and Darlow look on as Grandma Sarah cuts the cake at her 100th birthday party, Rose Villa Retirement Home, Portland, Oregon, August 9, 1962. Portland Oregonian.

Dorothea stayed in Kodiak for nearly a month, during which time Dad showed her everything—even exploring some of the backcountry military roads from the latter years of World War II. She met many of the family friends, and the family had the opportunity to get to know and appreciate her. She was a quiet person, a philosopher and a poet, and, on the last Saturday afternoon of her visit, after a picnic lunch on the front lawn at Sprucehaven, she spoke of the seven planes of existence of yoga, her current interest. It was a sunny day, warm enough to be comfortable outdoors, and the discussion was a nice family affair—interesting and informative—I remember it well. The next day, she departed to begin her return to Cape Town.

✳ ✳ ✳

IN MID-SEPTEMBER, having learned that the Hinckels would be leaving Kodiak, the Johnsons invited thirty folks to a cocktail party at Sprucehaven to bid them adieu. Two days later, they attended another farewell party put together by Emil Kraft. Hinckels had become good friends, and an important part of the community.

The Achesons and the Schotts, who had been friends for years, and the Bullocks, who arrived in Kodiak in 1962, became the most frequently seen of the folks' friends. Bob Acheson, the manager of Donnelley and Acheson's (D&A's), formerly the Erskine Company, was an alert, openly pleasant man, who was honest and efficient. His wife, Betty, was an outgoing and ambitious hostess, who took special pains to bring folks together in her home, for meals and games, and had introduced the Johnsons and others to Kodiak newcomers. Ivor Schott had been the School Superintendent since the construction of the new school. He was a quiet, conscientious man with a twinkle in his eye, which revealed his lurking sense of humor. His tiny, energetic wife, Helen, was the much-loved kindergarten teacher of our first three children. Don Bullock was the first Episcopalian minister in residence, a jolly fellow. His wife, Evelyn, was a dynamic woman who was active in the community.

Still chairman of the Planning and Zoning Commission of the borough, Dad attended a public hearing on November 14, at which the Comprehensive Community Development Plan was passed in public hearing, the culmination of many hours of commission work.

In December, Dad assumed one more responsibility. He attended a meeting to form Kodiak-Baranof Productions, a nonprofit corporation to produce the "Cry of the Wild Ram," and to assume the management of other, and future, activities of the arts in Kodiak. The proposed Articles of Incorporation and By-laws were reviewed and approved. Dad was nominated and elected to the twelve-member Board of Directors. He didn't need another volunteer task, but joined to lend moral support to an otherwise rather daunting undertaking.

Chapter 30

Rotary District Governor

1962–1964

R OTARY, founded in 1905, was the first service club in the world, a cross-section of business and professional men (and women, eventually) united by the motto, "Service Above Self."

A. Holmes Johnson, District Governor, Rotary District 504, 1962–63.

This year, 1962, was the first year of his tenure as Rotary Governor of District 504, which included most of Canada's British Columbia and parts of Northwest Washington State, in addition to Alaska. In July, he and mother would start club visitations. He, in his official capacity, she, as his indispensable aide and social secretary. He was to monitor their performance, answer their questions, and encourage them to uphold Rotary's mission. This would include reports of his findings to them and to Rotary International by the end of the Rotary year.

Fostina Johnson, Aide and Social Secretary to the Governor, 1962.

But during the first six months of the year, he still had work to do at home. On January 5, there was a conference of an Overall Economic Development Plan for Kodiak, to build a consensus for future growth. Dad continued as chairman of City Planning, which he pursued until the formation of the borough the following year, when City Planning became part of the Planning and Zoning Commission. He had pictures taken for Rotary International, to be published with a list of incoming district governors, and began a study of world religions, with the idea that Rotary was a practical application of the best in all religions. He studied the organization, regulations, and procedures of Rotary International, and put together several talks on important aspects of Rotary, and a longer speech for presidents and secretaries at the next district conference.

In March, he wrote to the State Local Affairs Agency to inquire about borough government, and laid plans for a public meeting to look into the prospects of a borough for Kodiak, which would function as an agency for governing the larger Kodiak area. The Kodiak Island Borough was formed the next year (1963), taking over area-wide powers of taxation, education, planning and zoning, health care, and waste disposal.

In May, Dad and Mother went to Seattle and boarded a plane for New York, to attend the week-long Rotary International indoctrination of incoming district governors from all over the world, before taking the governors' train to the International Assembly in Los Angeles. There, on a Sunday night, he and mother found themselves among 26,000 other folks at the opening session in the Hollywood Bowl. The convention speakers, including the Rotary International president, were experienced stalwarts who had "been there, done that," and reminded those assembled of the many ways Rotary had fulfilled their motto through hundreds of programs all over the world. Each speaker was inspiring. During the final session, candidates from over 100 countries were elected district governors. Then they departed, vowing, "to make a difference."

On July 26, Dad mailed the visitation schedule to all clubs. He and Mother left for Seattle, and drove north, to attend his first visitation—the board meeting, dinner, and club assembly of the Vancouver Rotary Club, where he reviewed the club organization and committee goals. The club vice-president felt Dad's presentation was excellent—that he had been tactful, but pulled no punches. This was just what Dad wanted to hear. He gave his first message on "Rotary and Its Relationship to Religion" the following day, somewhat apprehensively, not knowing how well it would be received. When there was protracted applause and he was surrounded by a crowd of enthusiastic Rotarians, he was relieved. He hoped that it would inspire Rotarians to raise the priority of service in their everyday lives.

His message, as Rotary Governor, was an important part of this process. It began with a quote by Dana Greeley: "In this one world, living under the threat of atomic annihilation, it is folly for one race or nation to be uniquely righteous, or for any single religion to claim the one way to salvation. World understanding can never come about until the inherited patterns of segregation are put into proper perspective. We need an experience of brotherhood that can transcend racial and religious barriers."

He continued: "Rotary is not just another luncheon club. It has a message and a destiny. When a man joins Rotary, and becomes imbued with the spirit of service, he becomes a better man. He finds a new satisfaction in life and a new zest for living. He becomes aware of a new meaning to existence. He becomes dedicated to an important task.

"There are men in Rotary who have not missed a meeting in twenty or thirty years, a few, in a lifetime. There are men, in Rotary, who have risen to great heights in their relationship to the world about them, by seeing needs and helping to fill them, and having a great-hearted sympathy for all mankind. And there are Rotary clubs all over the world, in 128 countries, that have been of great benefit to their fellowmen and society.

"Of course, as in any organization, every man is not automatically a true Rotarian, in this sense. It takes time to learn the meaning of its motto. It takes time to sense that the dignity of man depends upon knowing that service to others is more important, and more satisfying, than serving one's self. It may be months before a member can say, 'The important thing is not what I can get out of something, but what I can contribute—where I can be of most use!'

"Rotary teaches the golden rule in personal, business, community and international life. This teaching marks its relationship to religion. What do all religions teach? Simply stated, is it not a belief in God and some form of golden rule?" He further stated that the ability to agree upon the fundamentals of all religions should be a great influence toward world understanding and world peace."

This was followed by a summary of each of the world religions, including their origins, a brief history, a statement of their primary goals, and some reference to philosophy, showing that the basis for all of them was some form of the Golden Rule. "It seems quite evident, in this day of expanding frontiers of knowledge, that all knowledge is tentative in character and that certainty must be impossible. We should, therefore, not worry about certainties, but be satisfied with the progressive correction of knowledge, through continued inquiry and new discoveries. Ultimate meaning can be seen as a continuous creation. We must not waste our time looking for security, but must realize that security is impossible, with freedom—even security of thought.

"Albert Camus, feeling that religion must be focused on the kind of life a man leads here and now instead of emphasis being placed on preparation for a future life, took 'Love' as his religion, and 'Service' as its means. He felt that faith and happiness are not in worlds to come but in our present life. He said, 'It has become man's primary responsibility to do nothing that might increase suffering and unhappiness; conversely, he must neglect nothing that might prevent or alleviate misery. Man's duty, in this world, is to man.'

And in conclusion, "After all, what brings happiness and satisfaction?

Is it money? Is it success? Is it position? These all help the ego but they cannot bring deep-seated content. It is most satisfying to man, to be of service to others, and the more each of us does this, the more we have a deep sense of being right and honest, we gain an inner glow of true contentment. That is why Rotary, with its emphasis on the ideal of service, with its insistence on ethical standards and complete honesty of purpose, with its application in all four avenues of service, and its whole-hearted belief in these principles is, if not a religion in itself, an excellent practical application of all religions."

There followed an intense five months of club visits, three to five a week, until the end of the year. They completed the southern B.C. clubs by the end of August, the Washington clubs through September, and the northern B.C. clubs by mid-October. The Alaska clubs followed, and were completed in time for them to attend a District Assembly in Vancouver. There, six hundred fifty Rotarians met in the Princess Elizabeth Playhouse on the 17th of November, to hear the first Asian Rotary International President speak. His message inspired the listeners to remember to put, and keep 'Service' in the forefront of their everyday activities.

Dad stopped in Seattle long enough for a report of his routine medical exam before returning to Kodiak on the 20th where, to his delight, he was met by nearly all of the Kodiak Rotarians and escorted to their regular noon meeting before going home.

Once home again, they couldn't let the old year end without some celebration, so they accepted an invitation from the Bakutis's on the 30th of December for cocktails, where they found the Achesons. This was followed by bridge at the Achesons, which was so much fun they agreed to continue at Sprucehaven the following night, which they did, and they had a gay time playing bridge until 1962 ran out and 1963 had a good start. They called it a day at one o'clock in the morning.

New Year's Day, dad mailed his January first Governor's Letter, composed his mid-January letter, and got ready to complete the club attendance reports so that by evening he and mother were ready to relax a bit. In the first half of the year, he spent about half his time preparing, and sending, reports of his club visits to each club and to Rotary International.

He continued as chairman of Borough Planning, School Board, Red

Cross, and involvement with mother in Eastern Star, Rainbow Girls, etc

He continued surgical consultations, and performed surgery: to remove an inherited Meckel's Diverticulum and untwist the small intestine that had wound around it to produce obstruction in a youngster; to close a ruptured duodenal ulcer and treat the resulting peritonitis; to remove a ruptured, gangrenous gall bladder and treat the resulting severe peritonitis. He remarked that all did well, quite happily, since the resulting peritonitis was quite serious.

Most cases of peritonitis resulted from ruptured organs (including appendices) which occurred in patients from remote locations who, coming to Kodiak by boat, often arrived too late to prevent rupture. Most did well; however, partly because dad didn't hesitate to open and drain abcesses when they occurred, and partly because bacteria remained sensitive to penicillin and sulfa drugs, the two antibiotics available.

He completed his reports of club visits and mailed them to the clubs and to Rotary International by June, thus completing his task as Governor of District 504.

✳ ✳ ✳

DAD AND MOTHER, having befriended a number of Aussies and New Zealanders at the previous two Rotary conventions, planned to go to the next International Convention in Auckland in February of 1964. Early in January, Dad obtained passports, made reservations, contacted friends, and developed an itinerary.

January was a busy month. Dad and a plumber replaced the galvanized plumbing in the garage apartment with copper. He audited the Eastern Star Books, and he and Mother installed the officers of Eastern Star. He conferred with the mayor on city planning business, and attended a joint meeting of the Kodiak and Anchorage Chambers of Commerce to discuss a State Ferry System, which was considering the addition of Kodiak to their itineraries. Then, he took a day off: "Aside from filling the wood box, I spent the day reading a large pile of Frostie's love letters I had saved which emphasized our early pure love for each other."

He prepared and submitted a report of the Library Board to the City Council with the request, "for a paid librarian and a new building," which gained approval and provided a salary of $7,000 for a librarian.

He assisted me on a caesarian section at 4 o'clock the following morning, and an appendectomy that afternoon, in addition to several surgical consultations. He was busy with the Planning and Zoning Commission and the Platting Board, who were anticipating the institution of an Urban Renewal project for downtown Kodiak.

On February 6, Bruce Keers delivered Marian of Gary, Dad's fourth grandson.

On February 18, mid-winter in Kodiak, Mom and Dad began their trip to New Zealand, via Honolulu and Fiji. In Auckland, they and others who had come for the conference were met by the Rotary District Governor and introduced to their host families, who then took each of them home—a custom at Rotary conventions. They attended conference sessions over the next few days, and were shown about New Zealand in their free time. Then they flew to Australia, and began their tour of that continent. For two weeks, they toured Australia, and were hosted by Rotary families throughout the country, seeing most of what made the country special, in cities and in the wild. Dad spoke at Rotary Clubs and to schoolchildren about Alaska and Kodiak.

On March 28, they took a particularly memorable trip. Their flight took them over the plains into what was called the Outback. They passed over wheat fields and vineyards, then sheep stations and salt lakes, touching down at a coal-mining town, ultimately landing at an airfield adjacent to a circle of hills. Through a cleft, and within the hills, lay Alice Springs, a modern city in the middle of nowhere.

In the evening, when they were about to turn off the radio and retire, they were shocked by a disturbing newscast!

Chapter 31

The Good Friday Earthquake
1964

IT WAS GOOD FRIDAY, March 27. The sky was thinly overcast and the air was soft and springlike, though a crust of snow remained on the roads and the ice had only begun to thaw on the lakes. The townsfolk were looking forward to a long Easter weekend. Cars buzzed up and down the roads, some stopping at the post office, the grocery store, and the barber shop on their way home. The crab season had just ended and most of the fishing fleet had returned to the harbor, a few entering or still unloading at canneries along the Pillar Mountain shore. A Widgeon circled and touched down at the entrance to the boat harbor and taxied up the channel to its hangar. The evening Pacific Northern Airline Constellation took off from the Base and flew over town on its way to Anchorage. Some folks were already at home, preparing dinner, on this typical, early spring evening in Kodiak.

The boat harbor in Kodiak from Pillar Mountain, late afternoon, March 27, 1964, just before the earthquake hit.

Marian was on her way home from the airport with three of the children, having seen Craig and me off on that Constellation to Anchorage. As she approached the slide area, there was a sudden rumbling and the Volkswagen began to leap and shake. Thinking she had a blowout, she stopped and got out, to find the earth shaking so hard that she had to hold on to keep from falling. The rumbling seemed to come from deep in the earth, and visible waves were rolling across the surface of the ground. The bushes on the hill above were wildly swishing back and forth, and some dirt and rocks tumbled down onto the highway.

Downtown Kodiak and (right) the boat harbor parking lot, before the earthquake.

People erupted from their houses. Cars had stopped at all angles, and people were outside hanging on to keep their footing. The power lines were thrashing to and fro, tree branches waving wildly, rocks and dirt falling onto the highway from the hillside. Wires on the poles were singing under tension and there was shouting, and noisy splashing of the water in the boat harbor creating a cacophony of noise accompanied by that deep-throated rumbling in the depths of the earth. Marian was frightened.

In what seemed a long time but really was only a few minutes, the violent shaking eased, the rumbling and tremors began to subside. She jumped back in the car with one thought—to get the children and herself safely home. Mother and Dad and I were gone and, though it had not yet occurred to her, she was alone. She got home safely.

It was low tide. The water in the boat harbor started draining out fairly rapidly as the tremors subsided. In ten or fifteen minutes, the sea began to rise again, quite rapidly but not violently. Many fishermen had come down to check their boats. As the water continued to rise higher and faster, several boats got under way and left the boat harbor at full speed, heading for deep water. The breakwater had broken and a section of it sank. Other boats followed as fast as they could. The water rose further and began to flood the parking area next to the harbor, where a number of folks were trying to move their cars out of harm's way. A few succeeded, but many did not, as the water rose rapidly to flood the whole Kodiak downtown. Some buildings floated off their foundations. A Widgeon roared down the channel and took to the air. It was 6 in the evening. The tide slackened, then began to ebb—gradually at first, then rapidly—soon becoming a rushing torrent, slewing cars about in the parking area as it returned to the sea. Boats still leaving the harbor, aided now by the rushing current, were swept into the channel where they battled swirling currents as they careened through the channel to the north.

Fifteen or twenty minutes later, residents on Pillar Mountain witnessed a giant thirty-foot wave roar into and through Near Island channel from the north. As it reached the harbor entrance, a huge, swirling eddy curled back and slammed into the floating docks, where many vessels were still tied. There was a terrific grinding, cracking, and crashing as floats, pilings, and boats were crushed together and swept into adjacent floats and up into the parking lot and lower downtown. About a hundred boats, floats, piling, buildings, and debris flowed into the downtown area. Dusk was falling as this, the second of a series of tsunamis, began its return to the sea, leaving about half of the debris behind, while it roared through the boat harbor carrying the rest out to sea.

The earthquake registered 9.2 on the Richter Scale, the most violent ever recorded in Alaska. It was the result of the slipping of a fault that extended from Anchorage, through Seward, Resurrection Bay, and to and through the end of Narrow Cape on Kodiak. It caused the northern end of the island to sink nearly six feet and initiated a series of tsunamis, the first of which was the largest and, luckily, had occurred at low tide, or the damage—if it could be imagined—would have been considerably more.

The boat harbor in Kodiak in the early evening, following the first tsunamis, without boats, floats, or anything.

Anchorage had also experienced severe damage. The control tower at the Anchorage Airport had collapsed during the quake, and the Constellation had returned to Kodiak before dusk. We noticed a few buildings shifted off their foundations as we drove through town. We found the approach road to Sprucehaven under water and had to backtrack and take an alternate route to tie into Mission Road on higher ground on the west side of the lake and drive through a homestead on the north end of the lake. We parked in the woods and walked to the house, finding it intact and Marian and the other boys at home. They were marooned, because of the submerged road. We arrived just before the big wave that had created havoc downtown, and it created havoc for us, too. It rushed into the lake with great force, where the quake had fractured the ice into sixteen-inch floes, building a thundering crescendo as more and more floes were tumbled over one another through the lake and into the woods. After it crested, there was quiet for a few minutes until it began its return, gaining speed until it thundered back to the sea, taking with it many of the ice floes, our dock, our well house, our telephone and power poles, and what was left of the road. We were left without water, power, or telephone.

The newscast that disturbed the folks, announced a severe earthquake in Anchorage, on Good Friday—the day before—that had caused considerable damage. There had been no word from Kodiak. The folks did not sleep well that night. They contacted the American Embassy in Canberra, first thing in the morning, and the embassy was able to reach Anchorage, but got no word about Kodiak.

For four days, communication to Kodiak was not open and no information was forthcoming. On April 1, they called Marian's folks in Seattle, and learned that everyone was safe, which lifted a great load from their minds. There was no report of the amount of damage, however, so this remained an unknown. They canceled the rest of their plans and flew on to Seattle, where they were welcomed at the James's residence, where they read Marian's and my letters and all the newspaper accounts that had been saved. They felt relieved to some extent, knowing that their home still stood, but realized the future lay somewhat in doubt.

Mission Lake after the earthquake and tsunamis, 1964.
The land sank with the earthquake, and the lake became a tidal flat,
cutting off road access to Sprucehaven (on the ocean side).

We were able to talk by telephone, and I described the problems caused by the tsunamis in as positive terms as I could, and the steps taken, so far, to cope with them. They were able to fly in to Kodiak two weeks after the Good Friday disaster. They were shown the *Windbird*, which had been dismasted, rescued, and towed to Woman's Bay, on Base, where she rested safely against a big rock on shore. Dad wrote that they went "on a personally conducted tour of the damaged areas. It was beyond description: 100-foot boats hurled several hundred yards inland, others out to sea; most of the business section gone; much of Sprucehaven's earth gone and (the) lake replaced by a malodorous tidal flat."

The fault had cut through Narrow Cape on the east shore, and the whole island west of the fault had tilted so that the our end of Kodiak sank nearly six feet, and the south end titled upward a bit. In addition to this, the tsunamis had washed out all the low-lying land separating the south end of Mission Lake from the sea, where our access road had traversed a log bridge over the brook that drained the lake. The road and brook were no longer, and the sea had claimed the lake as a tidal inlet. We drove around the north end of the lake to reach our property.

Downtown Kodiak in the early weeks following the tsunamis, spring 1964.

Both families had to heat with fireplace fires, flush toilets with salt water carried in buckets from the sea, bathe and wash clothes at friends' homes, and use rain water, supplemented by fresh water, hauled from town, for drinking. Electricity was restored within a week. Within two months we had rigged an emergency pressure system that was fed from a 2,000-gallon tank truck, hauled in periodically for the purpose, and had become fairly self-sufficient. We drove in the back way for a year, before five other residents around Mission Lake signed a note to assist in the construction of a breakwater and a tide-gate to restore the lake and the approach to Sprucehaven.

Mother and Dad were, certainly, shocked by what they encountered, but they went to work to establish a life style that would fit the circumstances, and allow them to participate in the restoration of the community. One of Dad's first chores was to go through stacks of mail, separating that which had arrived since the tsunami from the others, many of which enclosed checks for the relief of those who had suffered loss. Sunday, he walked the property and found high tide encroaching, somewhat, on the lake side, and a number of foot-thick ice floes in the low lands, but, except for the losses already described, Sprucehaven was relatively intact. In the afternoon, he and Mother called on some folks to see how they had fared.

On Wednesday, Dad wrote letters to those concerned, summarizing the disaster, and thanking those who had sent funds to help those needing assistance. Thursday, the Chamber of Commerce convened at the Montmartre, since the Island Fountain downtown was no longer usable. Mid-meeting, there was a severe aftershock, which sent everyone, pell-mell, out of the club, some leaping over the backs of booths. It lasted only 5 to 10 seconds, and when we returned, we felt a little sheepish, for there was Dad—still sitting in the booth—peacefully smoking his cigar. Friday, there was a meeting of Spruce Cape residents concerning a water supply. Most of them were on wells, many of which were not functioning well, and Sprucehaven, of course, was without a supply at all. Saturday there was a meeting of the new Borough Planning and Zoning Commission, of which Dad was elected chairman by acclaim, and that evening the Commission had a joint session with the City Council to hear representatives from the Alaska Housing Authority and Urban Renewal. Sunday, Dad convened an eight o'clock meeting of the commission at City Hall, "to settle some problems, and get recovery under way faster."

The next week he was going in all directions at once. He called on Captain Gee at the Base to thank him for "storing" the *Windbird*, met Admiral Riera, the new commandant, and picked up a package for me at their post office, which was handling the mail until ours could get back in business. In town, he started plans to assess the *Windbird* damage, arranged some repairs to the apartment house, and approached the city regarding possible restoration of Mission Lake.

In the next several weeks, there were frequent meetings of the Planning and Zoning Commission, which was involved in the urban renewal project for downtown Kodiak as well as in restoration in the outer areas. There was a lot to do and Dad was in the middle of it. He had some minor stomach discomforts from time to time, which did not concern him, but since his return, he had developed symptoms that concerned me. Thus, on the first of May, I performed an upper gastrointestinal X-ray series on him, which was normal.

In the next few days, he began to work on a commencement address for the forthcoming Kodiak High School graduation. He had always felt that education was the most important ingredient of a rational society and that, without it, the inanities of human nature would prevail, to the detriment of all of us.

Chapter 32

The Final Chapter

1964

DAD'S INTESTINAL SYMPTOMS seemed more frequent, and he began to refer to them as gall bladder symptoms. We performed a gall bladder X-ray series, which also proved negative. Symptoms did not abate, but there were days when he felt "much better." I was beginning to feel quite uncomfortable with his condition and told him I thought he should go to the Mason Clinic in Seattle to go through a thorough investigation to be sure he didn't have something serious. But he had too much to do and—being who he was—felt that no one else was capable of doing it! Apparently, he was not ready to do this.

On May 19, he gave his talk to the graduating class, "The Need for Education Today." Captain Fulp, retired submarine commander, whose family had remained in Kodiak and become friends, told him, "It was Churchillian," which, for Dad, was the highest compliment.

I did a colon X-ray series on him, and no abnormalities were seen at fluoroscopy, and inspection of the films was normal. But I was getting more concerned as, I suspect, was Dad.

Dad wrote, "GB symptoms getting worse. Have complete lack of ambition." He had "ulcer and GB pains during the night."

Thursday, Dad was feeling a bit better, but rested all day. He held a Planning Commission meeting in the Johnson Building in the evening with folks from the Housing and Home Finance Corporation. The last day of May, Dad attended an urban renewal meeting that evening, where the first phase for restoration of downtown Kodiak was decided. At the Rotary meeting on Tuesday, Dad was presented with the Annual Robbins Award for outstanding community service, through the Alaska State Medical Association, and received prolonged applause that he found "most gratifying." He continued working with the Planning and Zoning Commission for several days, and then, on the June 6, wrote, "Bob has been wanting me to go out to Clinic from the start and, as it is holding on so long, it is not fair to him not to go—so have decided."

He completed his deskwork in the next couple of days, and flew to Seattle on Tuesday, June 9, to the Virginia Mason Hospital. He was examined by an intern, who, "left more bewildered than not." All the tests that I had performed and many others were conducted during the next week without finding any answers. As a last resort, the hospital psychiatrist visited and determined, in half an hour, that there was "nothing in his line" that was wrong. Dr. Baker then decided they must resort to the old method of an exploratory laparotomy—a surgical look-see into the abdomen—to find the problem, and the family was informed that surgery was scheduled for the next morning.

Mother caught a plane that evening, and went to the hospital. She was able to see Dad before surgery. I called at 8 o'clock that morning to wish him well, and he went into surgery an hour later. After surgery, he was kept sedated the remainder of the day. On Thursday morning, "Joel Baker called and gave us the news—cancer of the body of the pancreas, too far advanced to cure." The worst possible! According to Dad, "All took it well, and Frostie and I were able to talk things over sanely for her future. I have no fear of death—would greatly prefer it to continued pain, and my only fear is that I will not die soon enough, and will go on to unendurable pain, and be a burden to my loved ones—the one thing I wanted to avoid.

And, the following day, "I'm really the lucky one, as I will not have to grieve when my loved ones go first, and I'll be the first freed from worry and responsibility, which I was glad to assume until this illness, but now, simply, do not have the energy." On the fourth postoperative day, Dad made an attempt to describe the character of his recurrent distress: "The bad symptoms are out of proportion to the pain. The same pain across the upper abdomen and at the rib margins, right and left, and across the back could be stood handily were it not for the physical and emotional collapse that accompanies it, as of one in shock."

He was discharged a week after surgery, and remained in town until full recovery from surgery, and was kindly made at home in the James's downstairs apartment. As expected, he was not very chipper. I had been in touch with Dr. Baker and had talked to mother, and knew that he was having a lot of pain, so called him on Sunday; and he wrote: "Talked to Bob, who wanted me to have a splanchnic block before returning, so decided for Monday, since I am weaker every day."

He had the injections, but was depressed when he had relief on one side only. The other side was reinjected the next day and he "began feeling better mentally and emotionally before returning to the room, and when the pain failed to return, he was much relieved and happy! "This should keep me pain free for six months to a year and, according to statistics, I should be dead by then. This is a most satisfying miracle and we [he and Mother] are overjoyed!"

July 3, they boarded the PNA jet which departed to Anchorage at 7 o'clock, he boarding in a wheelchair, on a lift, and when they arrived in Anchorage, they were escorted to the crew quarters to await flight time when the captain, himself, drove them to the Constellation bound for Kodiak. Dad wrote, "Met by Bob before eleven o'clock in Kodiak and driven home where his wonderful surprise was his impressive, working, central water system. We chatted a while before he left for work but I was exhausted after that stimulation stopped."

The next few days were free of pain and this allowed Dad to speak with the accountant and the attorney to transfer funds, and make some changes to his will. Friends came to visit, daily, at first, and when it was clear that he was tiring, were considerate enough to leave. When he felt best, he would work crossword puzzles, and, sometimes, watch television, but he tired more and more rapidly, and waned. He spent his day in a chaise lounge, on the sun porch, and the night, in bed. He required more and more narcotics for pain, graduating to injectable Demerol toward the end of the month.

On July 17, Dad wrote, "Bob in, and Frostie, of course, and I was quite perky. They are the only ones I really want to see, and Marian sometimes. I love them all greatly. No one ever had a truer wife." On the eighteenth, the Sisters came to visit. He had had many a spirited discussion with Sister Hilary, and even though he was not Catholic, he had a high regard for these women. He enjoyed their visit, but tired rapidly, and they left him with a prayer for his strength and comfort.

On the twentieth, he wrote: "Have been getting some wonderful letters from folks all over. Such thoughtfulness makes one humble, and makes me think that the world might be better for my having lived in it."

From then on, he began to sleep more, and required less pain medication. His last note was on August 2: "Bob in, off and on, during day. Frostie stayed with me, like the loving wife she is. I do love her, too, and Bob and Marian and the grandchildren. Father Bullock wanted to see me about governor's visit. Each ten minutes seemed like an hour. Betty Weir (nurse) going to stay with me nights for a week. "

He became more and more lethargic and began sleeping most of the day, requiring about 100 milligrams of Demerol several times a day. He neither spoke nor rose from bed again. He died quietly, in the morning of August 21, 1964.

Mother sent no Christmas cards that year, since she did not wish to send the news of Dad's death at that time of celebration. Instead, she answered each card she received and included the following editorial, written by Bill "Wooley" Lamme—good friend, fellow Rotarian, and editor of the *Kodiak Daily Mirror*:

His Influence Will Remain
August 27,1964

The many friends of Dr. A. Holmes Johnson will mourn his passing, and residents of Kodiak, old and new, will feel his influence in the years to come.

His influence on Kodiak is timeless, for he has brought many of this generation into the world. He has cared for their mothers and also their fathers, even the offspring of the younger generation. But this is not what we mean when we say his influence will be timeless.

Oftentimes the influence of a man on a community and his fellowmen is in no way connected with his vocation. Though (remembered) as a doctor, and particularly a surgeon, Dr. Johnson will probably be remembered as a citizen, quick to see the civic needs of the community, and willing at all times to give of his precious time to foster anything that in any way would be of benefit to his beloved Kodiak.

He was not a crusader in the ordinary sense of the word, but he worked quietly, efficiently, and effectively, and with great good humor in service clubs and other groups in civic undertakings, ever willing to serve in any task he was given. He appreciated, perhaps more than most, the historical background of Kodiak, its buried artifacts, its little known history.

But, A. Holmes was too filled with the business of living, too cognizant of the future to spend all his thoughts and energies in recreating the past, important and interesting as it was. He looked keenly to the future. He saw Kodiak's great potential. He saw the commercial value of this seaport town, but he also sought to steer the thinking to aesthetic values. The library to him was most important. Education, too, he saw as a real necessity in the town's growth and well being. If there is any memorial set up for him, and there should be, it is the proposed new library. Nothing could be more fitting than for it to bear his name.

Kodiak has lost a voice that was outspoken in its praise wherever he went. He often stated on his return to Kodiak after his many trips throughout the world, that he found no place as beautiful or that he liked so well. Kodiak was always home to him.

The influence of his presence has been stilled, of course, but his deeds and efforts in Kodiak will remain monumental and effective for years to come. We mourn the passing of Dr. A. Holmes—a good friend and a first-rate citizen!

Epilogue

MOTHER WAS DEVASTATED. She had lost her life companion and her *"raison d'être"* as well, for she was an integral part of a "missionary" partnership that had occupied all her adult life. Darlow and Alta came to stay with Mother at the log cabin, and were a great comfort through and beyond the memorial service, after which Dad's ashes were scattered over St. Paul harbor from a Kodiak Airways plane.

Friends and relatives all over the world wrote to her, expressing sympathy, and commenting on the contributions she and Dad had made during their lives together.

She had, with Sister St. Hilary, founded the Kodiak Library in the old Community Center and had become the volunteer librarian when it was moved to the Manual Training building of the old school house. After she regained some sense of control over her life, she reassumed this task.

Dad had a hand in Rotary's purchase of some downtown property several years before his death, which was to become the site of a permanent library. This was within the urban renewal area, however, which placed that prospective use in jeopardy. As fortune would have it, the Felder building with our clinic was destroyed by fire in the spring of 1965, and the Grey Nuns allowed Dr. Keers and me to erect a prefabricated structure next to the hospital to serve as a temporary clinic.

When downtown was leveled and filled, it was subdivided into lots, one of which encompassed that library property. It was a good location for a new clinic, with adequate space for parking. I purchased the Rotary property and the remainder of the urban renewal lot, and built an attractive building to house the Holmes Johnson Clinic. In 1968, Rotary donated that money, and, with a grant from the state, supplemented by the city, the A. Holmes Johnson Memorial Library was built.

Mother stayed on as director of the new library for the next seven years. As one who had an abiding interest in history, she also functioned as a research historian until her retirement in 1975. She continued as organist in the Community Baptist Church and as volunteer in many community organizations. She received the Alaska Volunteer of the Year award by Governor Jay Hammond in 1982. In mid-1980, dementia crept in and she gradually lost her sense of time, but, to the gratitude of the family, she remembered each of us. She insisted on staying at home until her death, with a daily private attendant, until, one morning, twenty days before her ninety-fourth birthday, she drew her last breath.

Within minutes after her death, there appeared a wild doe in her front yard, the first ever seen at Sprucehaven. She was seen several times in the next few days, but never again. It was tempting to imagine this beautiful animal as a spirit, sent by Dad, to escort Frostie to him in the nebulous Great Beyond.

* * *

DR. KEERS, A PERFECTIONIST, decided he just wasn't cut out for general practice, and in l965 he left Kodiak to do a radiology residency. It took me eleven months to find a surgeon and a generalist to help in the practice. The community continued to grow rapidly, as did the practice. A new hospital was built in 1968. The system outgrew the Grey Nuns, who retired in 1978 after thirty-four years of invaluable service. After the king crab fishery waned in the mid-1980s, the growth of the Kodiak population slowed, and in 1998 it stabilized at about 14,000 people. I retired in 1994, and the Holmes Johnson Clinic retired with me.

Kodiak finally became part of the Providence Hospital System, and a new hospital was built, leaving the 1968 structure to function as a nineteen-bed extended care unit, with a cafeteria, administrative offices, and specialty clinics for the use of resident and visiting specialists. The Kodiak Area Native Association built an Outpatient Clinic, and Providence formed a foundation, which built a Community Health Center in conjunction with the hospital. There is a small Public Health Center, three private clinics in town, and one for personnel of the Coast Guard Support Center. At the time of this writing, Kodiak's hospital and medical facilities provide sophisticated, Level 3 medical services, employ 700 people, of whom are 26 physicians and 8 paramedical practitioners. These, plus several alternative care providers, supply health care for everyone in the greater Kodiak community, regardless of their financial status.

Chronology

Arthur Holmes Johnson

1894:	Arthur Holmes Johnson born, October 18, Mapleton, Iowa
1912:	AHJ's documents (diary and letters) begin
1914:	Editor and printer, North Douglas Herald, Drain, Oregon
1916:	Served in U.S. National Guard, Mexican Border Service
1917:	African Methodist Episcopal Mission, secretary to the Bishop
1918:	Student, Morningside College, Sioux City, Iowa, B.A. degree
1918–19:	Lieutenant, Tank Corps, American European Forces, WWI
1920:	University of Oregon Medical School, Portland, B.S. degree
1923:	Northwestern University Medical School, Chicago, Illinois, M.D. degree
1923–25:	Surgical internship, Brooklyn Methodist Hospital, New York City
1925:	Married Fostina "Frostie" Bishop, March 12
1925:	General practice begun, St. Helens, Oregon
1925:	Son born, Robert Holmes Johnson, December 25
1929:	Surgical practice begun, Portland, Oregon
1937:	Summer physician, Libby cannery, Bristol Bay, Alaska
1938:	General and surgical practice begun, Kodiak, Alaska
1941:	Hospital practice begun, Kodiak, Alaska
1942:	Sprucehaven Lodge completed in December
1955:	Father and son joint practice, Kodiak, Alaska
1962:	Semi-retirement
1962-63:	Rotary District Governor
1964:	Died of pancreatic cancer, August 21

About the Author

Robert Holmes Johnson

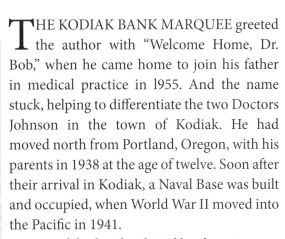

THE KODIAK BANK MARQUEE greeted the author with "Welcome Home, Dr. Bob," when he came home to join his father in medical practice in 1955. And the name stuck, helping to differentiate the two Doctors Johnson in the town of Kodiak. He had moved north from Portland, Oregon, with his parents in 1938 at the age of twelve. Soon after their arrival in Kodiak, a Naval Base was built and occupied, when World War II moved into the Pacific in 1941.

Beyond high school, Bob's education was outside Alaska. He had always pursued music and studied piano, and during his first year at Willamette University in Salem, Oregon, he played with jazz groups, which helped fund his education. In 1944, he enrolled in the U.S. Merchant Marine Cadet Corps, served nine months in basic training and sea duty in the South Pacific, and shipped as Third Mate with the U.S. Lines until the end of the war. He obtained a B.S. in biology from Willamette, an M.S. in zoology from the University of Michigan, and an M.D. from the University of Washington.

He married Marian James, from Seattle, in October of his second year in medical school. They had their first child six weeks before driving across country to intern at Methodist Hospital, Brooklyn, New York, where his father had trained thirty years earlier.

His father died in 1964, a few months after the Alaskan Good Friday earthquake and tsunami. Bob and A. Holmes Johnson had practiced nine years together. Forty years later, he discovered his father's diaries and correspondence. At the turn of the century as he approached his eighties, he decided that all this information should be written down as this biography.

Index

— A —

A. Holmes Johnson. *See also* Kodiak medical / surgical practice; medical / surgical practice
    changing name to, 85–86
    death, mourning, and scattering ashes, 300, 301, 303
    influence as a first-rate citizen, 301

A. Holmes Johnson Memorial Library, 183, 303

Africa, 1917. *See also* Old Umtali Mission; Rhodesia
    Boer War graves, 21
    Cape Town, 20 (photo)–21, 29, 34, 39, 262
    decision not to return, in letter to his parents, 1922, 64
    Dorothea marriage and remaining in, 60
    Karroo, 21–22
    Khama country, 22
    passport via England, 18
    visit by Arthur and Fostina in 1958, 261

African Methodist Episcopal Mission. *See* Old Umtali Mission

Alaska. *See also* Bristol Bay
    Albrecht, Dr., Commissioner of Health, 145, 175
    Alice Springs, 287
    Basic Science Act, 180
    Bristol Bay area, canneries around, 96–97
    fur trade, 98
    Good Friday earthquake effect on, 291
    Koggiung, cannery, 94–95 (photo)
    military involvement during World War II, 132 (photo)–134
    Outback, 287
    shipwreck and snowstorm, 1947, 199–200
    statehood, planned, 181

Alaska Association of School Boards, and presidency, 256, 257, 261, 267
    talk on "Education in Europe and America," 270

Alaska Commercial Company, 209

Alaska Lines, costs to move Fostinia, Bob, and the dog Simba to Kodiak, 113

Alaska Music Trail
and Mr. Schapiro, 225
Winter Concert Series, 268

Alaska Natives in Kodiak, 98, 99 (photos)

Alaska State Medical Association

as president, 234
Dutch Bailey attendance at meeting, 209
Robbins Award for outstanding community service, 297

Alaska Steamship Company, 121

Alaska Territorial Medical Association, paper, in 1946, 179–180

Aleutian Campaign in World War II, 133–134

Aleutian Homes, government housing project, 256

Alta (Darlow's wife), 5 (photo). *See also* Darlow

with Arthur and Fostina in Oregon, 77, 79, 87
staying with Fostina after Arthur's death, 22
visit with Sarah in 1949, 212

Armed Forces Television, 257

American College of Chest Physicians, Fellow and governor, 123, 165

American College of Surgeons, Fellow, 123

American Literature, authors, 167

Anchorage Times, and publisher Atwood, 181

The Arctic Trader (Madsen), 105

army

Army Communication Corps, 216
Camp Colt Officers Training School, 38–39 (photo), 40
induction center in Missouri, 37
Jefferson Barracks, 37 (photo)–38
Tent village induction center, 37 (photo)

Army Medical Corps reserve duty, 1929, 82

Asian cannery workers in Alaska, 93

Association of National School Boards, attending in Miami, 257

Australian wounded soldiers, 34

Aunt Ethel, 50–51

Aviation Signal Corps, 36

— B —

Bailey, Dr. Clarence "Dutch"
    arrival at hospital and indoctrination, 189, 195, 206
    bear hunt, 195–196
    move in 1949 and residence in, 215, 250, 269
    shared practice with, 189, 202, 205, 209, 210, 211

Bank of Kodiak, 194, 215, 256
    merger, 270
    president Bill Smith, 242
    welcome to Robert in 1955, 251 (photo)
    Torgeson as president, 256

Baptist Mission in Kodiak, 121

Baranof and shipmates, 101–102, 117
    Captain Ramsauer, 111

Baranov Museum, 225 (photo)

Beecher, Ward, 135–136

Bishop (Arthur's father)
    in African mission / Old Umtali, 14–15, 17, 27–29 (photos)
    death in 1939, 122
    eighty-seventh birthday at Sprucehaven, 122
    financial help to son during hard times in Oregon, 89
    health issues, 1929–1934, 87–88, 90
    in Iowa National Guard (photo), 13
    at Morningside College Glee Club, 12 (photo)
    officiating at Arthur and Fostina's wedding, 73
    retirement in Portland, 122
    son's fond feelings for and from, 149
    summer cabin on Fire Island, New York, 75 (photo)

Boeing Aircraft Company / William Boeing, 174

Botha, Graham and Dorothea, 60

Botha, Hilary Graham, 5 (photo)

Bristol Bay (in 1937)
>   canneries around, 96, 97
>   Good Samaritan Hospital, 91, 94, 95, 97
>   Native Indians around, 96, 97
>   Swedish fishermen around, 93
>   travels around, and scenery, 96, 97
>   weather, 92–95

Brook Farm (Unitarian), 167
>   Brooklyn Methodist Hospital
>   Bruce Keers as intern, 256
>   Dr. Goodrich and Miss Duryea compliments, 66
>   Fostina, meeting and romance, 69, 71 (photo)
>   internship of Arthur, 65, 73 (photo)
>   internship of Robert, 246
>   reminiscing about, 251
>   RH transfusion procedure, 254

Brownsville, Texas, during Mexican Border War, 13–14 (photo)

Buckner, General, 133 (photo), 145, 154, 160, 219

Butler, Major General (Air Force), 133 (photo)

— C —

Calvanism, 167
>   Camp Colt and Officer's Training School, 38–39 (photo), 40
>   motorcyclist at, 206

Camp Dodge, Iowa, 13

canneries in Alaska, 156
>   Asian workers in, 93
>   Ekuk, 96
>   at Koggiung, 94–95 (photo), 96
>   summer medical internship at, 93, 95–97

Cape Town. *See* Africa
>   cars, 147
>   Chevrolet, 117, 120, 121

Clark's Garage / Basil Clark, 155
Pontiac, 211, 212, 213
Volkswagon during Good Friday earthquake, 290

Catholic presence
Father Fitzgerald, Alaska Catholic Bishop, 180
Father Gallant, 160–161, 165, 241
Father Mahar, 241
Sister Hilary, 299
Sisters hospital at Aberdeen, 193
Sisters of Providence in Anchorage, 180
Sisters of St. Anne in Juneau, 180

Christmas
in 1947, 199–200
in 1949, 216
in 1957, 253–254

City of New York ship, 35 (photo)

City Planning Commission chairman, 275, 282

Civil Defense and Hospital Units, chairman, 215

Coast Pilot, 224

Community Baptist church, 127–128, 160, 242, 249
Fostina as organist, 303

Community Center, and Board, 177, 181, 182–183, 195, 199, 207, 215, 224, 270, 303

Coon, Louise and Merrill, 242

Cordova ship, 115, 134, 153, 183

Corlett, General Pete, 133 (photo), 141, 146, 219
recommendation for Medical Corps, 159–160

Cosmopolitan article on oceanic yacht race. 38

Council, Dr., Commissioner of Department of Health, 102–103, 107, 108, 158

Craig Holmes
birth, 246
grandfather's first meeting, 251
on Piper Super Cub crash, 252

Crane, Fish and Wildlife ship, 181

Crutcher, Marshall, bank president, 182, 198, 242, 250

— D —

dancing / square dancing, involvement in, 67, 155, 166, 177, 183, 194, 207, 225

    Darlow (brother). *See also* letters
    as editor / printer and minister in Oregon, 10
    at Fremont Methodist Church, Portland, 144
    at Sarah's one-hundredth birthday, 279 (photo)
    staying with Fostina after Arthur's death, 303
    visits with Arthur and Fostina after their move to Oregon, 77, 79, 80, 90
    visits with family
        in 1947, 194
        in 1949, 212
        in 1958, 261
        in 1960, 274

Darlow Botha, 217
    and bride Beverly, 218

De Beers Diamond Company, 23

Deep Sea floating crab processor, 257

Denali ship, 145, 171

dogs
    Pataud, 244–245, 248
    Simba, 113, 117, 119
    Smoky, 157, 244, 245 (photo)

Donnelley and Acheson's (D&A's), 280

Dorothea (sister), 5 (photo), 39, 211. *See also* letters to Dorothea
    concerns about "Daddy's" illness, 87
    marriage to Graham Botha, 60
    poet and philosopher, and yoga interest, 263, 279 (photo)
    second husband Frank Spears, and Spearhead boats, 262–263
    son Darlow Botha, 217
    sons Hilary and Johnny, 263
    visit to Sarah from South Africa, 212, 278, 279 (photo)
    visit from Arthur and Fostina in 1958, 262–263

Douglas, Earl, doctor prospect, drafted, 143

Dupler, Paul, Kodiak town lawyer, 242

— E —

earthquake. *See* Good Friday earthquake

education. *See* schools

Ekuk, Alaska, cannery and clinic, 96, 97

Ellis Airlines / Bob Ellis, 254

England
    stopover in 1918, 42–43
    Sunderland, stay in, 49–50

Episcopalians, thoughts on, 64

Erskine, William (Billy), and family, friends, 103, 106–107, 108, 109, 112, 123, 138, 219
    Babe (B.A.B.), 175
    house, then museum, 225
    Nellie, illness and death in 1948, 208–209, 219
    Leisha, second wife, 197, 207, 209
    Nellie, first wife, death, funeral, and grave, 141–142, 197, 209
    supporters of, 144
    terminal illness and death, 197, 198, 219

Erskine Company / store, 118 (photo), 120, 121, 166, 280
    purchase by Mr. Donnelley and Bob Acheson (Donnelley and Acheson's, or DI&A's), 208, 219, 241

Ethel, Aunt, in England, 50–51

— F —

fatherhood with Robert, 1925 (photo), 75

Felder Building, and destruction by fire, 268, 303

flight training and practice
    in the 1950s, 247
    on Link Trainer, 171
    pilot on Piper Cub crash, 252–253

Fostina (Frostie). *See also* letters
as Acme Fast Freight employee, 89–90, 115
after her husband's death, 303
aide and Social Secretary to Governor, 282 (photo)
Alaska Volunteer of the Year in 1982, 303
at Brooklyn Methodist Hospital as student nurse, 69 (photo)
in Business and Professional Women's Club, 225
Christmas events, decorations, and spruce trees, 216, 253–254
courtship, marriage, and honeymoon with Arthur, 69–70, 71 (photo), 72, 73–74
death at age ninety-three, 303–304
diary entries
about Arthur's health in 1929, 87
about liking Portland, 85–86
of training completion at Brooklyn Methodist Hospital, 73
Eastern Star involvement, 171, 243 (photo), 268, 270, 286
and Florence Welch as helper, 246
garden, 184 (photo)
Grey Ladies and Hospital Auxiliary involvement, 156
at Holmes Johnson Clinic grand opening, 267–268 (photos)
hysterectomy at time of forty-second wedding anniversary, 255
library director and research historian, 303
Medical Association auxiliary, president, 240
organist, 303
pregnancy and birth of Robert (Bobby), 78–79
selling Portland house, 108–109, 111–115, 117
visit to family in New York in 1947, 191–192
on *Windbird*, 237 (photo)
worry about husband's illnesses in 1953, 244–245

France
Château de Fompeyres / Castillon, 47–48 (photo)
church attendance description, 45–46
response to father's disappointment with him there, 59–60
with friend Harris, 43–45
Kennedy, Bob, in Amiens, 47
MacLean, description of post-war visit, 47
Mme. Nicard as cook, 46
as officer in, 43–44, 45 (photo), 46–48

friends, close
Bullock, Don (Episcopalian minister), 280
Acheson, Bob and Betty, 208, 219, 241, 242, 254, 277, 280, 285
Hinkels, 279–280

Hoag, Dan, 183, 199, 217, 218
Lowry, Captain 163, 165, 171, 174, 177, 185–186, 192

Friesland ship to Africa, 261–262 (photo)
Gordon and Mary Ibbotsen on, 279

— **G** —

Good Friday earthquake
Arthur and Fostina return from Australia to Alaska after, 293
boat harbor at Kodiak before and after earthquake, 289, 290 (photos)
Kodiak downtown after earthquake, 290, 294 (photos)
restoration after, 295
Richer Scale register of 9.2, 291
and tsunamis, 291, 294

Good Samaritan Hospital, Internship Training at Bristol Bay, 91

Gorgas (ship), 96

grandchildren
Gary, 287
Jimmy, 273

Great Depression, effect on medical practice in Portland, 85–87

Grey Nuns of the Sacred Heart, 161, 162 (photo)–163, 175, 180
Mother House and Sister Mary Leo in Philadelphia, 192
retirement, 304
temporary clinic after fire, 303
tenth anniversary, 248

Griffin, acting governor Edward W., 131

Griffin Memorial Hospital, 131 (photo) –132, 161–162 (photo). See also Kodiak hospital

Gruening, Governor, 173, 180, 217, 240

— H —

Hammond, Governor Jay, 303

Hewlett (Hew), Fostina's brother, 73, 81, 191, 192, 246

Historical Society president, museum planning, 258

Holland-American Line, 261

Holmes Johnson Clinic, 303
grand opening, 267–268 (photo)
retirement from in 1994, 304

hospitals /hospital practice. See also Kodiak hospital
early in Kodiak, 131–132, 141
at Fort Richardson, with Dr. Albrecht, 145

Hygiene ship, 185

— I —

Illinois National Guard, 13

illnesses (Arthur), chronology
in 1949, 217–218
in 1953, 244–245
gall bladder symptoms, 297
cancer of pancreas diagnosis and surgery (Dr. Baker), 298–299
and death in 1964, 300
notes and changes to will, 299

influence, widespread, 301

Iowa. See also Morningside
Camp Dodge, 13
Patrick's Boarding House, 11

Iowa National Guard, Bishop in, 12, 13 (photo)

Isenberg, Al, and motorcycle, 206, 207

— J —

James, Lloyd and Isabel (Marian's parents), 240, 269, 293

Jefferson Barracks, Missouri, 37 (photo)–38

Johnson
   Alta, 5 (photo), 10. See also Alta
   (Samuel) Darlow, 5 (photo), 10. See also Darlow
   Dorothea, 5 (photo). See also Dorothea
   Ebenezer Samuel, 3 (photo). See also Bishop
   Robert. See Robert
   Sarah, 4 (photo), 17, 23, 29, 34. See also Sarah
   William, 49

Johnson Building, and Sears Roebuck lease, 271–272
   joint medical practice with Robert
   planned, 220
   beginning / early, 252, 253, 257

Jones, Dr., orthopedist, practice with, 109–110, 111, 121, 144, 148, 152–153, 148, 158

— K —

Kearns, Kenneth and Maile (Marian's relatives), 274

Keers, Dr. Bruce and family, 256–257, 258–259, 267 (photo), 269, 273, 287, 303
   leaving Kodiak 304

Kincaid, Admiral Commandant, NOB, 133 (photo)

"King Crab Capital of the World" and festival, 257, 258 (photo),
   waning in 1980's, 304

Kirby, **Dr.** See medical practice

Kiwanis involvement, 81

Kodiak, Alaska, 120 (photo), 121. See also schools
   animals and environment, 221
   Armstrong, Karl, jailer, 121

Baptist Mission, 121. *See also* Community Baptist church
Baranof Hotel and Baranof Apartments, 182
Blinn's Pool Hall, 121
boat harbor before and after earthquake, 289, 290 (photos)
cannery, 121
City Council, favorable to Arthur, 169
first house, 119, 120, 121
fishing industry, 196–197
Fostina and Bob, and Simba moving from Portland, 117–118, 119
generator and /light plant problems, 151, 153, 155, 156, 157, 165
after Good Friday earthquake and tsunamis, 294 (photo)
Gilmore, Tim, 118
guide Sid Olds, 195
Kodiak Electric Association, 165, 272
Kraft, general merchandise store, 117–118
Louie Thompson's Transfer Company, 121
military / navy base in 1942–1943, 132–133
Montmartre Inn, 146, 205, 295
moving to, in 1938, 101–102
newspaper, and editor Gene Dawson, 127
office-home in, 110
Overall Economic Development Plan, 282
Pacific Northern Airlines (PNA) flights, 123
Planning and Zoning Commission, 282, 287
Platting Commission, chairman, 271, 287
population in 1995
radios, 121
Red Cross, and director Art Larkin, 155, 176, 177
religion, history in, 160
Shriners, 171
Standard Oil Company, 121
stores and companies, 121
Sunbeam Hotel, 103, 182, 268
Taylor, Warren A., town lawyer, 121
Thompson Transfer / Louis Thompson, 156
Totem Igloo Curio & Gift Shop, 182
Union Oil Company, 256
Wakefield Fisheries / Howard and Lowell Wakefield, 257
during World War II, 132–133

Kodiak Airways, and Bob Hall, pilot, 179

Kodiak Area Native Association, 304

Kodiak-Baranof Productions, 280

Kodiak bear, 106, 207

Kodiak borough. *See* Kodiak Island Borough

Kodiak Chamber of Commerce / and president, 154, 165, 173, 182, 195, 224
    after Good Friday earthquake, 295
    joint meeting with Anchorage Chamber of Commerce to discuss a state ferry system, 286
    President John Gibbons, 257

Kodiak Daily Mirror, 124–125

Kodiak Island Borough, 277
    chairman, 285, 295
    formed in 1963, 282
    Planning and Zoning Commission, 280, 295, 296, 297, 298

Kodiak fishing fleet, 255

Kodiak hospital
    accusations of incompetence and libel lawsuit, 169
    Christofferson, Harry, Board chairman, 169–170
    doctors leaving, 154
    "Dutch" Bailey, 189, 195, 206
    first operation, private, 132, 141, 141
    Grey Nuns and Sisters, 161–162 (photo)–163, 196, 210, 304
    new in 1941, 131 (photo), 147
    new in 1968, 304
    planning, 103, 106, 123, 131
    problems in, 157–159, 163–164
    in Providence Hospital System, 304
    Public Health doctor and problems, 158
    Sister Mary Monica Brennan, administrator, 161, 171, 180
    sophisticated modern, in 2013, 304

Kodiak Library and Sister St. Hilary, librarian / library board, 183, 269, 270, 286, 303

Kodiak medical / surgical practice. *See also* joint medical practice
    early, 107, 111, 122

cases in 1940: 125–126, 129–130
"fish poisoning," 127
"throat painting," 128
cases in 1941–1942: 138–139, 141–142, 144
cases in 1943: 147–148
cases in 1944, most difficult year, 150–151, 159
cases / heavy workload in 1945: 167–170
cases in 1946–1947: 181–182, 185, 188–189
cases in 1948–1949 (shared with Dutch Bailey): 197–199, 205, 210, 211, 215
cases (solo again) in 1950, 1951, and Arthur's illness, 217–218, 222
cases and heavy workload in 1952, 244, 245
description of clavicle fracture treatment, 258

Kodiak Mirror, Sig Digree, editor, 269

Kodiak Realty Company, 182
Kodiak Village in 1937, 97 (photo)–98
Natives, 98, 99 (photos)

— L —

Latin terminology, vs. common English, diary entry about, 128

letters, all chronological:

letters to Bishop, father
in response to upset about experiences in France, 59
about University of Oregon Medical School expenses and schoolwork, 59, 60–61
after transfer to Northwestern and Chicago, 62–63
about decision not to return to Africa, 64
of thanks to an exceptional father, 65
about Methodist Hospital, Brooklyn, 65–67
about his love for Fostina, 72
about young "Bobby," 80
from St. Helens, Oregon, 80–81
about Fostina's job with Acme Fast Fright, 89–90
about Portland Yacht Club, 90–91
letters to Darlow
about medical work and syphilis in Rhodesia, 30–31
about induction into army, 37
about relatives in Sunderland, England, 50
from Oxford, 50, 53
from University of Oregon Medical School, 59–60

about Northwestern and Chicago, 63
about father's death, 122–123
letters to Dorothea
about Dr. Cadman speech and dancing, 67
about missing her and Graham, 68
letters to Fostina
about effects of financial problems beginning in 1929, 86–87
during move to Kodiak, 101–102
after his arrival in Kodiak in 1938, 103, 108
describing new office-home in Kodiak, and what she should bring,
111–112
about Portland house sale and money, 112
awaiting her arrival in Kodiak and getting a home, 115–116
during her vacation in 1942, 134–140, 146
presenting two rings, 186
letters from Fostina
to "Daddy, about baby Robert, 79–80
about putting Portland house on the market and moving to
Kodiak, 108, 111, 113–115
about cold winter in 1947, 186–188
about weasels and rats, 220, 221
to her husband, his rereading above love for each other, 286
letters to Robert from dad
expressing feelings for, 148–149
philosophical, 172–173, 186
regret at not being able to attend graduation, 179
concern with medical school preparation, 209
about upcoming vacation in 1949, 211–212
letter from Robert to dad
during visit to Oregon, 136
letters to Sarah, mother
about Robert's birth and infancy, 79
about financial worries and health in Portland, 85, 88
letters from Sarah
about Bishop's illness, 87, 88
Libby, McNeill & Libby cannery, 93–95 (photo)
at Koggiung, Alaska, 94–95 (photo)

library, personal, 270

Logan, Adjutant General of State of Iowa, 36

Lowry, Captain, 163, 165, 171, 174, 177, 185–186, 192

— M —

MacArthur, General Douglas, 229

Madsen, Charley, hotel owner, 105–106, 142, 182, 207, 247

Mandisozda, David, interpreter, 28

Marian, Robert's girlfriend, then wife, 226, 240
    birth of Gary, 287
    birth of Jimmy, 273
    on Piper Super Club crash, 252 (photo)
    on *Windbird* voyage, 227, 237 (photo)
    at grand opening of clinic, 267 (photo)

marriage, Fostina and Arthur
    officiated by "Daddy" Johnson, 73
    and honeymoon, 73–74

marriage / wedding, Robert and Marian, 240–241
    parents at, 240, 241
    wedding party, 241 (photo)

Mashona tribe at Old Umtali Mission, 26 (photo)

Masons / Masonic Lodge involvement, 81, 171, 268, 270, 274

McKinney, Mr., Assistant Secretary of the Interior, 240

Medical Corps, application, endorsements and rejection, 159–160

medical experience and training. *See also* Oxford
    beginning in Umtali, 29–31
    University of Oregon Medical School, 59
    Northwestern University Medical School, M.D., 62–63 (photo)–65
    Brooklyn Methodist Hospital, 68

medical / surgical practice. *See also* joint medical practice with son
Robert; Kodiak medical practice
    early days in Kodiak hotel, 106, 107–108, 109
    at Emmanuel and Good Samaritan Hospitals, 82

license to practice permitting problems, 157–158
in St. Helen's, Oregon, 77–78, 81–82, 85–86
in Portland, with Dr. Cable, 82–83, 85–86
University of Oregon Medical School staff, 82

medical providers / doctors / nurses

Doctors
Beech Barrett, 223
Bill Mills, itinerant clinic, 257
Cable (Portland), and his recommendation, 82, 85, 86, 89, 114
Douglas, 179
Earl, 156
Gray, 145
Joel Baker, Virginia Mason Hospital, 180
Johnson (town doctor), 121, 144
Jones (town doctor), 121
Kraft, 103, 117, 144, 148, 158
Louise Ormand, 226, 239
MacFarlane (husband and wife), 243, 244
Milo Fritz, 218, 257
Sullivan, 170
Leisha Flood, 142, 143, 145
Marion Lynch, Public Health nurse, 242
Miss Curtis, Territorial Nurse, 176
Miss Oslin, 158
Miss Spencer, Territorial health nurse, 130

medical summer internship in Alaska, 96, 97

Megantic, 41, 42 (photo)

Methodist Episcopal Mission / Church, 3, 15

Methodist Hospital. *See* Brooklyn Methodist Hospital

Mexican Border War, 12–13

military. See also navy
in 1942–1943, 145, 132–133
friendships with "Doc" and Harriet McKechnie and Rear Admiral and
Mrs. Caldwell, 270, 271, 272, 276
in Kodiak during World War II, 147

Mission Lake
flood, in 1947, 188
after Good Friday earthquake and tsunamis, 294, 295

Missouri, Jefferson Barracks, 37 (photo)–38

Missouri Pacific Railroad, 10

Molletti, Reverend John, and Mrs. (receptionist), 243, 249

Montana, selling bibles in 1913, 10

Montgomery, Admiral, 205

Morningside College, Iowa, 11–12 (photos), 33, 36
    B.A. in liberal arts, 61
    Miss Quinton's accident, 33
    Patrick's Boarding House and roommates Earl Hicks and John and Jim, 11

motorcycle rides with son and Al Isenberg, 206–207

Motor Transportation Corps option, 46, 47

murder cases in Anchorage, testimony at / Judge Heloenthal, 144–145

— N —

National Bank of Alaska, merger, 269, 270

National Guard in Mexican Border War, 12, 13, 68
    Bishop in, 14 (photo)

Natives, Alaska / Kodiak, 97, 98–99 (photos), 107
    in Alert Bay, 229
    around Bristol Bay, 96
    doctors serving, 185
    at King Cove, 236
    Malutin, 166
    schools established for, 160

Natives, Rhodesian: tribe, pastors, and teachers, 22, 26, 27 (photo), 29 (photo), 31

Naughton, Judge, and Naughton's Bakery, 121, 246

naval stations / Naval Air Station (NAS) / Naval Operating Base (NOB), 107, 123, 124, 132–133, 147, 151, 219, 245, 276
    Captain Lowry, 163, 165, 171, 174, 177, 185–186, 192
    flight training on Link Trainer, 171
    Fort Greely, 133
    friends

"Doc" and Harriet McKechnie and Rear Admiral and Mrs. Caldwell, 219, 270, 271, 272, 276

Hobbs, NOB admiral and commandant, 256

Navy League / Navy League Conference, 268, 272

Seadragon atomic submarine, 273

Nebraska, ranching in, 1912, 7–10

Beebe, minister, 7, 8, 9, 10
Bussy, Mr., rancher, 8–9
Daniels, Reece, rancher, 7–8, 9
Rosebud Reservation and Sioux Indians, 8
Yankee Robinson's Circus, 8

New Zealand, trip to, and return after earthquake, 1964, 286

North Coast ship, 127

Northwestern University Medical School, 62–63 (photo)–65
M.D. Degree from, 65
sexual promiscuity in Chicago, displeasure with, 62
letter to Darlow about Trinity Church and Episcopalians, 64
transfer to, in 1921

Northwind Coast Guard cutter, 273

— O —

Officers Training School, Camp Colt, 1918, 39 (photo)–40

Old Umtali Mission, 21, 23–24, 25 (photo)

Advance publication for, 26, 29, 31, 33
Bishop's health in 1929, 87–88
Borland, Swedish nurse, 29
Gates, Mr., District Superintendent of Missions, 22, 23, 33
Mandisozda, David, interpreter, 28
Mr. Roberts, 25
Native pastors and teachers, 26, 27 (photos)

Oregon, 1914. *See also* Portland; University of Oregon Medical School

Darlow as Methodist minister and editor and printer in, 10
North Douglas Herald, 10

Oregon, 1925

beginning medical practice with Dr. Ross, 77
new home with Fostina, 78
Sarah's visit to, 81

Oregon visit to Salem in 1947, and Robert's KJ musical quartet, 194

Otsego (ship), 93

Oxford

    Alice Elsmore Atkin, girlfriend, 57–58
    American Expeditionary Forces scholarship, 48
    application and acceptance, 48, 51
    Divinity School building, 52 (photo)
    Elsmore, punting companion, 57
    Knotty Ash Camp, 49
    lekkers (lectures), 56
    Mr. Chattaway chemistry lecturer, 53
    Mr. Whiston, tutor, 51, 52
    punting, rowing, canoeing notes, 53, 57–58
    "sitter" and "bedder," 53, 55
    St. Catherine's Sports Club, 51–52, 57
    St. John's Street living quarters, 49–50 (photo), 53–56
    undergraduate life, 56–57

— P —

Pacific Northern Airlines (PNA), 179, 213, 289

Pan Pacific Surgical Conference in Honolulu and State Tuberculosis Hospital, Board member, 274

passport, 1916 (photo), 18

pastoral work
    in Africa, 30
    in Nebraska, 8

Paul Bunyan ship, 181

Perry, Admiral, 205

Pershing, General, 44

Piper Super Cub, 252 crash in Mission Lake, 252 (photo)–253

Portland. *See also* medical practice; Oregon
    Chamber of Commerce president, 81
    City Club membership, 86
    Dr. Bowman, First Presbyterian Church, 79
    Dr. Kirby's office, in joint practice with Dr. Cable, 85
    Emmanuel and Good Samaritan Hospitals, 82

financial problems during Great Depression, 85

Good Samaritan Hospital, 193

house sale in 1938, 117

move to, and purchase of new home on Wisteria Avenue, 82–83 (photo)

move to Klickitat Street in 1932, 89

physicians Dr. Peace, Dr. William Mayo, Dr. J.W. Thompson, and Dr. MacCollum, 80

surgeon partner Dr. Cable, and his recommendation, 82, 85, 86, 89, 114

YMCA, Physical Education Committee chairman, 86, 101, 193

Portland Yacht Club, 88 (photo)–89, 90–91, 193, 220

Presbyterian Church / United Presbyterian Church, 174

Sheldon Jackson, Alaska minister, 160

printing jobs

for Old Umtali Mission, 23, 25–25, 26, 29, 30, 33

in Oregon, 10

Princess Marguerite ship, 227

Problem Island book, 201

psychiatry and Freud, thoughts on, 201

— Q —

Quinton, Miss, in Umtali dispensary, 33–34

— R —

Red Cross, 285–286

Rhodes Scholarship / Cecil Rhodes, 23

Rhodes, Wes, teaching how to upholster furniture, 269

Rhodesia

Chimanyika people in, 23, 26

leaving for military service, 30

medical work in, 29–31

Mr. Roberts, head of agricultural department, 25

Old Umtali Mission in, 25 (photo)

syphilis in, 30–31

Rhodesian Mission Press, 26, 30

RMS *Balmoral Castle*, 18 (photo), 19–20

Robert ("Bobby"), author of biography. *See also* letters
    appointment by Judge to U.S. Merchant Marine Academy, 153
    Boy Scout, in Portland, 108
    expressions of fond feelings from father, 149
    joint medical practice with father, 220, 252
    externship with dad, 243
    graduation from Kodiak High School, 134
    internship completion in 1955, 251
    joining dad in practice, 251. *See also* joint medical practice
    motorcycle rides with father and Al Isenberg, 206–207
    practice with Bruce Keers, 256–257
    Rh transfusion as new procedure, 254
    University of Michigan, 216, 218
    University of Washington Medical School dean recommending his
      withdrawal, 239
    Willamette attendance, 134
    Windbird boat, 223–224 (photo), 226

Roberts, Avery, dentist, 123, 125, 126, 213, 219

Roosevelt, President Franklin Delano, death of, 170

Rotary / Rotarians, 154, 157, 159, 165, 169, 170–171, 173, 177, 181, 183, 195
    in Anchorage, 213
    Australia / New Zealand visits and return after earthquake, 1964, 286, 287, 293
    convention in St. Louis, and President LeHarry, 277–278
    land purchase for library, 202

Rotary International
    Asian President, 285
    District governor, 182, 275, 281 (photo) 282–283, 286
    headquarters in Switzerland, tour, 264
    New Zealand trip, 286, 287
    talks / speeches, 282, 283–285

Russian America / Russian Orthodox Church / Russian Easter Week, 119 (photo), 121, 160, 166, 234, 246

Russian-American Company, 98, 209

Russian parsonage fire, 270–271
    Priest Roman Sturmer and wife Xenia, 271–272

— P —

Salazar, Dr. Louis, Ketchikan surgeon, 97, 255

Sarah (mother), 4 (photo)
    cold baths at age ninety-six, 215
    one-hundredth birthday, 278, 279 (photo)
    retirement in Tigard, near Portland, 122, 143, 211, 212, 274
    visits
        to Oregon, 81
        to Kodiak, 127–128, 171–172 (photo), 174, 176, 255–256
        from son and wife in New York in 1947, 191, 193, 194
        with family at Villa Ridge Drive in 1958, 261
        to Kodiak at age 96, 268
        to Arthur and Fostina in 1960, 274
        from Arthur and Fostina in 1962, 278

schools / School Board and president, 106, 122 (photo), 212, 216, 217, 222, 224, 242, 270, 285
    enrollment after occupation of Aleutian Homes, 250
    high school commencement speech, "The Need for Education Today," 296
    Ivor Schott, Superintendent, 242, 256, 280
    Parent Teachers Association inception, 242–243
    Territorial School Board Convention in Petersburg, 1957, 254

Sears Roebuck lease in Johnson Building, 271–272

Seattle, vacation stops in, 192, 212, 213

semi-retirement chronology
    planned, 259
    initial depression, 267
    Holmes Johnson Clinic, 267, 268 (photos)
    peritonitis cases, 276, 286
    skull fracture, 277

Seven Storey Mountain (Merton), 217

Shell Oil Company, 173–174

ships and boats
    Balmoral Castle, 18 (photo), 19–20
    Baranof, 101, 117
    City of New York, 35 (photo)
    Cordova, 115, 134, 153, 183
    Crane (Fish and Wildlife), 181

Denali, 145, 171

Friesland, 261–262 (photo)

Gorgas (Libby ship), 96

Hygiene (Public Health), 185

Megantic, 41, 42 (photo)

"MV Afrika" tour ship, 264

North Coast, 127

Otsego, 93

Paul Bunyan, 181

Princess Marguerite, 227

Shuyak and owner Bob von Scheele, 156

Spencer, 200

Starr, 103, 112, 117

Yale, 43

Yukon, 117–118

Shrew sailboat, 88 (photo)

Shuyak delivery ship, 156

Sioux Indians in Nebraska, 8

Sitka Mount Edgecumbe Sanatorium and surgeon Dr. Phil Moore, 246, 255

Skonberg family survivors of ship accident, 200

South Africa. *See* Africa

Spencer grounding at year end, 200

Sprucehaven log cabin home, 145, 146 (photos), 150, 151

    animals around, 221

    Bishop's visit to, 222

    Christmases at, 216, 199–200, 253–254, 269

    Crawford, Cyril, work on house, 153

    evolving, 216

    generator/light plant problems, 151

    Knut Solberg, builder, 136–137 (photo), 139–140, 143

    Leo Sears, roofer, 140

    maintenance, 207. See also Sutliff

    planning and building 124–125, 126, 127, 128–129, 134, 136, 143

    Vinnie Root, plumbing and heating, 216

    Wolff, lumber work, 140

    upkeep and changes, 156, 171

SS Friesland, 261

Standard Oil, 174

Starr, (ship) and Captain Tronsen, 103, 112, 117

state senate candidacy, 271, 272, 274

St. Helens, Oregon, *See also* Portland; Oregon
  medical practice and commute, 77, 81, 83, 85–86
  Chamber of Commerce president, 81
  Kiwanis involvement, 81
  Masons involvement, 81, 171
  midsummer festival planner, 81

Stiles, Tom, and Tom Stiles Road, 222

Sullivan, Gene, dentist, 186

surgical practice and skill, 259. *See also* Kodiak medical / surgical
  practice
  acceptance by American College of Surgeons, 89
  as Brooklyn Methodist intern, 73 (photo)
  on bull's fracture, 273
  with Dr. Cable in Portland, 85, 86, 89
  consultations in joint practice with son in Kodiak, 253
  in semi-retirement, 287

Sutliff
  Charley, caretaker, 184, 196–197, 208 (photo), 213, 221–222, 273–274,
    275
  Hazel, 196, 213, 225, 239, 249 (death)
  Norm, owner of lumber supply business, 143, 196, 249, 273
  Windbird care, 239–240, 247, 248, 250, 259

— T —

Tank Corps, American European forces, WWI, 38, 44, 46–47, 68, 160
  at Camp Colt, 38–39 (photo)
  end in Cohons, France, 46
  induction center at Jefferson Barracks, Missouri, 37 (photo)
  Whittingham, Captain. 38

Tent village induction center, 37 (photo)

Territorial Medical Association, 180

Taft, President, 12

Torgerson, Oscar "Torgy," 123, 142, 152, 165, 177, 181
    bank sale and move to California, 185, 219
    return to Kodiak, 250, 256

"Torgy's shack" / Torgy's cabin / retreat, 134, 137, 139 (photo)–140, 156, 248, 249 (photo), 252
    Robert and Marian leaving, and improvements to, 275

Transcendentalists, 167

tuberculosis / Tuberculosis Control Officer Robert Fraser in 1957. 54

Tuthill, H.J. (Hazel Sutliff's father), 222

— U —

Union Oil / Jack Hinkel, 256, 279–280

Unitarian Church, 167, 174

United Nations, visit to, 264

University of Minnesota Hospital and Dr. Owen Wangensteen, 191
    University of Oregon Medical School
    B.S. degree from, 62
    chemistry, difficulty with, 61
    clinical instruction of surgery in 1929, 82
    expenses / costs, letter to father, 60–61
    letter to Darlow, 59–60
    pre-med entry in 1919, 59
    romance and love musings, 62
    YMCA room and theft, 59, 60

University of Washington Medical School, and Dr. Dean Turner, 239

U.S. Commissioner Gil Bubendorf, 121

U.S Merchant Marine Academy, appointment for Robert by Judge Anthony J. Dimond, 153

USS Yale, 43

— V —

vacation, in 1947, 189, 191
    in Anchorage with Drs. Walkowski and Romig, 191
    to Boston's Lahey Clinic & Dr. Frank Lahey, 192

at Mason Clinic and Drs. Baker and Capaccio, 192–193

in Chicago, University of Chicago Billings Hospital, and Dr. Lester Dragstedt, 193

in Minneapolis / University of Minnesota Hospital with Dr. Wangensteen, 191

to Philadelphia and Grey Nuns Mother House, 193

in Rochester, Mayo clinic and St. Mary's Hospital, 191

in Seattle, 192

to Temple University Hospital, 192

to Washington, D.C. and Lowrys, 192

vacation, in 1949

to Salem, 212

to Seattle, 211, 213

in San Francisco, 213

in Southern California, 213

along Alcan Highway and Canada with son, 213

in Anchorage, 213

vacation in 1958

first at Alaska Territorial Association of School Boards in Ketchikan, 261

in Africa, 262–264

to Switzerland and United Nations, 264, 264

to France, 264

to Spain, Belgium and Netherlands, 265

at Oxford, England, with relatives, 265

back to Kodiak and semi-retirement, 265

— W—

weddings

to Fostina, 74–75 (photo)

Robert and Marian, 241 (photo)

William (father's brother) and family in Sunderland, England, 49–50

Wilson, Woodrow, 12–13

Windbird boat, 223–224 (photo), 247

in cradle, 243–244

after earthquake, rescued and stored, 293, 285

moorings, 239, 240, 241–242, 255

slides of cruise showed at Robert & Marian wedding, 241

and Tutti Frank, mechanic, 226

upkeep and improvements during semi-retirement, 269, 274–275

Windbird voyage in 1952, chronology
   departure from University Boat Mart, 227
   in Canadian port, 227
   near Chatterbox Falls, 228
   in Alert Bay, 229
   weather after Safety Cove, British Columbia, 230 (photo)
   through Inside Passage, 231
   in Ketchikan, 231
   encountering dolphins and whales, 231
   visiting Mendenhall Glacier, 232
   Icy Strait and Gulf of Alaska, 232
   Indian Cove and Icy Bay, 233
   at Montague Island and Resurrection Cape, 234
   down Kenai Pennisula coast and Nuka Passage, 235
   seeing orcas and sea lions, 236
   arrival back at Kodiak, 235 (photo), 236, 237 (photo)

Wooden Shoe tug, 95 (photo)

Woodley Airways, 179

World War I armistice, 46. *See also* France

World War II, 17–20
   Alaska as part of Pacific theater, 132, 170
   bombing of Dutch Harbor and occupation of Kiska and Attu, 133–134
   end of war in Pacific, 174
   victory declared in 1945, 170
   VJ (Japanese surrender) day, 173

— Y —

yacht racing, 38

Yukon (ship), 117–118